CROSSING
the
DIVIDE

JOHN WESLEY
THE FEARLESS EVANGELIST

CROSSING
the
DIVIDE

JAKE HANSON

SHILOH RUN PRESS
An Imprint of Barbour Publishing, Inc.

Member of the
Evangelical Christian
Publishers Association

Printed in the United States of America.

Dedication

To Abigail, Evangeline, and Susannah
Psalm 22:23

Contents

Introduction:
Crossing the Divide

I now stood and looked back on the past year,
a year of uncommon trials and uncommon blessings.

By 1749, the ministry of forty-six-year-old John Wesley was beginning to expand greatly, but so, too, was opposition to it. He was banned from preaching in most churches and was met with mobs and destructive violence in several of the towns he visited.

Many preachers would cower in the face of such resistance, but Wesley saw opportunity. On October 18, when he arrived in Bolton, just north of Manchester, he was met by a mob of protesters whose "rage and bitterness" he "scarce ever saw before, in any creatures that bore the form of men." When Wesley entered his host's house, it was quickly surrounded by angry citizens who closed off every street and means of escape. One of Wesley's companions who ventured out into the mob was beaten. Then one of the rioters threw a rock through a window near to where Wesley was sitting, and the mob then broke down the door and entered the house.

By this time in his life and ministry, Wesley was well seasoned in facing opposition, and the violence he encountered in Bolton came as no surprise to him. After all, he had faced a similar mob in nearby Rochdale earlier that day, and the people of Bolton had tried to silence him as he preached the last time he had visited their town. But what he did in response to the trials he faced is indicative of a ministry that turned calamities into opportunities.

As the rabble poured into the house, one of Wesley's traveling companions warned them of the coming "terrors of the Lord," while another spoke with "smoother and softer words." Finally, Wesley saw his chance and stood before his audience. As he stepped onto a chair to raise himself above the crowd where he could be seen and heard, he looked upon the aggressors with a "heart filled with love, eyes with tears, and mouth with arguments." As Wesley later recorded in his journal, the response of the angry throng was surprising: they were "amazed, they were ashamed, they were melted down, they devoured every word."

So radically did his words transform the crowd that they disbanded peaceably, only to return at five o'clock the next morning and once again overflow the house. But this time they came to hear the evangelist speak; at their urging, Wesley was "constrained to preach longer" than he was accustomed. Seeing that the people wanted more, he arranged to preach again at nine o'clock in a nearby meadow. His sermon that morning was titled "All things are ready; come unto the marriage."

On New Year's Eve in 1762, Wesley reflected in his journal about the past year: "a year of uncommon trials and uncommon blessings." A survey of his life suggests that such years for Wesley were anything but uncommon.

Controversy, trials, and crises followed John Wesley throughout the course of his six decades of ministry. His times were rife with ecclesiastical divisions, ministerial turf wars, and predicaments that could easily deflate the spirits of even the hardiest soul. Not only that, but he encountered a world that was in disarray, with multitudes in need of help to make it through their own crises of poverty, sickness, and spiritual darkness. So how is it that Wesley's ministry thrived in the midst of endless trials to become one of the most successful and far-reaching evangelistic efforts the world has ever known?

Wesley's unflinching refusal to back down, even in the face of severe opposition and dissension, testifies to his remarkable ability to find within almost every situation an opportunity to spread the transformative message of the Gospel.

But Wesley was not an overnight sensation. It took the first thirty-four years of his life before he encountered his own transformation, even though he had been raised in a minister's home with a very religious mother and had been an ordained minister himself for thirteen years.

Wesley's "awakening" set the stage for his conviction that *every* person needs a transformational encounter with the Gospel.

John Wesley was a remarkable man with a remarkable mind who led a remarkable life. Resolute in his convictions, he was ever gracious to his many opponents. There was no person to whom he would not minister. There was no method of ministry he would not employ, unless it was prohibited by scripture. No one was too rich or too poor, too sick or too healthy; too young or too old, too religious or too irreligious for Wesley. Even his most ardent critics were not immune from the reach of his ministry.

His message and methods still speak to readers in our day who face growing disputes over traditional church teaching as well as societal rejection of biblical morality and justice, and who wonder how to engage with a world in which the ground seems to be shifting under their feet.

John Wesley was a controversial figure in his own day—and remains controversial today, 225 years after his death. Modern readers are likely to find some of his teaching unpalatable, or even wrong, just as his contemporaries did. Indeed, his life illustrates the need for an abundance of caution in the areas of doctrine and practice. But just as his contemporaries found much to learn from the ministry of this man of God, modern-day critics may find in Wesley a path for the Gospel to reach beyond the complicated controversies and divisions of our own day.

John Wesley lived in an age of division, partisanship, and violence of a degree as yet unknown in the West today. He serves as a model for our generation to not merely lament the difficulties and disputes, but to view opposition as an opportunity to transform a world that is spinning out of control.

Part I

The Transformation of John Wesley

Chapter 1
Controversial Fires

*'Tis like a coward to desert my post
because the enemy fire is thick upon me.*

Late on the night of February 9, 1709, the Wesley family was awakened when the Epworth rectory, already half engulfed in flames, began to collapse around them.

The children, asleep in an upstairs nursery along with a maid, were the first to be alerted as fire fell onto one of the children's beds. Almost immediately, their parents, Samuel and Susanna, awoke and began to sound the alarm. Susanna's first few attempts to escape were blocked by the flames, but eventually she was able to run from the house, though slightly burning her hands and face. The maid and the elder children had carried the toddlers as they fled down the steps and out into the garden. At last, everyone was safely accounted for, except for one—five-year-old John.

In all the commotion, no one had noticed that John was sleeping soundly in the nursery behind his bed curtain. When he finally awoke, he saw streaks of fire on the ceiling. Running to the door to escape, he found it blocked by the raging fire. He retreated to the second-story window, found a chest on which to stand, and called out to the neighbors who had gathered below to watch the house going up in flames.

When Samuel realized that John was not outside with the others, he ran back in to see if he could rescue him. But the flames were too hot. By then, the neighbors had calculated that time was too short to fetch a ladder to rescue the young Wesley boy from the upper story, and they had resigned themselves to his fate. Samuel led the gathered assembly in prayer, commending his young son into the hands of God. It seemed that John was destined to the same fate as nine other Wesley children—and some 30 percent of English children in the eighteenth century—who died before reaching adulthood.

But even as young John Wesley stood at the window of his burning home, not knowing that his family now counted him as yet another child lost, the neighbors had not given up. One man leaned himself against the burning building while another climbed onto his shoulders to try to snatch the boy from the window. The first attempt ended with the would-be rescuer tumbling from the shoulders of the other man. But on their second try, they were able to rescue John from the flames an instant before the roof collapsed right above where he had been standing. It was a trial by fire that no one in attendance that night would ever forget.

Even before the flames that destroyed the rectory had died down on that tragic winter night, some were accusing Samuel Wesley of setting fire to his own house to receive financial aid from the Church of England. Indeed, the blaze was the third—and worst—to have struck the property in a span of ten years. But although accusations and suspicions would linger, the Wesleys suspected that a serial arsonist was intent on driving them away—or worse.

Controversy was a familiar theme in the history of the Wesleys. Samuel Wesley had begun his ministry with difficulty in 1697 at Epworth, a farming town of two thousand residents in Lincolnshire. Low pay and a growing family forced him to accrue unbearable debts, part of which were loans to begin a farm (at which he proved inept), and part of which resulted from the collapse of his barn shortly after his arrival. The financial trials were exacerbated in 1703 when a private letter written by Samuel twelve years earlier was published without his approval. The letter—an insider's negative portrayal of the Dissenting Academies, which had educated him for most of his life—was seen by many as a base, unforgivable attack on a popular movement.

The hornet's nest he inadvertently stepped on stemmed from the long-smoldering English Reformation, which had fragmented the religious class into two main camps. On one side were the Established

Churches, the Church of England, led by the British monarch—whose line of succession was established "for ever" as Protestant by the Settlement Act of 1701. The other side comprised a diverse group of Nonconformists, or Dissenters—including Catholics, Puritans, Presbyterians, Congregationalists, Baptists, and Quakers among others—who refused to subject themselves to the religious authority of the crown. As the Dissenters were squeezed out of the political process and educational system, they began establishing their own Dissenting Academies, which included the institutions that Samuel Wesley had criticized.

In the century and a half after Henry VIII ignited the English Reformation with his annulment of his marriage to Queen Catherine in 1533, the Dissenters suffered various levels of persecution. Ancestors of both Samuel and Susanna Wesley were leaders and pastors in the Nonconformist movement. As a child, Samuel saw his dissenting father imprisoned and forced to flee for extended periods—likely leading to his premature death. Samuel was financially supported by Nonconformists and educated in the Dissenting Academies, but when he matured into adulthood, he turned his back on his heritage and his acquaintances and joined the Established Church.

But even though he had switched camps, he never meant to attack his former associates in the Nonconformist movement, and he was grieved by the publication of his captious letter. The firestorm continued to grow, reaching a fever pitch in 1705 when some local Dissenting politicians to whom Samuel had pledged his support became publicly critical of the Established Church. When he rescinded his pledge, a band of gun-toting rioters gathered in front of his church and rectory.

Shortly after the election, and likely as punishment for failing to keep his promise, Samuel was served by a creditor with a demand for immediate payment of a debt of £30 or else he would be thrown into debtors' prison. When he could not pay his obligation, he was sent to Lincoln Castle jail. While he was there and apart from his family, vandals in Epworth stabbed several of the Wesleys' cows, rendering them milkless; broke the door locks at the Wesleys' home; and nearly cut off a leg from the family dog, who staunchly, and loudly, defended the property. Clearly, some within the town were trying to drive the Wesley family away. But the rector remained undeterred. With a steely resolve that he would pass along to John, and fortified by Susanna's even greater determination to stand firm in the face of persecution, Samuel wrote a letter from jail to his concerned archbishop:

> *Most of my friends advise me to leave Epworth, if e'er I should get from hence. I confess I am not of that mind, because I may yet do good there; and 'tis like a coward to desert my post because the enemy fire is thick upon me. They have only wounded me yet, and, I believe, can't kill me.*

Samuel was soon released from debtors' prison and returned to Epworth to minister to these same souls until his death in 1735. But it was not easy.

John Wesley was the fifteenth of nineteen children born to Samuel and Susanna. At the time of the rectory fire, eighteen children had been born, including Charles, the future hymn writer, but nine had died at an early age.

Throughout his life and ministry, John Wesley reflected regularly on the fateful fire of February 9, 1709, often saying of himself, "Is not this a brand plucked out of the fire?" This quote from Zechariah 3:2 became something of a life verse and motto for Wesley. In that nearly tragic event from his childhood, he saw a providential deliverance and a call on his life to help deliver those who would otherwise be engulfed in the spiritual flames of the wrath of God to come. But first he needed to find his own spiritual deliverance—or rather, to be "found" by the almighty Deliverer.

Chapter 2
Almost Christian

I doubted not but I was a good Christian.

After surviving the fire of 1709, John Wesley set out on a twenty-year journey to determine what it meant to be a true Christian. It took as long for him to discover what his erratic spiritual life suggested—he was not an "altogether Christian."

Observing his outward life during this decades-long quest could give a false impression of his spiritual condition, and that is perhaps the main point of John Wesley's ministry. Raised in a devoutly Christian home, the pastor's son exhibited every reasonable sign of authentic Christian faith. He read the scriptures and prayed twice daily through most of his schooling; he participated in intense Christian fellowship as a young adult; he was ordained as a deacon and then as a priest; he served as curate at one of his father's parishes; and he even traveled overseas to America as a missionary. As Wesley himself later wrote, "I doubted not but I was a good Christian."

Immediately after the Epworth fire, the Wesley children were dispersed to the households of family and friends. This separation would have been difficult for any mother, but even more so for Susanna, whose watchful eye controlled every aspect of the children's secular and religious education and training in a highly regimented way. Her system was designed "to conquer their will, and bring them to an obedient temper." The tragedy of separation left the family matriarch out of control for nearly two years as the rectory was rebuilt.

But through that trial, she gained a new appreciation of her role and heightened her dedication to the spiritual well-being of her children.

Throughout the rest of their childhood, she met with each child individually one night a week in order to "discourse...on something that relates to its principal concerns"—namely religion. John fondly reminisced and, in adulthood longed for, the Thursday evening times set aside with his mother, saying that it had formed his judgment and regularly corrected his heart.

Though Susanna had ten children to care for, she did not overlook the significance of John's miraculous deliverance. She set her eye on this "brand plucked from the fire," knowing that God had purposefully preserved him. Susanna wrote a note in her devotional book shortly after the family reunited on May 11, 1711, demonstrating not only a mother's concern, but also her recognition of the sovereign providential hand of God on John's life:

> *I do intend to be more particularly careful of the soul of this child, that Thou hast so mercifully provided for, than ever I have been, that I may do my endeavour to instill into his mind the principles of Thy true religion and virtue. Lord, give me grace to do it sincerely and prudently, and bless my attempts with good success!*

Even though so much was poured into John Wesley's spiritual upbringing by both his father and mother, at the age of thirty-four he reflected negatively on his childhood, "having been strictly educated and carefully taught that I could only be saved 'by universal obedience, by keeping all the commandments of God.'" It took until young adulthood for John to realize the error of this salvation-by-works teaching—a teaching that the Protestant Reformation had sought to destroy.

In 1714, his spiritual journey took a detour when, at the tender age of ten, he entered Charterhouse Academy, southwest of London and two hundred miles from home. Charterhouse eventually opened the door for him to continue his studies at Christ Church, Oxford. At these two schools, the pendulum of faith swung from the strict upbringing of his Epworth home to a place where "outward restraints being removed," he was "almost continually guilty of outward sins. . .though they were not scandalous in the eye of the world." His view of salvation began to shift from an impossible "universal obedience" to the much more manageable road of finding salvation by comparing his minor misdeeds to the more heinous misdeeds of others. To add to his sense of security, he rested on his kindness for religion, all the while striving through the spiritual disciplines of Bible reading, prayer, and regular attendance at Holy Communion. Nevertheless, he later lamented, he had no "notion of inward holiness."

Even though his spiritual detour led him from the error of salvation by works to other, opposite errors, he was an engaged student and acquired a first-rate education that laid a broad and solid foundation for his unique ministry in later years. He learned Hebrew, Greek, and Latin—the latest of which he could converse in and write with near fluency. Knowledge of these languages not only opened doors into the scriptures for the young student but also into classic literature and philosophy, which he used throughout his life and writings to offer comparative lessons and witticisms to drive home his points.

After six and a half years at Charterhouse and another five in Oxford, new seeds had been planted in his heart, though they would not come to fruition for another decade. Still, they began to set the stage for a vibrant ministry.

After graduating from Christ Church, John sought election as a fellow at Lincoln College, Oxford, and also considered entering into holy orders—receiving ordination as a deacon in the Church of England. When Samuel Wesley learned of his son's intentions, he asked him to wait and instead return to the family home to help with a work on the book of Job that Samuel was trying to finish. He told John that this would help to prepare him for ordination.

Susanna, however, thought differently. "My dear Jacky," she wrote, referring to him by his nickname, "I heartily wish you would now enter upon a serious examination of yourself, that you may know whether you have a reasonable hope of salvation by Jesus Christ." Such critical self-examination, she said, "deserves great consideration in all, but especially [for] those designed for the clergy."

While his father cautioned him to slow down the process of ordination, his mother urged him to speed it up. "I think the sooner you are a deacon the better," she wrote, skeptical of "trifling studies." She believed that serving as a deacon "may be an inducement to greater application in the study of practical divinity, which of all other I humbly conceive is the best study for candidates" for the priesthood. Susanna's advice won out.

Preparation for ordination led him to two authors who challenged his thinking and gave him insight into inward holiness and true religion "seated in the heart." He had already been convinced by William Law's book *A Serious Call to a Devout and Holy Life* that one could not be a "half Christian." Now *The Christian Pattern*, Thomas à Kempis's classic fifteenth-century work, raised questions about whether the godly are destined to be "perpetually miserable" in the world.

Wesley shared these questions with his mother, whose practical wisdom was fused with a theological mind that had few equals. Thomas à Kempis "is extremely in the wrong in that impious—I was about to say, blasphemous—suggestion," she replied, "that God by an irreversible decree hath determined any man to be miserable in this world."

When he encountered difficulties concerning another classic writer, Jeremy Taylor and his *Rules for Holy Living and Dying*, Wesley once again sought his mother's opinion, this time concerning Taylor's view of unattainable humility. What followed was an extraordinarily thoughtful examination of the definition and application of humility, which—Susanna wrote in a several-page letter to her academically inclined son—"is the mean between pride, or an overvaluing of ourselves, on one side, and a base, abject temper on the other." Their correspondence over the following months shows her to be a great mentor who shaped him deeply, examining issues related to predestination, the providence of God, evil in the world, faith, salvation, and various other topics.

John Wesley was ordained a deacon in September 1725. Six months later, he was elected as a fellow of Lincoln College, Oxford, a position he would hold for the next twenty-five years.

In April 1726, the new Lincoln College tutor had no pupils, so he asked for and received a leave from Oxford for the summer to assist his father in serving the two churches under his charge in Epworth and Wroot. When John returned home, he entered into a family controversy. How he responded gives an early indication of how he would deal with controversy, sin, and sinners for the rest of his life.

The issue concerned his older sister Hetty, who had fallen in love with a lawyer whose character raised Samuel's suspicions. Frustrated by Hetty's meddling father, the suitor took her away for an entire night. This of course outraged Samuel, and when Hetty returned home the next morning, she was embarrassed and ashamed, and the relationship was ended. There are various accounts of what happened next, some of which require reading between the lines of the Wesleys' correspondence. What is clear is that Hetty left the family, breaking contact for several months, and eloped with another man.

Samuel, the family patriarch, was "inconceivably exasperated against her" and spoke ill of her whenever her name came up. Most others in the family felt disgraced by Hetty's behavior. Believing that her subsequent displays of penitence were feigned, they disowned her.

When John arrived at home, he was concerned that his family was being too harsh, judgmental, and unforgiving with Hetty, who had been "innocent enough" since her marriage. The young Lincoln College fellow made his convictions clear, which inevitably led to friction with his father.

Perhaps John's compassion was driven in part by his own personal struggles with sinful passions. His private diary from that summer records an ongoing and escalating struggle with young women, the details of which would likely have been as scandalous as Hetty's situation. Indeed, the scandal would have been greater, as John was serving as the acting curate of the church in Wroot. This struggle—even when he did not act on his passions—haunted him and racked him with guilt for at least another twenty years.

So whether or not he was defending his sister as an expression of how he would want to be treated, he was moved to publicly declare his vision for the treatment of "wicked men." In late August, he completed a sermon on "universal charity" that he had been thinking about for nearly a year. The next week, he preached on "rash judging," with the suggestion that even the vilest sinners were entitled to some measure of charity. He read the first sermon to his mother, who afterward observed, "You writ this sermon for Hetty." He later confessed as much in a letter to his father: "One great reason for my writing the...sermon was to endeavour, as far as in me lay, to convince them that even on supposition that she was impenitent, some tenderness was due her still."

The fallout from these sermons on such a particularly sensitive situation was an escalation of tension within the Wesley family. Samuel, in particular, was enraged at such a public renunciation of his stated position—and from his own pulpit! When John learned of his father's great displeasure, he wept at Samuel's feet, asking for forgiveness. But perhaps his message had the desired effect. That autumn, Susanna visited Hetty, with Samuel's permission, to pursue reconciliation. But Hetty wasn't interested in burying the hatchet, and she responded coldly to her mother's efforts. Though some of the hostility waned over the years, the family relationships were never quite set right. But perhaps because of the tenderness that John expressed to Hetty—whose unwise choices led to a somewhat unhappy life and marriage—in the years before her death she found in his ministry a place in which she could be reconciled to God.

John resumed his duties in Oxford in 1726, but he returned to Wroot in 1727 to assist his father. Having now been ordained to the priesthood, he served as his father's curate for the next two years before his role as a fellow at Lincoln College forced him to return once again to Oxford to tutor students and lecture, which he did for the next six years. During this time, his direction and impulse shifted from academic pursuits to the role of spiritual adviser, a crucial turning point in his life.

Back in Oxford, John was reunited with his brother Charles, who had been a student at Christ Church since 1727. Like his elder brother, Charles had left home at a young age for an education at Westminster School in London, where the eldest Wesley sibling, Samuel Jr., took him under his wing. When Charles first arrived at Christ Church, he was swept away by the excitement of university life and the prospect of meeting young women, but he soon found these pursuits at odds with his desire for a personal reformation. He wrote to John, seeking help and encouragement: "Christ Church is certainly the worst place in the world to begin a reformation in; a man stands a very fair chance of being laughed out of his religion at his first setting out, in a place where 'tis scandalous to have any at all."

John relished the idea of assisting his younger brother, even though his own soul was similarly divided. He enjoyed the collegiality of the other fellows and their intellectual pursuits in their exclusive meeting place, the Senior Common Room, but the tensions of the world and his growing pursuit of inward religion would very quickly clash.

In October 1732, he invited his brother and two companions to come to his room at Lincoln College, and they began reading classic literature together on weekday evenings and books of a religious nature on Sunday evenings. This gradually led to less reading of the classics and more devotional reading, Bible study, and prayer, as well as regular attendance at public prayer and the Lord's Supper. They began to call themselves The Holy Club because they were pursuing holiness together.

The Holy Club tried to return to the "ancient, if not apostolical" practices of the church, as John came to believe that there had been more spiritual vibrancy in the church before Constantine established Christianity as the Roman Empire's official religion. Following the practices of the early church, he led the others in fasting two days a week—Wednesdays and Fridays—and they began visiting prisons, the sick, and the poor, and performing other acts of charity. Their aim, according to Wesley, was to have nothing less than complete holiness: "a constant ruling habit of soul; a renewal of our minds in the image of

God; a recovery of the divine likeness; a still-increasing conformity of heart and life to the pattern of our most holy Redeemer."

All the while, they continued to meet for prayer and reading, as well as for accountability, reading self-critical questions to point out sinful attitudes, actions, and omissions. They eschewed the company of others who would lead them astray. This radical pursuit caught the attention of others at Lincoln College and the university. Some began to derisively call them The Godly Club. Others referred to them as "Methodists" because of their rigid methodical rules and expectations. This latter name is one that would stick for this small group of devoted young men (no more than seven at a time), which included John and Charles Wesley and George Whitefield, a young, lazy-eyed, gifted orator from Gloucester, who joined the club in 1733 and went on to become the greatest evangelist of his day.

The derision faced by the members of The Holy Club as a result of their practices deeply affected John's progress as a fellow. Pupils looking for a tutor were told—by the school's rector, among others—to avoid John Wesley, lest they become too strict in their "notions of religion." The activities of The Holy Club hurt not only John but also the reputation of Lincoln College, leading potential students to choose other colleges.

In time, John Wesley became less welcome among his colleagues and students—and less comfortable in their presence. It became clear to John, Charles, and a few others that their ideas of holiness were impossible to achieve in the academic climate at Oxford—though John would soon realize that it was the state of his own soul, not the environment, that kept him from holiness. Several years later, in a reflection on these rigid pursuits—and something of a confession to the Oxford community—he declared:

> *I did go thus far for many years, as many of this place can testify;*
> *using diligence to eschew all evil, and to have conscience void*
> *of offence; redeeming the time; buying up every opportunity of*
> *doing all good to all men; constantly and carefully using all the*
> *public and all the private means of grace; endeavouring after a*

26

*steady seriousness of behaviour, at all times, and in all places;
and, God is my record, before whom I stand, doing all this in
sincerity; having a real design to serve God; a hearty desire to do
his will in all things; to please him who had called me to "fight
the good fight," and to "lay hold of eternal life." Yet my own
conscience beareth me witness in the Holy Ghost, that all this
time I was but almost a Christian.*

This conviction did not come easily for the rigorous religious leader.
And it did not come at Oxford, but rather through failure and rejection
in a new venture.

By 1734, John's father was begging him to return to Epworth to pastor
the church there. Samuel's health was failing, and the end of his ministry was drawing near. But John would not accept the offer. He argued
that his own holiness was at stake, and that this holiness could best
be achieved not in Epworth, but among the young men of The Holy
Club, who have "according to their power renounced themselves, and
wholly, absolutely, devoted themselves to God."

On April 25, 1735, John and Charles attended the bedside of their
dying father. "The Christian faith will surely revive in this kingdom,"
Samuel told them. "You shall see it, though I shall not."

For John and Charles, however, the next several years of their journey would take them away from England to a new venture in North
America, where General James Oglethorpe was developing a new colony called Georgia. Two previous chaplains to the colony had either
died or failed, so Oglethorpe asked John to fill the role, with Charles
assisting him as secretary. If Epworth did not afford the potential to
make John holy, perhaps a journey to minister to the Indians of America
would.

Anticipating his upcoming adventure, John began to idealize the
new colony and its native inhabitants. Simplicity, lack of diversions, and
absence of the temptations of women all greatly appealed to his desire

for purity of devotion. Furthermore, he believed that the natives, unlike the academics of Oxford, were open to the things of God:

[They] have no comments to construe away [the Bible]; no vain philosophy to corrupt it; no luxurious, sensual, covetous, ambitious expounders to soften its unpleasing truths, to reconcile earthly-mindedness and faith, the Spirit of Christ and the spirit of the world. They have no party, no interest to serve, and are therefore fit to receive the gospel in its simplicity.

His idealism and hopes were about to be crushed.

Questions for Self-Examination

1. Am I consciously or unconsciously creating the impression that I am better than I really am? In other words, am I a hypocrite?
2. Am I honest in all my acts and words, or do I exaggerate?
3. Do I confidentially pass on to others what has been said to me in confidence?
4. Can I be trusted?
5. Am I a slave to dress, friends, work, or habits?
6. Am I self-conscious, self-pitying, or self-justifying?
7. Did the Bible live in me today?
8. Do I give the Bible time to speak to me every day?
9. Am I enjoying prayer?
10. When did I last speak to someone else about my faith?
11. Do I pray about the money I spend?
12. Do I get to bed on time and get up on time?
13. Do I disobey God in anything?
14. Do I insist on doing something about which my conscience is uneasy?
15. Am I defeated in any part of my life?
16. Am I jealous, impure, critical, irritable, touchy, or distrustful?
17. How do I spend my spare time?
18. Am I proud?
19. Do I thank God that I am not as other people, especially as the Pharisees who despised the publican?
20. Is there anyone whom I fear, dislike, disown, criticize, hold a resentment toward, or disregard? If so, what am I doing about it?
21. Do I grumble or complain constantly?
22. Is Christ real to me?

Chapter 3
Contrary Winds

I can conceive no difference comparable to that between a smooth and a rough sea except that which is between a mind calmed by the love of God and one torn up by the storms of earthly passions.

On October 15, 1735, John and Charles Wesley, along with Oxford Methodist Benjamin Ingham and Charles Delamotte, the son of a Middlesex magistrate and businessman, boarded the *Simmonds* at Gravesend to embark on a transatlantic voyage. Their stated purpose was to become "better Christians" and to spread the gospel of Jesus Christ to the Native American Indians in the newly established colony of Georgia in North America. John Wesley, who had "dreaded and abhorred the sea" since his youth, moved ahead in the face of some of his greatest fears.

After sailing down the Thames and making its way through the English Channel, the *Simmonds* encountered a rolling sea and difficult winds just off the coast of England, stalling the journey almost as soon as it had begun. Additionally, the man-of-war that was to protect them on their journey was not yet ready to sail; and when it was, the winds remained contrary, delaying their departure for several weeks, wasting necessary provisions and squandering the most valuable season in Georgia for labor. Even so, the Wesleys took the delays in stride, making the most of every opportunity to minister to their fellow travelers. Charles also preached onshore at local congregations. Finally, after nearly two months of delay, the two ships carrying 227 men, women, and children departed in mid-December.

The journey across the Atlantic took a southerly route down to the nineteenth parallel to take advantage of the trade winds. There they found subtropical temperatures and met with violent storms. As they approached the American coast in late January 1736, they encountered a series of five frightful and violent storms in a two-week period. One of the storms ripped through the mainsail, and another tore the foresail. John Wesley described the force of this storm in frightening detail:

> *The winds roared round about us, and (what I never heard before) whistled as distinctly as if it had been a human voice. The ship not only rocked to and fro with the utmost violence, but shook and jarred with so unequal, grating a motion, that one could not but with great difficulty keep one's hold of anything, nor stand a moment without it. Every ten minutes came a shock against the stern or side of the ship which one would think should dash the planks in pieces.*

Fear gripped his soul. "What if the Gospel be not true?" he asked himself as he pondered his seemingly imminent death. Even as such questions tormented his mind, he observed a group of twenty-six German passengers on the ship. They were Moravians, a pious German Christian sect led by Nikolaus Ludwig von Zinzendorf and based in Herrnhut, Germany. The Moravians, in the midst of a great, decades-long spiritual renewal, were sending missionaries around the world.

Wesley took note of how the Moravians remained calm and composed in the midst of the terrifying storms. Rather than cry out, they sang hymns and were prepared for death at a moment's notice. The authenticity of their faith intrigued Wesley and caused him to question the genuineness of his own convictions. He wrote in his journal concerning the distinction:

> *I can conceive no difference comparable to that between a smooth and a rough sea except that which is between a mind calmed by the love of God and one torn up by the storms of earthly passions.*

On February 5, they reached the relative safety of the American coastland—an island at the mouth of the Savannah River. Still, they were weeks away from their final destination—the settlement of Savannah, fifteen miles upriver—and were shortly welcomed by a heavy Georgia rain shower, which "before we could get one hundred yards," Wesley noted, "wetted us all from head to foot." It would be another month before he could begin his ministry in Savannah.

By March 7, 1736, the fearful storms of the sea were behind him, but the drastic temperatures and powerful Georgia storms were not. Moreover, he could not foresee the great personal, social, and ministerial storm into which he was entering. Before long, his reputation would be left in tatters and he would be seen as "a sly hypocrite, a seducer, a betrayer of...trust, an egregious liar and dissembler."

When John Wesley arrived in Georgia, he had already conquered his great fear of the sea. He came as a pioneer to the British colony settled by James Oglethorpe only three years earlier as a slave-free colony—out of practicality, not morality. Composed of rivers, marshes, wild woodlands, and savannahs, "the low, watery meadows which are usually intermixed with pine-lands," the Georgia territory served as a buffer between the Spanish colony of Florida to the south and the British Carolinas to the north. By settling Georgia, the English hoped to fend off the Spanish from encroaching northward. They established a London-based commission of trustees who initially planned to send debtors and other poor folks to settle the lush lands of Georgia, which received almost 70 percent more rainfall per year than England. Along with the increase in rainfall, Wesley was astounded by the extreme temperatures and "terrible" thunderstorms in the Americas.

Charles Wesley came to the colony to serve as Secretary of Indian Affairs for General Oglethorpe. This role placed him at Fort Frederica, strategically positioned on St. Simon's Island some one hundred miles south of Savannah, which served as an outpost to keep an eye on the movements of the Spanish to the south. So although the two brothers had traveled the ocean together, they were now separated by up to a five-day journey by boat. Without daily contact and brotherly encouragement, John found comfort in his relationships with Benjamin Ingham and Charles Delamotte; the latter came as a servant and proved an invaluable partner in ministry—particularly to the children and youth of the newly formed colony. Charles Wesley, however, was stranded at Fort Frederica without any support.

Though John had come to Georgia with hopes of reaching the Indians, his main ministry at first was to the "importunate" needs of the people of Savannah, many of whom he had begun serving on the journey from England by leading prayer and Communion services, and through counsel and preaching. He began his ministry in Savannah with a mixture of conviction and doctrinaire arrogance, which the people at first tolerated but soon found eccentric and insufferable.

When the people gathered for their first service in the courthouse—no church building having yet been built—John read a notice to the congregation that set the stage for nearly every battle that lay ahead. In the notice, he made clear that he would admonish the parishioners for their faults both publicly and privately; that though many Church of England parishes often overlooked the rubric of the 1662 Book of Common Prayer, he intended to follow its regulations as "a servant" rather than a "judge" of the Church of England. For Wesley this meant that he took seriously the regulation that a participant of Holy Communion give at least a day's notice to the parson before receiving the sacrament—a move intended to maintain the purity of the church. He also made it clear that in accordance with the prayer book's rubric on baptism, any children "who were well able to endure it" would be dipped into the water rather than sprinkled or poured over. This included infants. Furthermore, he maintained that he would only accept participants to the Lord's Table who had been baptized by a minister ordained through apostolic succession. This meant that he rejected the baptisms of Dissenters of the Church of England, whom he believed practiced de facto lay baptism. These oft-overlooked rubrics of the church would not be ignored by this cocksure young parson.

The first challenge to Wesley's administration of the sacraments came in early May when the second bailiff and his wife refused to have their baby dipped in the water. Wesley informed the parents that he could only pour water over the child if they certified the child was weak.

This they refused to do. Instead, the couple found a minister in a nearby town to baptize the child, resulting in long-standing ill will between them and Wesley. Still, Wesley did not back down, apologize, or show any remorse over the exchange.

At Fort Frederica, Charles faced more immediate trials. John's junior by three years, he was of a more sensitive disposition than his more rigid and decisive brother. While many of John's trials in Georgia were of his own making, Charles was more innocent and found himself embroiled in a bewildering array of unimaginable lies and intrigue, including the possible discovery of an adulterous love triangle.

The trouble began on Sunday, March 21. Oglethorpe had stipulated on more than one occasion that no shooting was to be done on Sundays because it would profane the Lord's Day. But during Charles's morning sermon that day, a gunshot sounded outside the meeting hall. When the constable ran out of the service to investigate, he found that the shooter was the town doctor, Thomas Hawkins, and confined him for three days until the governor returned from a hunting trip and could adjudicate the dispute. The doctor was enraged to be treated as a "common fellow," and his wife was even more incensed. Though Charles had nothing to do with the confinement, the Hawkinses put the blame fully on him, citing his meddling and invasive religious beliefs.

In the midst of this turmoil, Charles learned of an alleged affair that the doctor's wife was having with General Oglethorpe. This allegation came from Mrs. Anne Welch, who also confessed her own infatuation with the governor. Furthermore, Charles learned that Mrs. Hawkins had been whispering to the governor that John Wesley had "kissed her a thousand times" during the overseas voyage on the *Simmonds*.

The veracity of these claims came into question a few days later when Charles learned that he himself was being accused of inappropriate relations with one of Mrs. Hawkins's maids. However, when Oglethorpe returned from his hunting trip, he apparently believed all of the accusations against Charles, lost all confidence in him, and treated him very coolly. As a final blow, Oglethorpe stopped sharing necessary resources with Charles and stripped him of what he already had—including his bed.

By late March, Charles was lonely, in despair, and believing that he "could not be more trampled upon were I a fallen minister of state." He was rejected, isolated, hungry, and sick, and his hut was infested with biting flies—all of which proved a great personal trial.

In April, word of his brother's despondency reached John in Savannah, so he went to visit Charles to bring him encouragement and direction. When John arrived, the two stole away into the woods, out of the earshot of the "spies and ruffians," and spoke together in Latin, in case anyone else happened to overhear.

Fully apprised of the situation, John asked for a conference with the governor, at which Oglethorpe maintained his innocence of the charges of adultery. Charles was dubious of the governor's claims until the source of the rumors, Mrs. Welch, changed her story. Apparently, she and Mrs. Hawkins, both of whom confessed to be in love with Oglethorpe, had concocted a plot to rid themselves of the meddlesome parsons by accusing the Wesleys of indiscretions. As a result, they had turned the governor and much of the fort against the Wesleys. When John and Charles learned of this scheme, they were both "utterly confounded."

It took a week before Charles could begin to clear the air with the governor and another month before he was received entirely back into his good graces; but by then, the damage to his ministry had been done. In mid-May, John relieved him of his ministerial duties in Frederica for a month, and Charles replaced John in Savannah for that time.

In the end, Charles never returned to Fort Frederica. He later wrote in his journal: "I was overjoyed at my deliverance out of this furnace, and not a little ashamed of myself for being so." Charles, the guileless young secretary, resigned from his post on July 25, just over four months after beginning his service in the colony. He left the American continent in August, still confused at his utter failure.

John was left to pick up the pieces at Fort Frederica. He continued to try to meet with Mrs. Hawkins, the chief accuser and enemy. Wesley believed that none were beyond the reach of God, and therefore there was no one to whom he did not have a duty to serve as a minister. He attempted to placate her until she confronted him in her home, with a pistol in one hand and a pair of scissors in the other, and attempted to shoot him "through the head. . .with a brace of balls." Wesley was able to grab her wrists to avoid these assailments, but she forced him down to her bed, screaming, "Villain, dog, let go my hands!" until a crowd gathered. Though physically restrained, Mrs. Hawkins began biting at Wesley's cassock, bit off his sleeves, and finally bit his arm before someone pulled her away.

John was delighted when General Oglethorpe ordered Mrs. Hawkins and him never to utter a word to each other again. In a typically heroic reflection, he wrote in his journal: "Blessed be God, who hath at length given me a full discharge, in the sight of man and angels, from all intercourse with one 'whose heart is snares and nets, and her hands as bands.'"

As difficult as Mrs. Hawkins was, and as much as the conflict torpedoed the Wesleys' reputation in Frederica, she was not the one who would undo John's ministry in Georgia.

John principally intended for his ministry in Georgia to reach the Indians of North America. From his academic perch in Oxford, he could think of no better way to purge himself of the world than to devote himself to the simple, uneducated—and therefore, to his mind, undefiled—indigenous people who dwelt in the American colonies. His idealized notions of such a mission were never tested, for when he approached General Oglethorpe about ministering to the Indians, he was refused permission. Though he subsequently had some formal hearings with Indian tribe leaders in Savannah, his ministry was confined to European settlers in and around Savannah and Frederica. Oglethorpe had argued that if a Wesley-led delegation were to leave the settlements to reach the Indians, they would potentially be intercepted by the French and either imprisoned or killed. Furthermore, if John left Savannah, it would create an unacceptable ministerial vacuum there. While the strong-headed minister considered going out anyway, contrary to the wishes of the governor, his heartstrings were beginning to be pulled by the "more serious parishioners [of the colony] to watch over their souls a little longer."

In Georgia, Wesley established an exacting method of ministry, much as he had at Oxford. He visited as many of the parishioners as he could, entering deeply into their problems and into the civic issues and disputes of the colony. He catechized children and young people on Saturdays, in addition to what his colaborer Charles Delamotte did during the week. He also led the more zealous parishioners in regular morning and evening prayers, in addition to their normal Sunday morning and evening services. Not a moment seems to have been wasted as Wesley noted every hour of his day in his private diary and graded his sense of religious zeal on a scale from one to ten. He labeled this scale *Grace*.

Wesley was diligent in the pursuit of the five hundred or so souls who then resided in Savannah. In March of his first year, with the counsel of Benjamin Ingham and Charles Delamotte, he decided that he must visit his parishioners weekly, particularly those who were communicants—a resolve consistent with the rubric of the Church of England. It also led him to begin ministering to a young woman soon to turn eighteen by the name of Sophia Christina Hopkey—or Sophy for short.

Sophy was the niece of Thomas Causton, the chief magistrate of Savannah. She had come to Georgia in 1733 with her uncle and aunt as some of the original pioneers under General Oglethorpe's charge. By 1736, the familial relationships had become strained as Sophy grew from a teenager into an independent young woman. She tired of the uninterrupted guests—and would-be suitors—who descended on the magistrate's house. The Caustons apparently reciprocated her feelings as it was their stated desire that she marry and move out.

Wesley's ministry to this blossoming young woman tested his initial resolve "to have no intimacy with any woman in America." It would also test the distinction between his ministerial duties and romantic passions—a division Wesley believed he could maintain, but one that would crumble over the next year and a half. The fact that Sophy's uncle was of one of the more powerful men in the city led to an uproar that would thrust Wesley out of Savannah.

Chapter 4
Georgia Storm

I can't take fire into my bosom and not be burnt.

John Wesley very often used controversies and trials as opportunities for ministry. But in regard to Sophy Hopkey, he unwittingly turned a ministerial opportunity into a controversy. Blinded at first by the denial of his passions, he entered the relationship with a "single eye" toward Sophy's spiritual well-being. But as time went on, he grew enamored of her.

During that first spring of ministry, he met with Miss Sophy once a week—never alone—and appears to have treated her no differently than any other communicant. But after John returned in June from five weeks in Frederica covering the ministerial duties of his brother Charles, Sophy was in a crisis. She had engaged herself to a young man, Tommy Mellichamp, a "notorious villain" who was taken to prison in Charleston for forgery. Sophy was despondent over the developments, and when the parson—John Wesley—returned to Savannah, Mrs. Causton begged him to reach out to her niece.

At the end of June and into early July, Wesley commenced meeting with her weekly, but by mid-July, he was seeing her daily. It was during one of these meetings that John first kissed Sophy, whereupon a major shift took place within him. "From this time," he later reflected, "I fear there was a mixture in my intention, though I was not sensible of it."

In late July, John left for Charleston to see Charles, who was returning to England. At the same time, Tommy Mellichamp, who had been released from prison, returned to Savannah, apparently with the desire to return to Sophy's good graces. Afraid of reconciling with a man who had proved himself not worth marrying, she fled to Frederica and remained there for several months.

In the late summer and fall of 1736, John made two extended trips to Frederica. The first was to sort out the mess created by his brother's departure. During this period, from mid-August to the beginning of September, he tutored Sophy in French, read prayers with her and others, and generally spent a part of every day with her. All the while, his passions overwhelmed his good sense, as he kissed her on a few occasions but "immediately condemned [himself] as having done foolishly."

At the same time, he was impressed by her desire for spiritual growth. "There is no happiness but in holiness," she reflected to him to his utter delight. "So, the more holiness, the more happiness."

Wesley left Frederica in early September after he was assaulted by Mrs. Hawkins. Back in Savannah, he consulted with the Caustons about what he should do for their niece. In mid-October, he returned to Frederica—and to Sophy—with open-ended instructions to do what he thought best. The Caustons had seemed to imply that Sophy wanted—and indeed, needed—a husband, and that John would do.

In Frederica, the uncertain parson found Sophy disconsolate, regressing spiritually, and desirous of a return to England. He talked her out of returning to the homeland, but when he spoke with General Oglethorpe, he found that the governor had grown weary of the drama associated with the couple. Oglethorpe directed John to take Sophy back to Savannah. They traveled alone, except for a servant boy and crew, which put John in a compromising situation, as they were together while "none but the All-seeing Eye observed" them. Although they restrained their passions from "the great offense," they were not innocent of everything.

John's intense passions collided with his desire for holiness, and the sense of a divided soul is palpable in his writings at the time, as the minister tried to balance duty with desire.

The fall of 1736 proved to be a great struggle for Wesley. The Savannah pastor was falling in love with a young lady who had told him she would never marry anyone other than her former criminal beau. Wesley himself had pledged not to marry in America; but when he writes about Sophy, his descriptions are from a man in love. He was drawn to her simplicity in life, manner, and dress. He thought she was slow to speak, not angry or spiteful, and had a budding desire to serve God. When he consulted with his friends, he understood them to say that he should continue on in the relationship. Meanwhile, his tutoring sessions with Sophy continued to give way to physical caresses and kissing.

Riddled with guilt, more about the "insincerity" of failing to keep a "single eye" toward Sophy's well-being, Wesley resolved to break off physical contact with her. But his resolution failed after just ten days. Unable to control himself, he found in Sophy a willing partner through the next few weeks into December. If they ever went beyond hand-holding, embracing, and kissing, it is never revealed in his journals. What was at issue for Wesley, and what filled him with guilt, was his commitment to God and his sincerity before men—foundational values, in his mind, that were not to be broken.

In the spring and summer of 1737, Wesley committed a series of mis-steps that threatened any chance he had of a relationship with Sophy Hopkey and derailed his ministry opportunities in Savannah.

The year began with twenty days in Frederica. His reputation there was already in tatters as a result of his brother's falling-out. By then, he had concluded that all ministry was simply "beating the air." Even so, while he was in Frederica, his friends stoked the embers of his thoughts of marrying Sophy. They told him that even though Sophy had vowed to marry Tommy Mellichamp or no one at all, to them she had said she would marry "a very religious man." Wesley took this to mean that the only thing stopping Sophy from marrying him was his own weakening resolve not to marry. This struck terror in his heart and set the course for the decisions he would make over the next few months.

In late January, he left Frederica out of "utter despair of doing good." And, like Charles, he never returned. Back in Savannah, he began a time of discernment regarding his relationship with Sophy. However, imme-diately upon his return, they resumed "the familiarities" he had resolved to avoid, and he hinted at proposals of marriage. But this time it was

Sophy who raised objections to the idea of marriage. She thought it best for a "clergyman not to be encumbered with worldly cares."

Wesley was plainly confused and caught up in uncertainty from all directions. Was God really calling him to singleness? Was Sophy truly committed to singleness? And if not, was she committed to him? Further, there was confusion in his soul as to Sophy's suitability. Would she be a good mate for him? Would she help or hinder his striving after holiness? Could he continue to pursue what he believed his purpose was in reaching the Indians if he were married? All these questions flooded his mind and intersected with a complex mixture of his base passions.

To sort through the uncertainty, he consulted with friends he trusted. Even then he had trouble discerning the wisdom of their advice. He went to a Moravian pastor from whom he had been learning German and with whom he had sought insight into religion. When the German pastor suggested that there was no reason *not* to marry, Benjamin Ingham and Charles Delamotte "utterly disapproved" of the advice.

His colleagues' true thoughts soon became clear. Ingham in particular believed that Sophy was not what she seemed. He doubted her "sincerity in religion," chalking up Wesley's perception of piety to her "excellent natural temper," as well as her desire to enter into marriage with Wesley. Ingham therefore advised him to clear his head by leaving town for a few days to discern the situation without her presence. Wesley took his friend's advice.

Before leaving, he wrote a short note to Sophy explaining his departure: "I find, Miss Sophy, I can't take fire into my bosom and not be burned."

With a mind cleared of the noise that was building in Savannah, Wesley was once again able to view the situation less passionately. With the advice of his friends and his own reflection on the purpose for which he had come to America, he came to a decision. He would not marry Sophy, as it would "obstruct the design" of his going out among the Indians. Furthermore, he did not feel he was "strong enough to bear the complicated temptations of a married state."

When he returned to Savannah, he informed his friends of his decision and met with Sophy, telling her that he had decided not to marry "at least till [he had] been among the Indians."

Sophy in turn began to back away. She no longer came to his house alone and would no longer receive his tutoring. One consolation for Wesley was that he was able to visit her at her uncle's socially active home. But this was little comfort. These decisions set the relationship on a new and uncertain course. For most of February, their contact was more restrained, apart from a few, chance solitary encounters in which temptation once again took hold and they returned to their previous "familiarities."

Benjamin Ingham, who opposed Sophy most strongly, had left for England on February 26 to recruit more laborers. But when Charles Delamotte saw his pastor's resolve begin to weaken, he was greatly offended. With "many tears," he warned Wesley about the consequences of his actions and exhorted him to once again "weigh thoroughly the whole affair."

At Delamotte's request, Wesley reflected on the affair by prayer, fasting, and "deep consideration," but he was unable to "solve" the issue— or rather he lacked the strength to follow through with what he had already resolved. On March 4, he and Delamotte took three pieces of paper and wrote, "Marry" on one, "Think not of it this year," on another, and finally, "Think of it no more" on the last. After praying for half an hour, they cast lots to decide this issue of great importance. When the lot was cast, it said, "Think of it no more."

Wesley received this decision as "the goodness of God" but later wrote, "What [God] required of me was a costly sacrifice. . .such a companion as I never expected to find again, should I live a thousand years twice told." Though he initially embraced the decision, it did not end his burning desire.

Three days after the fateful casting of lots, the heartbroken lover was summoned to the chief magistrate's plantation. When he arrived, he saw

Sophy pacing outside, as if she were looking to speak with him. Despite his resolution not to speak with her alone, he went to talk to her. She immediately grabbed his hands, and they began a serious conversation that continued until they were interrupted by Mrs. Causton.

The next day, March 8, Wesley breakfasted with Sophy and Charles Delamotte, at which time he inquired about her relationship with her former suitor. She insisted she was no longer interested in Tommy Mellichamp. Wesley then inquired about another suitor, William Williamson, but Sophy insisted she had no inclination for him either.

Wesley wrote in his journal concerning his struggle to break off the relationship completely. He hoped that Sophy would be the one to end it, but in the blindness of his passion, he "saw less and less reason to expect" her to break it off. He felt captured, like a creature "who lay struggling in the net" unable to fulfill his resolve. But he was being deceived.

The next day, he was surprised to discover that Sophy had engaged herself that very night to William Williamson. He was, it seems, completely blindsided.

"I don't seem to be awake," he told Mrs. Causton when she informed him of the development. "Surely I am in a dream." But it was not a dream. Sophy had committed herself to a man who, according to Wesley's estimation, was "not remarkable for handsomeness, neither for genteelness, neither for wit or knowledge or sense, and least of all, for religion."

Wesley believed he could have scuttled the engagement by promising to marry Sophy himself—thus renouncing his pledge to God and the advice of his friends. But he restrained himself, and Sophy fled with her new fiancé to another town to be married just four days later on March 12.

Despite his own failures, foibles, and missteps, Wesley realized he had been deceived and lied to. His response to this is a complicated web that is impossible to untangle. Stating his willingness to overlook the personal insult of being spurned, he met with and counseled Sophy and her new husband half a dozen times through the spring and summer of 1737.

In his ministerial role, Wesley saw Sophy as a woman who had sinned and who was unwilling to repent, and he told her so. It is impossible to believe that, consciously or not, he wasn't driven to some degree by hurt feelings. Furthermore, Sophy was now in a new situation, and even if she would have preferred to have married Wesley, there was no advantage in making it known, either publicly or privately, that her husband was, in fact, her second choice.

Feeling attacked, she pulled away from the ministerial direction of her pastor, and her new husband understandably demanded that she no longer speak to Wesley. The problem with this was that the church had stipulated that anyone who desired to take Communion meet with the pastor the day before. Furthermore, at her husband's direction, Sophy had left off other practices as well to which she had once committed herself.

That summer, Wesley again entered into a period of discernment concerning Sophy. Could he in good conscience allow her access to the Lord's Table and thus overlook a sickness in her soul? Would he not be harming her soul by doing so?

His trusted companion Charles Delamotte encouraged him to "bear with her" and to continue to allow her to take Communion. But as Wesley continued to investigate and talk to others about Sophy—an act that makes him out to be a meddling gossip—he learned of the depths of her previous "dissimulations" and became even more concerned. Still, Delamotte encouraged Wesley to administer Communion to Sophy even as he confronted her in writing concerning her behavior. "The effect was not what I expected," Wesley noted. "However, if she die in her iniquity, 'I have delivered my own soul.'"

Eventually, Sophy stopped coming to receive Communion, and Wesley took careful note of this in his journal:

A new hindrance [to admitting Mrs. Williamson to Holy Communion] now occurred: she would not admit herself. Looking over the register, I found she had absented from it five times in April and May only; and in this month, June, four times more, viz., the 11th, 12th, 24th, and 29th.

By late summer, Wesley was making more enemies than friends in Savannah. In June, he had noted "the slippery ground" on which he stood. By August, his ministry was spiraling out of control.

The tipping point came on Sunday, August 7. Sophy had stopped attending services, including the Communion service, and she had not responded to the charges made by her pastor. Her uncle, the chief magistrate, chided Wesley for not dropping the matter, to which Wesley had replied, "Don't condemn me for doing in the execution of my office what I think it my duty to do."

Sophy came to receive sacrament of Communion for the first time in weeks; Wesley was surprised by her presumption. When she came forward to partake of the bread, Wesley "told her softly so that none could hear but herself, and in the mildest manner I was master of, 'I can't administer the Holy Communion to you before I have spoken with you.'"

"Repelled!" he wrote in his diary for the day. But Sophy, her husband, her aunt and uncle, and many others were outraged.

The fiercest storm that Wesley would ever see had begun to brew.

John Wesley insisted that his actions proved that he was not acting with respect to persons—that is, according special favor to the chief magistrate's daughter. Others insisted he was indeed acting with respect to one particular person—the one who had spurned his love. Though he had the law and the rubric of the church on his side, his actions made no common, social, or political sense. Instead, it appeared he was using the rubric of the church vengefully against someone who had hurt him personally.

On the following Monday, Sophy and her husband filed a legal complaint against the town parson for "defaming [her] and refusing to administer the Lord's Supper in a public congregation without cause."

The damages for which they demanded repayment was £1,000. Considering that Wesley's wages from the Society of the Propagation of the Gospel were £50 for his second year in Savannah, £1,000 was a vengeful amount to ask in damages. Nonetheless, a warrant was issued for Wesley's arrest, and he was brought before the bailiff on Tuesday. He denied the defamation charges and refused to accept civil charges on "purely ecclesiastical" matters. A court date was set.

In the meantime, people began to see Wesley as a hypocrite and a liar who was trying to break up marriages—a priest who admitted anyone to the Communion table except some out of spite and malice. Others were offended by what they viewed as Wesley's odd Christian practices and even heresy. Worse yet, he was seen as "a proud priest, whose view it was to be a bishop, a spiritual tyrant."

The issue divided the people against each other, revealing and magnifying already existing fissures. The environment in the city of Savannah was poisonous.

Sophy's uncle, Thomas Causton, was insulted and embarrassed by the entire affair. His house became the center of opposition against Wesley. As chief magistrate, the most powerful man in the city, Causton began to use his leverage against the man who had harmed his family, going so far as to bully anyone who would not stand against Wesley.

Two competing stories were circulating in Savannah. Wesley's camp contended that the minister had put the brakes on the romantic relationship and that his actions were not the result of being spurned. Sophy's camp insisted that it was she who had declined Wesley and that all his actions thereafter were the result of his "spite and malice."

Over the next several weeks, affidavits were signed by the various parties, a grand jury was convened—and enlarged, from twenty-six members to forty-four by Mr. Causton to "add weight" to their decisions and represent a "general sense of the people." Wesley believed that the numbers were increased in order to stack the jury against him.

Over the next few months, the grand jury met nearly a dozen times in the courthouse—the same building in which the weekly church services were held. On September 1, ten charges were issued against Wesley, including grievances stretching back to when he had refused to baptize the second bailiff's infant child by sprinkling. The next day, Wesley argued before the court that nine of the ten charges were ecclesiastical in nature, and thus not properly adjudicated in the courts. On the one "secular" charge—that of communicating with Sophy against her husband's consent—he requested a trial.

As if his legal troubles were not enough, Wesley's ministerial difficulties continued to spiral downward. Church attendance declined, and it became necessary for another minister to conduct services for the many citizens of Savannah who would not step inside the church as long as Wesley presided. Fearing that word of the case would soon spread to England, and especially to the trustees in London, Wesley began to consider leaving Georgia to get ahead of the accusations.

Some good news came when a dozen members of the grand jury sent a report to the trustees, calling into question all ten of the charges against Wesley. Even so, the case continued to be drawn out without going to trial, and by October, Wesley and his friends were seriously considering whether he should flee the colony.

Finally, in late November, seeing no hope of a fair resolution, the embattled parson announced his plans to depart. "Being now only a prisoner at large, in a place where I well knew every day would give fresh opportunities of procuring evidence for words I never spoke and actions I never did," he wrote on December 2, "I saw clearly I had nothing more to do but to fly for my life."

Shaking the dust of Savannah from his feet, he began the ninety-mile journey to Charleston to board a ship back to England.

"I went to America to convert the Indians," the defeated and failed missionary wrote dejectedly aboard the *Samuel*. "But Oh! who shall convert me? Who, what is he that will deliver me from this evil heart of unbelief?"

John Wesley departed America forever to return to the "beloved obscurity" of an Oxford fellow. During his time in Georgia, he had learned man's capacity for evil. But he also saw the evil in his own heart. He had gone to America a proud man; he left broken—uncertain not only of his calling, his mission, and his abilities, but even of his faith.

John Wesley squandered this early opportunity to serve the settlers of Georgia, and he was never able to fulfill the purpose for which he had gone—to minister among the Indians. But he was not the only one who had had a mission for the transatlantic trip. God used this failed endeavor to humble this very bright and devoted man and deliver him from a self-induced prison. Through Wesley's failure in Savannah, God began to set the stage to use him in new and powerful ways to reach multitudes with the hope of the Gospel.

Chapter 5
Strangely Warmed

How can you preach to others, who have not faith yourself?

John Wesley landed at Deal, on the Channel coast of England, on February 1, 1738. He returned to find a revival of religion taking place that would soon revive his own heart. Two years and four months earlier, he had left the same port brimming with confidence. Now he returned doubting human nature, himself, and—perhaps most important of all—his faith. For the previous few decades of his life, he had attempted to answer the question, "What must I do to be saved?" The progress he believed he had made in that time was lost all at once, and now he had to reexamine everything he knew and believed.

On his return voyage, he reflected on how he had been shaped by several teachings—the Lutherans and Calvinists, the English divines, the early church, and the mystics; but he also felt that they had misled him, as he was "tossed to and fro . . . with every wind of doctrine." The Lutherans and Calvinists, he believed, put an undue emphasis on faith over works and merit. The English divines—the founders of the Church by whom he had been trained and ordained—had a more balanced, middle way on that particular issue, but they failed to teach and practice church unity. He had been drawn to the teachings of the early church, viewing them as a unified and unadulterated representation of Christianity, and placed the ancient church on a "co-ordinate," or equal, authority with scripture. At the time, he failed to understand the complexities, diversity, and breadth of antiquity, but he was beginning to understand the diversity of teaching even during this early era. Finally, he had been drawn to the mystics' passionate love of God and withdrawal from the world, but soon found that they valued an abstract notion of love over obedience to God. He considered them "the most dangerous" of

Christianity's enemies and later called their notions "poisonous."

Now he turned to a different school—that of the Moravians, the pious Germans who had impressed him on his voyage to America, and with whom he interacted a great deal during his time in Georgia. It was in their teaching that he would find some of his answers.

In Georgia, he had become intimately acquainted with the intensity of the Moravians' faith. Now he made a careful study of biblical faith, which led him to write about his own desperate longings:

> *The faith I want is, "a sure trust and confidence in God, that through the merits of Christ my sins are forgiven, and I reconciled to the favour of God." I want that faith which St. Paul recommends to all the world, especially in his Epistle to the Romans; that faith which enables everyone that hath it to cry out, "I live not, but Christ liveth in me; and the life which I now live, I live by faith in the Son of God, who loved me and gave himself for me." I want that faith which none can have without knowing that he hath it (though many imagine they have it who have it not). For whosoever hath it is "freed from sin"; "the whole body of sin is destroyed" in him. He is freed from fear, "having peace with God through Christ, and rejoicing in hope of the glory of God." And he is freed from doubt, "having the love of God shed abroad in his heart through the Holy Ghost which is given unto him"; which "Spirit itself beareth witness with his spirit, that he is a child of God."*

The faith that John Wesley wanted was the faith he would soon receive and then teach for the next five decades.

Returning as a failed missionary, John Wesley was intent on resuming his academic fellowship at Oxford, but his plans were soon interrupted. Whether out of duty or to protect his reputation, he was "detained in London...by the Trustees [of Georgia]" and thus prevented from going directly to Oxford. At his first meetings with the trustees, he shared his observations of the colony and its issues and attempted to sabotage Thomas Causton, the chief magistrate of Savannah and Wesley's chief rival, by criticizing Causton's "mal-administration." But, before long, Wesley was answering for his own actions. Though historical evidence vindicates Wesley in some of the conflicts he had with the volatile colonists in Georgia, at least some of the trustees saw through to his hypocrisy and indiscretions.

Wesley was already mindful of his personal failings even as he reflected on the storm he had created and passed through in Georgia. Indeed, he resolved once again to control his time, conversation, and company toward the glory of God. His journals during this time reveal a palpable tension between his failures and his faith.

Though facing doubts deep within his soul, while he was stuck in London he was given multiple opportunities to preach, as there was a great spiritual hunger there. Indeed, his contemporary journal lists nearly twenty engagements from February to late May; and forty years later, he reflected that during this time he often preached multiple times a day—on weekdays as well as Sundays.

But then a new and peculiar thing began to happen. Churches that invited him and heard him banned him from returning to their pulpits. His messages were controversial, the people were stirred up, and the parish priests were unhappy with the disturbances. Of several parishes, Wesley wryly notes in his journal, "I was not to preach there anymore."

All the while, he wondered whether he should be preaching *anywhere*, not because he was getting kicked out of the pulpits, but because he was not sure he had an authentic faith. "Leave off preaching," he said to himself. "How can you preach to others, who have not faith yourself?" By preaching what he did not feel he had, he was guilty of violating one of his most treasured virtues—sincerity.

The steady Moravian influence in Wesley's life continued in London with the arrival of Peter Böhler from Germany in early February. Böhler had been ordained by Count Zinzendorf in Berlin in 1737—the count's first act after his own consecration as bishop of the Moravians. Böhler, as part of the Moravians' missionary endeavor, was headed to America, but he had stopped for several months in England on his way.

Though Wesley's junior by nine years, Böhler quickly gained his confidence. Wesley helped the young German find lodging in London, and in late February the two traveled together to Oxford, where Charles lay sick, fighting pleurisy. The journey gave the two men an opportunity to enter into deep conversation, culminating in a gentle rebuke by Böhler of his elder, Wesley: "My brother, my brother, that philosophy of yours must be purged away."

Wesley returned to London two days later while Böhler remained in Oxford with Charles, who seemed to be winning the fight with his illness. However, in early March, Charles's health took a turn for the worse, so John promptly returned to Oxford for what he believed would be his brother's imminent death. But by the time John arrived, Charles was on the mend, and John was able to resume his conversation with Peter Böhler. As these talks continued, John began to wonder about his own belief in contrast to the faith he saw in the German minister.

He asked his German friend if he should abandon preaching, to which the pious Moravian responded, "By no means."

"But what can I preach?" he asked.

"Preach faith *till* you have it," Böhler replied. "And then, *because* you have it, you *will* preach faith." This resolved Wesley's conflict temporarily, until one month later, on April 23, when he asked Böhler the same question again.

"Do not hide in the earth the talent God hath given to you," Böhler advised.

With this advice and comfort, Wesley continued to preach, despite his doubts.

At Peter Böhler's insistence, Wesley began preaching a doctrine that was entirely new to him: salvation by faith alone, which was a central doctrine of the Reformation. For the previous ten years, he had believed and taught that people are "justified by works." It had been the impulse behind all his religious activity and the reason for which he had cast aside the comforts of England to go as a missionary to America. But in all the activity, he had failed to achieve the intended goal, and the results in America had been catastrophic.

Though Wesley wanted the same powerful and sincere faith that the Moravians had—if it were true—he could not yet fully grasp or embrace the doctrine of salvation by faith alone. Nevertheless, he began preaching this faith. However, when the first audience for this new message was a prisoner under a death sentence with whom Böhler had insisted Wesley share this good news, his "soul started back from the work."

But if salvation by faith was a hard enough pill for Wesley to swallow whole, the necessary corollaries of instantaneous and deathbed conversions were an "impossibility" to one who had striven for salvation for most of his life. So, for three weeks, Wesley backed away from presenting the offer of grace to the condemned man.

On the day of the man's execution, Wesley returned to preach to and pray with him. Before the convict went to be executed, John saw him kneel down to pray, after which he rose up and declared, "I am now ready to die. I know Christ has taken away my sins, and there is no more condemnation for me." According to Wesley, the man went to his death in "composed cheerfulness" and "perfect peace." Still, Wesley, ever the rigorous moralist, could not accept the instantaneous nature of salvation by faith.

He began to investigate the three pillars of his understanding of truth: his church tradition, the scriptures, and the experience of others. Through the *Homilies of the Church of England*—foundational sermons disseminated throughout the church at its founding during the English Reformation—Wesley found that his own church's teaching was in line with what Böhler and the Moravians were teaching concerning salvation by faith alone. One of the homilies that deeply impressed Wesley, "On the Salvation of Mankind," asserts that true faith is not "only to believe that holy Scripture" and all the doctrinal teachings of faith are true, but that true faith is "a sure trust and confidence which a man hath in God, that through the merits of Christ *his* sins are forgiven, and *he* reconciled to the favour of God." More than merely propositional, it is a very personal faith.

In addition to the teaching of the Church of England, Wesley also turned to the scriptures, and what he found surprised him. In his study of the book of Acts, he found that Paul's conversion took three days, but virtually all other conversion descriptions were instantaneous. So the scriptural case was in favor of this "novel" doctrine. And finally, he met and heard the testimonies of multiple people who had experienced similar instantaneous conversions. These three pillars together—his tradition, his study of scripture, and his experiences—caused his defenses against the new doctrine to fall rapidly. The last line of defense was within his own heart.

If John Wesley was perplexed by the "new" doctrine, Charles was downright angry to hear his older brother speak of himself as having no faith and that instantaneous conversion was possible. But the anger set in motion some self-examination on Charles's part concerning whether he was "in the faith."

By early May, the brothers' chief instigator of these questions, Peter Böhler, was set to depart for his intended mission to America. Before leaving, he organized some devout men from both England and Germany into a society in which they would confess their sins and pray for one another per the command of James 5:16. The society was to be a large group meeting that was broken into *bands*—smaller groups of five to ten men who gathered weekly on Wednesday evenings. The society was open to any man who met criteria of transparency and striving after moral rectitude, and it soon grew into what was called the Fetter Lane Society.

Peter Böhler departed England on May 4, leaving the Wesleys to sort out their questions about faith on their own. But both brothers were becoming convinced of this new teaching, in spite of reservations deep within their souls.

In a letter John received on May 10, Böhler shows himself to be a man who cared deeply for Wesley's soul and prayed much for his transformation:

I love you greatly, and think much of you in my journey, wishing and praying that the tender mercies of Jesus Christ the crucified, whose bowels were moved toward you more than six thousand years ago, may be manifested to your soul; that you may taste, and then see, how exceedingly the Son of God has loved you, and loves you still, and that so you may continually trust in him, and feel his life in yourself.

This message was one that John Wesley was yet to fully receive. And because he had not yet embraced it, he continued to struggle with the appropriateness of his preaching. Writing to a friend, he bemoaned:

O why is it that so great, so wise, so holy a God, will use such an instrument as me! Lord, "let the dead bury their dead"! But wilt thou send the dead to raise the dead? Yea, thou sendest whom thou wilt send, and showest mercy by whom thou wilt show mercy! Amen! Be it then according to thy will! If thou speak the word, Judas shall cast out devils.

By early 1738, John Wesley was a man who appeared on the outside to be a model Christian—orthodox (enough) and obedient (enough)—but in his inner soul he had grave doubts. He was, in his later estimation, just a half Christian, or an "almost Christian" holding the "form of godliness" but lacking its power.

Charles was angry at first at questions about his faith and John's, but he was also the first to find resolution to his questions. That spring, as he battled yet another illness, he also came to the conviction that he was "without Christ." At the same time, like his elder brother, he became convinced of the scriptural teaching of justification by faith alone, which he discovered in the overlooked *Articles and Homilies of the Church of England* and confirmed in the writings of sixteenth-century German reformer Martin Luther.

On May 21, 1738, the Day of Pentecost, as Charles lay in bed in uneasiness of soul, desiring a word from the Lord, someone he could not see walked into his room and said, "In the name of Jesus of Nazareth, arise, and believe, and thou shalt be healed of all thy infirmities." While he sought to investigate who it was who had spoken the words, he wondered if it might be Christ himself speaking through the person, and he felt a "strange palpitation of heart" after which he became convinced that he now had faith.

When John heard these reports, he came to meet and pray with the spiritually renewed Charles, who continued to fight his sickness. During the prayer, Charles said that he "almost believed the Holy Ghost was coming upon" his brother John. This hope and expectation, however, was premature.

The turning point for John came two days later on the evening of May 24, when some friends persuaded him to join them for a society meeting at Aldersgate Street in the north of London. At the meeting, to which John went with some reluctance, a man was reading Martin Luther's preface to the book of Romans.

Of all the documents that could have been read, few would have intersected more appropriately with Wesley's own questions about faith. In the preface, Luther calls the book of Romans the "purest Gospel" of the New Testament. Before an explanatory outline of Paul's letter, he deftly defines its most important terms: *law, sin, grace, faith, justice, flesh,* and *spirit,* among others. One of the most important things the preface asserts is that all sin is ultimately seated in the heart, and because man's heart is inherently sinful, no outward act of obedience to the law is sufficient to fulfill the law of God. To fulfill the law, one's heart must be changed by the Holy Spirit, which can only happen by faith. The result of this faith, then, is a love of the law, which is demonstrated by obedience to it.

This preface was a powerful refutation of the previous ten or more years of Wesley's life. He had striven to fulfill the law of God through his rigorous self-discipline, and by most outward appearances seemed to be fulfilling the law—though even outwardly he was failing. What he needed to hear that night, and what indeed he heard, was that his heart—his innermost being—needed change. And it *could* be changed "through faith in Christ."

As the reading continued, that heart-level change began taking root in John Wesley. As he later famously wrote in his journal for this momentous day, "I felt my heart strangely warmed." What followed from this experience was a newfound peace in his soul and a new power over sin that he had not had before. As a result, he began to reflect on what was happening inside his soul.

The Church of England homilies that had been the subject of his study concerning the Church's teaching on faith describe salvation by faith as "a sure trust and confidence which a man hath in God, that through the merits of Christ *his* sins are forgiven, and *he* reconciled to the favour of God." Now Wesley was ascribing to himself this saving faith:

> *I felt I did trust in Christ, Christ alone for salvation, and an assurance was given me that he had taken away my sins, even mine, and saved me from the law of sin and death.*

The transformation of John Wesley had reached a remarkable climax that was about to shake the world.

Evaluating what took place on the night of May 24, 1738, is the subject of much speculation to this day. Indeed, it is difficult to accept the possibility that a man who had so thoroughly dedicated his life to God could really lack justifying faith.

But this is exactly what Wesley himself suggested in the aftermath of his experience at Aldersgate. His journal entry for the day—likely written as a memorandum some days later—is a lengthy appraisal and spiritual biography. After his return from America—he writes in that memo—he sought and prayed for "justifying, saving faith, a full reliance on the blood of Christ shed for *me*," rather than a reliance on his own righteousness. He made the same claims three years later—within a year of the publication of his first published journal describing this event—in a sermon suggesting that prior to this time, he "was but 'almost a Christian.'"

He was so adamant about his seemingly late conversion that three days after his Aldersgate experience, he caused a disturbance at the home of John Hutton after the host read a sermon to a religious gathering. In a moment of unchecked zeal, John surprised the group by standing up and insisting that five days earlier, he had not been a Christian. As a witness attested, "This he was as well assured of as that five days before he was not in that room." As if this were not enough to shock the sensibilities of those gathered, he also began to insist that all those gathered must recognize that they were not Christians either.

An argument immediately ensued, and the host charged Wesley to "have a care" not to disparage "the benefits received by the two sacraments," baptism and Holy Communion. This put the finger on the change that had taken place in Wesley's thinking. Herein, he believed, lay the grand delusion that he would spend the next several years of his life fighting—the teaching that at baptism a person is "born again" (as the Reverend Tipping Sylvester had preached at St. Mary's, Oxford, on February 26, 1738), and that a baptized person is saved unless he or she commits apostasy or a "mortal sin" and does not repent.

Elizabeth Hutton called Wesley "a great hypocrite" for having convinced everyone beforehand that he was indeed a Christian. She was greatly concerned not just about John, but about how he had influenced her grown children. She wrote a letter to Samuel Wesley Jr., John's elder brother, who was now headmaster of Blundell's School in Tiverton, informing him that "John seems to be turned a wild enthusiast, or fanatic," and asking Samuel to help "put a stop to the madness."

But there was no stopping John now; the "madness" was just beginning.

The question of how exactly John Wesley's experience at Aldersgate affected his salvation is one that only God can answer. From Wesley's point of view, the importance of that momentous day only became more muddled as the years went on. Indeed, if it was hard for his contemporaries to believe that he had not been a true Christian prior to May of 1738, it was also difficult for Wesley himself as he reflected on those years later in his life.

Beginning with the 1774 edition of his journal, written more than thirty-five years after Aldersgate, Wesley inserted clarifications and modifications to his narrative by use of a corrigenda and corrections to the text. The first such modification is found on February 1: "That I who went to America to convert others, was never myself converted to God." Here he adds a note: "I am not sure of this."

Later in the same journal, he adds notes to descriptions of doubts about his faith prior to Aldersgate by suggesting that, at the time, he "had then the faith of a *servant*, though not that of a *son*." This is a reference to a distinction he later made regarding his interpretation of the conversion of Cornelius in Acts 10, the book of Galatians, and his view of salvation. In all, these and a handful of other notes in his memorandum concerning his experience on May 24, 1738, serve to chip away at his original conclusions.

Why he inserted the modifications three and a half decades after the fact has been the subject of much speculation. One can only surmise, but here are three possible explanations.

First, during the intervening thirty-five years, his theology concerning faith shifted after he rejected the stringent and skeptical view of faith taught by the Moravians. As time moved on, he revised his thinking about how one experienced faith and what it really changed.

Second, thirty-five years is enough time to dull the acute pain of his seeming hypocrisy, which stood in such stark contrast to the dramatic relief he felt in 1738. The passage of time sometimes brings dispassionate clarity—or brings less clarity—to events of the past. Which of these outcomes more accurately describes Wesley's recollections is open to debate.

Finally, over the course of three decades, the emphasis of his ministry shifted from a primary focus on justification to the development of his distinctive teaching on entire sanctification. An experiential event, such as what occurred at Aldersgate in 1738, was not an end in itself, but merely the means to an end. As Wesley would later explain, repentance is the "porch," faith is the "door," and holiness is "religion itself." Some, by focusing on a singular justification experience, were rejecting his notion of true religion.

What is irrefutably important about Aldersgate is that it marked a significant transformation in Wesley's life. His personality, theology, and ministry were all affected. Some months earlier, he had come to a cerebral conviction that salvation came through faith alone; but at Aldersgate, he had embraced this faith for himself and gained the confidence to preach it. Thereafter, he dedicated his life to sharing the genuine faith that for so long had eluded him, and the faith that, he was convinced, the multitudes of professing Christians in England had thus far rejected. In Wesley's estimation, the Reformation truth of salvation by faith alone had not yet reached the masses. His own transformation, he hoped, would become a model for the transformation he would bring, by God's grace, to every highway and byway in England.

Part II

Controversies and Opportunities

Chapter 6
Closed Doors

For though a great door and effectual had been opened,
the adversary had laid so many stumbling-blocks before it
that the weak were daily turned out of the way.

The doors of John Wesley's ministry were quickly closing when he returned to England in 1738. Even before his Aldersgate experience in May, he had become, along with the other Methodists, an increasingly controversial figure in London and Oxford because he was drawing "unwieldy crowds" and because of his "unfashionable doctrine" of salvation by faith. But he was also controversial because of his teaching on free grace and on Christian perfection—that there is a state of Christian maturity in which a Christian is freed from willful transgression of the known laws of God. Furthermore, he was roundly criticized for the dramatic physical phenomena that accompanied his preaching—people falling down "as dead," crying or screaming out in agony, among other things.

Two and a half weeks after he had claimed faith for himself in London, Wesley returned to Oxford to preach at the University Church of St. Mary. His topic was "Salvation by Faith," and he chose as his text Ephesians 2:8: "For by grace are ye saved through faith." Before that august academic audience, he laid out his doctrine, warning against deficient views of faith, and explained his concept of layers of faith that would continue to grow.

The first layer is "the faith of the heathen"—who are required to believe that "God is" and that there is a coming judgment—that ultimately leads to a life of virtue.

The second layer is "the faith of the devil." The devil has received more special revelation than the heathen and believes that Jesus is "the

Holy One of God" (Luke 4:34) in addition to other objective realities. But this faith, too, is deficient in bringing salvation.

After noting these two incomplete layers of faith, Wesley asserted that a true, saving faith "is not barely a speculative, rational thing; a cold lifeless assent, a train of ideas in the head; but also a disposition of the heart." Therein lies the foundation of Wesley's teaching and ministry: religion is not simply a life of virtue, or of the mind; religion resides in the heart.

The message was received apathetically by the community of academics, who, according to one report, viewed Wesley as a little "crackbrained." The sermon itself, however, is a lucid explanation of his nascent doctrine. And even though the message had little discernible effect on Wesley's original audience, he published it at the encouragement of friends—the first of his post-Aldersgate published sermons. In every volume of collected sermons published in later years, he placed this sermon first, along with an edited collection of the *Homilies of the Church of England*, not merely because it was his first published sermon post-Aldersgate, but because he viewed it as the most important and foundational teaching he had. For Wesley, the doctrine of salvation by faith "is, and must be, the foundation of all our preaching; that is, [it] must be preached first."

Ever since his encounter with the Moravians on the transatlantic journey to Georgia, Wesley had determined to see the power of God at work with his own eyes. To do so, he had to go to the center of the revival, in Herrnhut, Germany. The fact that he had no pupils at Oxford and no parish under his authority made it possible for him to go in June 1738 on a three-month journey—along with Benjamin Ingham, who had also accompanied him to Georgia—to see "the place where the Christians live" in the "full power of faith."

Even though, in a sense he was enamored of these deeply spiritual people and greatly affected personally, Wesley went to Herrnhut with a degree of skepticism. When he arrived, he wrote in his journal that he "had now abundant opportunity of observing whether what I had heard was enlarged by the relators, or was neither more nor less than the naked truth."Though he doesn't openly answer this question, there is reason to suggest he was disappointed by what he found, even while being deeply impressed by a society whose very structure was centered on spirituality.

But even as he was evaluating the Moravians, the Moravians were evaluating him. According to the memoirs of James Hutton, an English Moravian and one of Wesley's first converts, the Moravian community's view of Wesley was less than flattering. With details not included in Wesley's own accounts, Hutton's memoir suggests that when Wesley and Ingham reached the Moravian settlement of Marienborn on July 4, the congregation there found Wesley to be "*homo perturbatus*"—that is, "a confused man"—whose "head had gained ascendancy over his heart"; therefore, they had denied him access to the Lord's Table, even while admitting Ingham.

Hutton, who later became the leader of the English Moravians, suggested that Wesley, in response to the slight, "brooded over" the offense and shared his discontent privately with others. Even at this time, Hutton suggests, Wesley "had a desire to be the head of a party" of his own.

If all of this is true, Wesley makes no mention of it. But fissures in his relationship with the Moravians were certainly growing. While in Herrnhut, he wrote letters to family and friends back home, reporting glowingly of the "spirit of meekness and love" of the German church. But by the time he returned to England in September, he had drafted a stinging letter to the Moravian church with questions and rebukes. However, not trusting his own judgment, he withheld the criticisms and never sent the letter. Instead, he allowed the embers to cool for two weeks before penning letters to the Moravian community in general, and another to their leader, Count Zinzendorf, expressing not criticism, but gratitude "for giving me to be an eyewitness of your faith and love and holy conversation in Christ Jesus."

Still, within two years, the gulf between Wesley and the Moravians would grow into an impassable divide.

Wesley returned to London on September 16 and immersed himself in ministering to the dozens of independent London societies that were meeting in homes and large rooms around the city. In particular, he returned to the Fetter Lane Society, the Moravian-style group of English Christians that Peter Böhler had founded during the spring. There he discovered that "though a great door and effectual had been opened, the adversary had laid so many stumbling-blocks before it that the weak were daily turned out of the way." There were "misunderstandings" and "evil-speaking," which threatened to tear "the little flock" apart. The society had grown to include more than fifty men and youths, who were further divided into smaller bands.

In addition, he found other society meetings in London at which he could preach to crowds that were swelling to some four hundred persons, and where he could "publish the word of reconciliation."

But the same could not be said for the London parishes. By October, he was banned from preaching in no fewer than a dozen churches, and the list continued to grow.

He spent most of November and into December in Oxford, where at first he found "a little revival of [God's] power." But soon he found doors closing on him once again. When one of his key supporters left Oxford, Wesley wrote to a friend in London, "There is none besides that joins with my brother [Charles] and me cordially."

The new year of 1739 proved no better. When John returned to London, the list of churches in which he and Charles could not preach continued to expand.

He was clearly frustrated.

Although most pulpits in the Church of England were increasingly closed to Wesley, he still found open doors to preach at societies in London and Oxford, as well as in the homes and building spaces of supporters of the new movement of evangelical preachers. In February, he reported gleefully to fellow preacher and friend George Whitefield, who was then in Bristol, "Our Lord's hand is not shortened amongst us." When churches such as at St. Katherine's and Islington in London opened their pulpits to Wesley, hundreds flocked to hear him expound the scriptures. Wesley observed that it was as "hot" spiritually as at other meetings, and "the fields after service [were] white with people praising God."

Private meetings such as the ones that Wesley and others conducted were generally tolerated prior to the burgeoning evangelical movement led by George Whitefield and others. But the growing revival soon threatened the authority structure of the Established Church.

Over half a century earlier, Wesley's grandparents had been persecuted as "dissenters" of the national church on account of the Act of Uniformity of 1662. The persecution had been mitigated in later years by passage of the Act of Toleration in 1689, which made private meetings legal if they were registered and if the leaders pledged allegiance to the royal authority. By the late 1730s, the political circumstances and purpose for which the laws had been passed had changed dramatically. Wesley argued that none of the meetings of which he was a part would threaten the monarchy. Furthermore, as a man who committed himself to the success of the Established Church for the rest of his life, he believed he was doing more to support it than many of the ministers who worked within the Established Church.

John's elder brother, Samuel, had already expressed concern about his younger brother's Aldersgate experience and resultant "enthusiasms," but by 1739 he was also worried that John would be seen as subverting the church's authority.

"You spoke in buildings not consecrated," Samuel charged in a letter to his unconventional brother. Further, he accused him of "not using the liturgy, and praying extemporarily"—the latter of which was an entirely new development for the newly reformed high church minister.

John returned to Oxford in March, but as a pupil-less tutor, he did not fully resume his duties and thus became ostracized among his academic peers. He did, however, find ministry opportunities elsewhere in town. At a gathering in a home in Oxford, he met a woman "who was above measure enraged at 'this new way.'" After a few minutes of fruitless and inflamed argument, he "broke off the dispute" and asked the woman to kneel with him in prayer. When she complied, she fell into "extreme agony, both of body and soul" before crying out, "Now I know, I am forgiven for Christ's sake." According to Wesley, "From that hour, God hath set her face like a flint to declare the faith which before she persecuted."

Wesley was reluctant to enter directly into personal controversy, but neither did he shy away from it. Two days after the miraculous transformation of the woman in Oxford, while Wesley was meeting with her and some of her neighbors, a man "of the same spirit she had been of" entered the gathering and was "labouring to pervert the truth of the gospel." Wesley, his reticence notwithstanding, "as the less evil of the two. . .entered directly into the controversy" of the "new way."

As Wesley declared the biblical case for justification by faith, a woman at the gathering "felt, as it were, the piercing of a sword" and began crying out in the street. Wesley led the gathered worshipers in prayer, and "no sooner had we made our request known to God than he sent her help from his holy place."

Though Wesley would never abandon argumentation altogether, he increasingly found that the power of his arguments were fleeting compared with the power of prayer and the power of the ever-persuasive God.

Despite these obstacles and discouragements, the fact that traditional forms of ministry were closing to Wesley soon led to his greatest opportunity.

Chapter 7
Open Fields

The word of God ran as fire among the stubble.

If by preaching at society meetings and in private homes Wesley was seen as pushing the envelope of his preaching authority, his friend George Whitefield was blowing up the envelope entirely with a practice hitherto unseen in eighteenth-century England: preaching outdoors, or field preaching, as it came to be known. Even as the churches closed their pulpits to the new, young evangelical preachers, it was becoming apparent that the church buildings could not contain the crowds that field preaching attracted. A church could hold a few hundred at most, but an open field could accommodate thousands—as far as the preacher's voice could carry. According to Benjamin Franklin, the famous American inventor and statesman, Whitefield's voice could be heard at a distance of sixty-five yards in a rough semicircle. And though Whitefield was just twenty-four years old in 1739, he delighted his vast audiences with his rhetoric and his delivery.

Whitefield had gone to Georgia in early 1738 to pick up the broken pieces left by the departure of the Wesley brothers, who had left in shame. For Whitefield, this was the beginning of an extraordinarily successful ministry throughout America. Not only was his preaching well received, but he also gained a vision for an orphanage for the many parentless children in the dysfunctional new colony.

By late 1738, Whitefield decided to return to England to raise funds for the orphanage. But like John Wesley before him, he soon found himself turned out of churches on account of his evangelical theology.

Though Wesley's mother had observed of him as a child that he "would not attend to the most pressing necessities of nature, unless he could give a reason for it," Whitefield was far less cautious. In February

1739, when pressed out of the pulpit in Kingswood, outside of Bristol, he began preaching in the open air to the rough, uncouth coal miners.

Whitefield's ministry in England sparked the beginning of the evangelical revival there. Still, his mission in the spring of 1739 was to raise funds for the orphanage and return to America as soon as possible. But he did not want to desert the blossoming work in Bristol without another laborer for the Gospel to take his place. So he wrote to John Wesley, whom he considered his friend and something of a mentor, and pleaded for Wesley to come relieve him of the ministry. "There is a glorious door opened among the colliers," he wrote.

For Wesley, there was much at stake in accepting the invitation to go to Bristol. First, he knew that by joining the evangelical movement to minister in place of his younger friend, he would cross the divide established by the Church he had dedicated himself to serve. Furthermore, he knew that imprisonment and even death were likely possibilities if he entered into this type of ministry.

By now, Wesley was dealing somewhat methodically with such weighty and timely decisions. When a "speedy determination" was to be made, he resorted to an interesting and controversial method of discerning the will of God. First, he looked for peace within his own soul. This he clearly did not have regarding Bristol. Lacking peace, he turned to the advice of trusted counselors, for whom he laid out all sides of an issue. Early in his ministry, he regarded the opinions and insights of others as almost more important than his own. He was deeply suspicious of his own motives and desires and believed others could temper his blind spots. This led him to his brother Charles and his spiritual brothers at Fetter Lane, all of whom expressed concern that going to Bristol could lead to John's death. But even concerns for his safety were not enough to settle a decision of such importance. In the end, after deciding that his trusted advisers could not be trusted as dispassionate on this issue, he resorted to two controversial methods he had learned from the Moravians: the practice of bibliomancy and casting lots.

Bibliomancy, or as Wesley called it, "opening the Bible," is a method of randomly turning to a particular page in the Bible and discerning God's will for a current situation based on the passage—or several passages—found there. His critics are often quick to note that this practice has no clear biblical precedent.

When Wesley finally turned to the third step and "opened the Bible" for answers about Bristol, he came to several passages related to death and persecution for the gospel. Though these passages encouraged him to persevere through persecution, they did not give him specific clarity about whether he should face that persecution in Bristol on this partic-ular occasion, rather than, say, London, Oxford, or anywhere else.

Finally, he turned to casting lots, a practice that, unlike bibliomancy, has clear biblical precedents—though some critics have noted that there is no record in the Bible of Christians casting lots after the apostles receive the Holy Spirit at Pentecost (Acts 2). Wesley throughout his life defended the practices of bibliomancy and casting lots, arguing that while scripture does not command the methods, neither does it prohibit them. This was a key determination for Wesley and a rejection of the Puritan rule of admitting nothing that the Bible does not explicitly teach.

By casting lots, Wesley determined that he should go to Bristol—a decision that marked "a new period" and a major shift in his ministry. If he wanted open doors for ministry, he would have to push them open himself.

When the reluctant preacher arrived in Bristol on March 31, he went to observe George Whitefield and "this *strange way* of preaching in the fields." He was clearly awestruck. In a letter to friends back in London, he writes, "Oh how is God manifested in our brother Whitefield! I have seen none like him—no, not in Herrnhut!"

That same evening, Wesley preached (indoors) to the Nicholas Street Society, choosing as his text the Sermon on the Mount, which he called "one pretty remarkable instance of *field preaching*." Whether he actively sought scriptural precedents for field preaching or not, he found it very clearly in the method of the Master. The Sermon on the Mount would serve as his first defense (if only for himself) of the practice he entered upon the very next day.

On April 2, 1739, Wesley, who had always been "tenacious of every point relating to decency and order," and who was usually more reticent and calculating, stood on "a little eminence" at a brickyard on the outskirts of Bristol and preached in this "unusual manner" to some three thousand souls (by his own estimation), thus stepping over a boundary and setting his course definitively away from ministry within the walls of the church that had nurtured him. In stepping out, he became a pastor to those who would never set foot in a church building. He had found the largest congregation of people in England—the congregation of the unchurched.

Preaching in the open air was explicit evidence that a preacher had been closed out from the local parish. And it was also a bold rejection of the authority of that parish. Wesley felt that tension. Before this "new period," he confessed, he "should have thought the saving of souls *almost a sin* if it had not been done *in a church*." He had already implicitly defended the practice by preaching on Jesus' own "field preaching" in the Sermon on the Mount, but now he needed to make a more articulate and spirited defense.

Perhaps the most extensive defense available is a letter he wrote to a critic whose identity is uncertain. The letter, addressed only to "Dear Sir," is to someone who had known Wesley since his Oxford Holy Club days, and who, like others, questioned Wesley's claim that he had not been a Christian before Aldersgate. To this critic, Wesley begins his defense of field preaching with an explanation of his recent spiritual journey and the need of true faith for the world. "If you ask on what principle, then, I acted," Wesley writes, "it was this: a desire to be a Christian, and a conviction that whatever I judge conducive thereto, that I am bound to do. . .and on the same [principle] am I ready now (God being my helper) to go to Abyssinia or China, or whither soever it shall please God by this conviction to call me."

His critical correspondent questioned why Wesley should not just return to Oxford as a fellow, or "accept the cure of souls" in parish ministry and "sit still" until such time, so as not to "invade another's office."

Wesley responded that these offices were closed to him. To another correspondent several months later, he wrote concerning the same critique, "I [cannot] be said to 'intrude into the labours' of those who do not labour at all, but suffer thousands of those for whom Christ died to 'perish for lack of knowledge.'"

In his initial defense to the first correspondent, Wesley turns to scriptural grounds for his ministry:

> *God in Scripture commands me, according to my power, to instruct*
> *the ignorant, reform the wicked, confirm the virtuous. Man forbids*
> *me to do this in another's parish: that is, in effect, to do it at all;*
> *seeing I have now no parish of my own, nor probably ever shall.*
> *Whom, then, shall I hear, God or man? "If it be just to obey man*
> *rather than God, judge you. A dispensation of the gospel is committed*
> *to me; and woe is me if I preach not the gospel."*

Wesley saw in scripture a command to minister everywhere, and to everyone. Man had claimed every locale by dividing into parishes England, Europe, Asia, America—even the Indians were under the parish of Savannah and Frederica. Wesley called into question the authority that the church claimed for itself when ministers attempted to supersede the clear commands of God. And then, after making his arguments, he made his most famous defense of his new ministry: "I look upon *all the world as my parish.*"

> *[In] whatever part of [the world] I am, I judge it meet, right,*
> *and my bounden duty to declare, unto all that are willing to hear,*
> *the glad tidings of salvation. This is the work which I know God*
> *has called me to; and sure I am that His blessing attends it. Great*
> *encouragement have I, therefore, to be faithful in fulfilling the work*
> *He hath given me to do. His servant I am; and, as such, am em-*
> *ployed according to the plain direction of his Word, "As I have oppor-*
> *tunity, doing good unto all men." And his providence clearly concurs*
> *with his Word, which has disengaged me from all things else that I*
> *might singly attend on this very thing, "and go about doing good."*

The fields were "white already to harvest." Wesley later reflected on the early days of his field preaching and the beginning of the evangelical revival that "the word of God ran as fire among the stubble." After he started field preaching at the brickyard, he remained in Bristol for the next five months, returning to London only for a week in June. He wrote to Charles on April 9, explaining the danger at Bristol: "The clergy here *gladiatorio anirno ad nos affectant viarn* [aim at us with gladiatorial intent]. But the people of all sorts receive the Word gladly."

Wesley made it his practice to visit and preach daily in the Bristol prison, but he was banned from this daily practice in mid-May. By July, he was prohibited from preaching in the prison at all. To add to the number of closed doors, the Baldwin Street Society—one of his main preaching venues—was not permitted to meet in their regular building and had to find another location.

His schedule in Bristol during this time is dizzying. He preached two or three times a day in locations that ranged throughout the Bristol area—Weavers' Hall, Pensford, Bath, Two Mile Hill, Baptist Mills, Newgate Prison, Hanham Mountain, Clifton, Rose Green, Baldwin and Nicholas Streets, Fishponds, and Conham. In short, he preached wherever and whenever he could.

In Kingswood, a small coal mining village outside of Bristol, George Whitefield had laid the cornerstone of a school before departing for London on his way back to America. In Whitefield's absence, Wesley oversaw the building to completion in July and would oversee its work for the rest of his life.

Throughout this time, he made the transition from aristocratic high churchman to plain—though highly educated and capable—minister to the people. Just a few years earlier, during his failed ministry in Savannah, one observer had faulted him for "a metaphysical discourse" that would have been "better adapted. . .to a learned audience than such a poor, thin congregation of people, who rather stood in need of plain doctrine." Now he had shifted his philosophy and practice of preaching.

"I design," he wrote in the preface to a collection of his sermons first published in 1746, "plain truths for plain people." He stripped his messages of intellectual phrases (for the most part) and doctrinal words that were incomprehensible to the masses while not abandoning the theological concepts behind the words. Wesley's spoken and written sermons were simple and thoughtful discourses delivered for "the bulk of mankind."

But preaching to plain people in the open air did not come without its problems. James Hutton, an English Moravian convert and Wesley contemporary, later wrote in his memoir concerning field preaching: "Here thieves, prostitutes, fools, people of every class, several men of distinction, a few of the learned, merchants, and numbers of poor people who had never entered a place of worship, assembled in these crowds and became godly." Still, Hutton noted, "It was all a jumble of extremes of good and evil—and so distracted alike were both preachers and hearers, that it was enough to make one cry to God for His interference!"

In particular, Wesley's meetings were filled with "outward signs which had so often accompanied the inward work of God." Listeners often shouted and howled in agony, falling down as dead, contorting, and in general making a scene. Labeled an *enthusiast* by some critics, Wesley spent considerable time defending these phenomena.

This type of preaching was exhilarating, especially compared with the disinterested listeners he'd found at Oxford and at churches such as St. Paul's Cathedral, where, he observed, "a considerable part of the congregation are asleep, or talking, or looking about, not minding a word the preacher says." Wesley wondered how such strong criticisms could be leveled against the practice of field preaching but not against the lifeless church preaching so prevalent in his day.

Even so, decades later, he wrote that "field preaching is a cross to me." Two decades after first preaching in a field, he reflected, "What marvel the devil does not love field preaching? Neither do I—I love a commodious room, a soft cushion, [a] handsome pulpit. But where is my zeal if I do not trample all these under foot, in order to save one more soul?"

To counter some of the drawbacks, he always looked for ways to enhance the effectiveness of his preaching. In a day without amplification systems, he was keenly aware of natural means of making his voice carry to reach more people. Diminutive in stature, he always preached from a prominence—a hill, a structure, a chair, a second-story window—or even, most famously, from his father's tomb. But he also employed more subtle techniques to gain acoustical advantage. Wesley historian Richard Heitzenrater notes that the evangelist "preached under tall spreading trees, in market places, tin mines, coal pits, in front of walls—any place that would give him a good sounding board and a veritable sound chamber." He wanted to get his message out to as many lost souls as possible.

Field preaching was a method that Wesley employed throughout the rest of his five-decade ministry. With the departure from Bristol of the phenomenally popular George Whitefield, Wesley not only shepherded the spiritually hungry crowds that Whitefield had generated, but he also began to organize them—exercising a particular gift of his, which helped sustain the evangelical revival for decades. But such a sustained effort had to include more than just open fields. He needed more permanent structures to more comfortably accommodate and regularly train up his faithful followers.

Wesley found the opportunity to pursue this vision in already established societies. Like London and other major metropolises, Bristol had multiple religious societies. Two in particular, the Baldwin Street Society and the Nicholas Street Society, teemed to overflowing when Whitefield or Wesley preached. When neither society proved able to contain the crowds, Wesley led a charge "to build a room large enough to contain both societies," thus uniting them into one larger group. This was the first of many United Societies that Wesley would take under his charge. On May 12, 1739, he laid the first stone in the Horsefair—a location in central Bristol brimming with both commercial and social traffic.

Such a building was a significant financial venture, and at first Wesley had little desire to be a part of it. He appointed eleven trustees, or *feoffees* as they were called, to administer the finances of the building project. But it soon became apparent that this arrangement was not only inefficient, but ineffective at raising the funds and finishing the building. At the advice of his friends, and with the agreement of the trustees—and in line with his controlling nature—Wesley took over management of the money and oversight of the project. This was his first major fund-raising enterprise. The building, called the New Room, was ready for use by July, and served as the center of Wesley's Bristol ministry for the rest of his life. It was his first step toward establishing a new and growing movement.

Closed out from traditional roles of ministry, Wesley pushed open innovative doors. In so doing, he reached people he never would have reached through ordinary ministry roles. He was at first disappointed by the closed doors, but it was in these that he found his greatest opportunities in the vast open fields of ministry that awaited him throughout the British Isles.

Chapter 8
Pursuit of Grace

Without utterly destroying the cause of God, I began to execute
what I had long designed, to strike at the root of the grand delusion.

After John Wesley's Aldersgate experience, his popularity began to soar as he rode the crest of the evangelical revival in England. The crowds increased and, even more importantly, Wesley began to develop methods for turning the fickle crowds into dedicated followers whose commitment would outlive the spectacular events of the revival meetings.

Events of the next ten years would force the budding evangelist to engage simultaneously in several complex but very practical theological issues. Discussions of faith, God's grace and election, Christian perfection, and enthusiasms—or religious fanaticism—were all issues that strained the unity of the evangelical movement and disrupted personal relationships with those he loved deeply. But the theological battles of the 1740s would lay the foundation for the rest of Wesley's ministry and shape a distinctive Wesleyan theology that centered on opening the door to receive more sinful men and women into right relationship with God.

The controversy that most distinctly shaped the structure and independence of Wesley's ministry was his disagreement with the Moravian Brethren, the German sect with whom he had associated so closely after his return to London, particularly in his association with the German-led Fetter Lane Society. The controversy centered on issues of faith and grace—Who has it? How does one receive it? What does it change for the one who receives it?

Issues of faith were paramount in Wesley's own journey. When he first met the Moravians on his journey to America in 1735, he was impressed by their fearless faith even in the face of death, which led him to question the authenticity of his own faith. But the same fearless expression of faith that initially drew him to the Moravians was the very notion that pushed him away in later years.

If he didn't see it at first, it had become abundantly clear by the early 1740s that the Moravians doubted the authenticity of almost everyone's faith. This is clear in how they questioned Wesley when he first arrived in America, and it became painfully obvious when he was denied Communion when he went to Germany after his evangelical conversion. Indeed, some of the Moravians in London taught that any hint of doubt, fear, or sin was indisputable evidence of a lack of justifying faith. Weak faith, according to these teachers, was no faith. Faith could not be partial or incomplete. It was either full or nonexistent. Wesley became increasingly uncomfortable with the harsh rejection of feeble but growing souls.

When Peter Böhler left England, the leadership void was filled by Philip Henry Molther, another German missionary sent by Count Zinzendorf. Like other Moravians, Molther intended to continue his journey on to America, but while in London he led the Moravian Brethren. Wesley and Molther butted heads, and though Wesley remained a member of the Fetter Lane Society until the early 1740s, he became increasingly skeptical of certain Moravian teachings—especially Molther's fullness of faith doctrine.

When Wesley returned to London from Bristol in November 1739, he was outraged at the upheaval caused by Molther's teachings among those who were previously "strong in the faith and zealous of good works." Rather than being lifted up in their faith, these people were being sent into a spiral of doubt and fear. Wesley's journal for November 7 records his concerns:

> *I observed every day more and more the advantage Satan had gained over us. Many of those who once "knew in whom they had believed" were thrown into idle reasonings, and thereby filled with doubts and fears, from which they now found no way to escape. Many were induced to deny the gift of God, and affirm they never had any faith at all; especially those who had fallen again into sin, and of consequence into darkness.*

As if the consignment of feeble souls to darkness was not enough, Wesley was perplexed and incensed by how the weak and wavering were told by the Moravians to receive faith—by being *still*. To the Moravians, stillness meant to wait on Christ and to look to Him alone for the gift of faith through His grace. No striving; no seeking; just waiting. Those who had no faith (according to the Moravians' exacting standards) were told not to seek it, especially through the Lord's Supper. This struck at the core of Wesley's sacramental tradition, learned within the Church of England, which teaches that the sacrament of the Lord's Supper is an "outward sign of an inward grace." To prohibit its use was to prohibit a means for God's grace to reach an individual who sought it.

Philip Molther believed that encouraging, or even allowing, those who lacked true faith to partake of Communion was tantamount to encouraging them to trust in their own works for salvation, rather than in Christ alone. Perhaps as an overreaction to this teaching, Wesley began giving examples of those who lacked faith before coming to the Lord's Table and who came to know Christ through participation in the sacrament—a teaching that goes outside of church tradition and teaching. Meanwhile, Molther even told believers that they had no obligation to participate in the Lord's Supper—a notion that Wesley rejected out of hand as a denial of the very commands of Christ.

But if those who lacked faith could not seek it through the Lord's Table—and most Christian traditions discourage such a practice—there were other "means of grace" that doubters were also told to avoid. Going to church, fasting, reading scripture, hearing it read, doing temporal good, and attempting spiritual good were all proscribed by Molther. All these restrictions flew in the face of Wesley's experience and history as one who had pursued God through these means for years before experiencing what he believed was his justification. As a result of Molther's teaching, many who had once claimed faith were thrown into confusion and doubt. And as a remedy for their doubt, they were told to do nothing—to simply be still. Wesley believed all of this to be contrary to the Word of God and the commands of Christ.

The incompatibility of the two men's teachings led to a major division, which Wesley spent the next year and a half trying to mend, to no avail.

To counter Molther's insidious teachings, Wesley ventured on a series of his own. He knew there was a kernel of truth in the Moravian doctrine— that indeed some members of the Church of England were trusting in their baptism, occasional church attendance, and participation in the Lord's Supper as "the means of grace" or foundation of their religion, rather than in life-transforming faith. The Moravians, however, were going to the opposite extreme in discouraging obedience to Christ's commands and discouraging opportunities to receive grace. So, on the one hand, in his critique of high church tradition, Wesley argued against a dead religiosity. On the other hand, he fought those who would reject the long-standing tradition of the church based on God's commands. Thus, he began to teach his hearers to "neither *neglect* nor *rest in* the means of grace."

Much of Wesley's time in 1739 was spent away from London, the center of the Moravian controversy, but he was kept abreast of the issues through reports from friends until he came to the Fetter Lane Society in November. When he investigated the issues on his own, he found the group filled with disputations and divisions. By late December, he had heard enough.

"I had a long and particular conversation with Mr. Molther himself," Wesley writes in his journal. "I weighed all his words with the utmost care; desired him to explain what I did not understand; asked him again and again, 'Do I not mistake what you say? Is this your meaning, or is it not?' So that I think, if God has given me any measure of understanding, I could not mistake him much."

As a result of his meeting with Molther, Wesley laid out an orderly chart, noting the differences between Molther's positions and his. "As to [X], you believe [Y]," he wrote in one column with dozens of Molther's beliefs, and "whereas I believe [Z]" was written in the other column. This methodical description of their differences served as a launching pad for the theological war that would rage over the next several months.

In the new year of 1740, Wesley split his time between Bristol and London and attempted a balancing act between intense debate over the Moravian doctrines and a desire for peaceful unity.

At the beginning of January, using Psalm 46:10 as his text, he taught the Fetter Lane Society members what he called "true, Christian, Scriptural *stillness*," in contrast to the passive, inactive stillness taught by Molther and others. The next day, preaching from Jeremiah 6:16, he implored the society to "stand ye in. . .the old paths" of salvation and set aside "idle controversies and strife of words."

But even if the Fetter Lane members were convinced by Wesley's teaching, the itinerant evangelist was losing his influence to other less transient leaders who took back whatever ground he may have gained while in London as soon as he left town again. Not only that, but Wesley also began to encounter the same disruptive teachings of the Moravians in areas outside of London, which was causing the same consternation, fear, and doubt among the recently awakened souls there.

In addition to the theological controversy, Wesley was broadsided that spring by an affidavit circulated throughout Bristol by Captain Robert Williams, who ripped open old wounds by reporting past indiscretions of Wesley's that had occurred while he was in Georgia. Williams added a dimension of controversy by suggesting that Wesley was an outlaw fleeing criminal charges in America.

Despite these growing personal trials, Wesley remained undeterred. The accusations set in motion the publication of his Georgia journals, which, while certainly containing his own biased accounts, are remarkably open about his failings. This installment of his journals, published in September 1740, was the first of twenty-one extraordinary installments covering five decades of ministry.

For reasons both good and bad, Wesley was becoming adept at facing controversy head-on—be it theological, personal, or practical. And he was learning to turn these issues to his advantage.

Like Wesley, James Hutton was an Englishman who was swept up in the revival of religion taking place in the 1730s. Hutton, too, was a member of the Fetter Lane Society. But unlike Wesley, who had grown apart from the Moravians, Hutton had become increasingly committed to them—and, as a result, hostile to Wesley. Hutton questioned Wesley's motives, believing that Wesley was looking for any cause to charge against the German Brethren because of a prideful desire to lead his own party. To Hutton, the issues were not so much theological as they were a struggle for power—a struggle that Wesley was clearly losing at Fetter Lane.

If Hutton had concerns about Wesley's motives, Wesley had his own concerns about the character of the Moravians. In the German religious society, he found a growing culture of "closeness, darkness, [and] reserve." He went so far as to charge them with using guile to achieve a spiritual purpose, by "describing things a little beyond the truth." This, to Wesley, was a fundamental breach of character.

During the late spring, while Wesley ministered in Bristol, two camps emerged at Fetter Lane and became increasingly toxic. Wesley's friends begged him to return to London for two weeks to minister to the "poor brethren at Fetter Lane [who] were again in great confusion" because of the "new gospel" taught by Molther. But as soon as he left London again, the situation spiraled out of control, making his eventual departure from Fetter Lane seem almost inevitable.

As a determined minister, Wesley would not give up without a final effort at winning over the leaders and the entire society. Returning to London in early June, he preached on the works-heavy epistle of James as a "great antidote against this poison" being taught by the Moravians.

Further meetings with Molther himself were thwarted by the German leader's illnesses, but Wesley began a barrage of teachings before the society to make his case.

"Finding there was no time to delay," he later recorded in his journal, "without utterly destroying the cause of God, I began to execute what I had long designed, to strike at the root of the grand delusion." Over the next eight days, he preached a series of sermons to refute the teachings of Molther and his followers.

Still, the fruitless meetings, discussions, and arguments continued as Wesley's teachings fell on deaf ears among a growing group that were entrenched "in their own opinions." On July 18, 1740, the Fetter Lane Society voted to prohibit Wesley from preaching there, claiming that the space should be reserved "for the Germans."

On July 20, John Wesley stood before the society for the final time and laid out his differences with the new teaching:

I believe these assertions to be flatly contrary to the Word of God. I have warned you hereof again and again, and besought you to turn back to the law and the testimony. I have borne with you long, hoping you would return. But as I find you more and more confirmed in the error of your ways, nothing now remains but that I should give you up to God. You that are of the same judgment, follow me.

He then led a small group from the Fetter Lane Society to begin a new independent ministry, through which he called on people to seek and pursue the Lord's grace and holiness through any biblical means, through righteous living, all done in and through faith.

The rejection by the Fetter Lane Society might have destroyed a lesser teacher. But for Wesley it was barely a setback. In fact, it became a launching pad for his London ministry. That summer, he purchased a vacated and "uncouth heap of ruins" that had been a foundry and royal arsenal before being severely damaged by an explosion in 1716. It sat on Windmill Hill, just to the north of Moorfields, the location of much of Wesley's London field preaching as well as the center of much of London's seedy activity and the shoddy living spaces of London's poor.

Wesley paid for the building to be repaired and suited for the needs of a preaching house, and it was affectionately dubbed the Foundery. It became the center of his London ministry for the next four decades and also served as a preaching house; living quarters for widows, itinerant preachers, and Wesley himself; and housed a book shop, a school, and a dispensary.

It was from the Foundery that Wesley began to spread the Gospel of grace and to reach out to the outcasts of London.

Chapter 9
Free for All

God will do what man cannot,
namely, make us both of one mind.

While conflict raged between Wesley and the Moravians in the Fetter Lane Society in London, he was simultaneously engaged in an equally taxing conflict centered 120 miles to the west in Bristol and Kingswood. But where the issues in London threatened to divide a religious society, the conflict in Bristol threatened to shatter the evangelical movement and quash the rapidly expanding revival. It also threatened to ruin the dear friendship between John Wesley and George Whitefield.

The controversy had begun in April 1739. Wesley had long been resistant to a teaching about salvation taught by most leaders of the Reformation, including Martin Luther and John Calvin. Often referred to simply as Calvinism after the French theologian, this teaching argued that Jesus had made atonement for sin *only for the elect* souls who were predestined. Therefore, God's grace of eternal salvation was available only for a limited or particular group, not for everyone.

That spring, contrary to the Calvinist doctrine, Wesley began preaching in Bristol and the surrounding area a sermon titled "Free Grace," in which he contended that "the grace or love of God. . .is free in all, and free for all." Based on his own reading of the Bible, he proclaimed God's *desire* that all souls be saved (1 Timothy 2:4), not just a predetermined, predestined group of "the elect."

Those who held to Calvin's teachings on predestination, he believed, were unable to resolve a greater tension—namely, if some were predestined to heaven, then others must logically be predestined to hell. Though most Reformed teachers were reluctant to allow that some were predestined for hell, Wesley saw no way around the double-edged sword. Indeed, he believed that such a teaching made God the "author of sin." He wrote to friends in London during this time, quoting from John Calvin's seminal work, *The Institutes of Religion*, and calling the teaching on predestination a "horrible decree." He contrasted this "horrible decree" with what he called "the great decree of God," that "he that believeth and is baptized shall be saved; he that believeth not shall be damned" (Mark 16:16).

This message was immediately met with both strong opposition and a warm reception. Wesley seems to have relished the controversy and was swept away by its reception. Some of his adherents encouraged him to print the sermon for publication to a wider audience. Still, Wesley knew that good Christian souls disagreed with him, so he looked to God to show him signs of favor.

By the end of April, he had some misgivings about continuing to preach so centrally on this theme. He wondered whether he should go forward with the publication of his five arguments against predestination from his "Free Grace" sermon. To determine the matter, he reverted once again to the casting of lots. Arranging four sheets of paper with four possibilities for the sermon—preach (or not), and print (or not)—he prayed "that if this were not the truth of God, he would not suffer the blind to go out of the way; but if it were, he would bear witness to his word." After prayer, he drew the lot: "Preach and print."

Later that spring, he printed his sermon along with his brother Charles's hymn "Universal Redemption." In so doing, he became fully entrenched in the controversy, but with the conviction that God was on his side.

"I hear, honoured sir," George Whitefield wrote from London on June 25, "you are about to print a sermon against predestination. It shocks me to think of it."

A few days later, Whitefield, who himself was aligned with Calvinism, wrote again from Gloucester: "I confess my spirit has been of late sharpened on account of some of your proceedings." His heart was "quite broken," he continued, over his friend's decisions and how they were dividing evangelicals in Bristol and beyond.

Wesley did not heed Whitefield's request to cease proclamation and publication of his sermon. By the time Whitefield's requests were received, the proverbial ship had already sailed for Wesley and his message. The divide between these two friends would be further complicated in August when Whitefield set sail for America on a year-and-a-half journey. The physical distance and lack of direct contact set the stage for a transatlantic debate that disrupted clear, timely communication and amplified misunderstandings.

What ensued was a frenzied two-year free-for-all.

Wesley had long been convinced that the Calvinists' rigid view of predestination was wrong. His mother, Susanna Wesley, was perhaps the first to plant seeds in his head that such a teaching made God the author of sin. But his teaching was not strictly a negative reaction to Calvinism. His conviction that God's grace was free for all who would receive it propelled his ministry to go to the highways and byways so that all *may*—but not necessarily will—come in. Indeed, he could understand no reason or motivation to go forth to proclaim the Gospel if only those who were already elect would receive it.

Over the next five decades, Wesley developed a refined understanding of God's grace, sharpened by debates that inevitably flared up throughout his life. His position was attacked by critics as overly optimistic about the goodness of humanity and our ability to choose faith on our own—a notion Wesley thoroughly rejected. He came, as he said, "to the very edge of Calvinism" and never differed more than a "hair's breadth" from it. As with Calvin, he rejected any merit or goodness in humans without the grace of God and also affirmed the total depravity of humanity. Further, he rejected any notion of free will "antecedent to grace." Still, his view of grace was more positive. He believed not in human potential but in the amazing power of God's grace to transform.

His mature teachings suggest that there is a sequence or "method whereby God leads us step by step toward heaven." The first step is what he called "preventing grace," or what is often called *prevenient grace*. This God-given grace gives an individual "the first wish to please God, the first dawn of light concerning his will, and the first slight transient conviction of having sinned against him," which leads to "convincing grace" or repentance. Finally, he taught that one would continue on this sequence by encountering justifying grace, which brought one to saving faith followed by sanctifying grace. Wesley summarized his views, saying, "By justification we are saved from the guilt of sin, and restored to the favor of God; by sanctification we are saved from the power and root of sin, and restored to the image of God."

Wesley's view of grace had many critics, especially regarding *sanctifying grace*. But right or wrong, his view of grace fit with his growing hope, not in the native ability of humankind but in the great power of God to restore souls to His divine image. He believed that the Moravians, with whom he had long done battle, beat people down with their unattainable view of faith. The Calvinists, he believed, closed the door for others to the possibility of receiving this grace. The grace that he taught was, in the words of the hymn written by his brother Charles, "so free, so infinite," and for all.

From the very beginning, George Whitefield's relationship with John Wesley was filled with a warm love, tempered by a very respectful circumspection.

Each man was committed to the truth as he saw it, but both men were nearly equally committed to Christian unity. These two ideals in juxtaposition caused great tension at times.

In March 1740, Whitefield wrote to Wesley from America, saying that since leaving England, he was "ten thousand times more convinced" of the doctrine of election and final perseverance. Even so, arguing over these matters could only "destroy brotherly love and insensibly take from us that cordial union and sweetness of soul. . .between us."

Though they held these loving sentiments of respectful disagreement, fissures remained, which were exacerbated by their followers.

The two leaders were about to become acutely aware of the out-of-control wildfire that their very public debate had ignited among their followers.

The first puffs of smoke appeared in Kingswood when John Cennick, a Wesley subordinate and one of the teachers at the school, came out against Wesley's teachings on free grace and Christian perfection. This led to a division within the Kingswood School and spilled over into the recently united Bristol Society. In response, Wesley reprimanded some of his opponents in what became a failed effort to try to snuff out the growing fire.

"God is sending a message to those on either side [of the predestination debate]," the battle-weary preacher wrote to Whitefield in August, hoping his friend would step in and squelch the dispute. "But neither will receive it unless from one who is of their own opinion." Flashing a ray of hope for doctrinal unity, Wesley told his Calvinist friend, "But when His time is come, God will do what man cannot, namely, make us both of one mind."

Whitefield likely had not received this conciliatory note from Wesley before sending an unusually heated letter of his own in September, critiquing his friend's teaching on Christian perfection and election. But Whitefield's missive also charged Wesley with setting "the nation a-disputing" and called his decision to cast lots "rash and precipitant."

Whitefield seemed to have moderated his views a bit when he wrote, just over a month later, that though he still strongly disagreed with Wesley on some matters, "I am willing to go with you to prison, and death; but I am not willing to oppose you." This promise would soon ring hollow.

The winter of 1740–41 proved to be a breaking point between Wesley and Whitefield, as well as between their respective camps.

Seeing how disruptive the theological feud had become, the Wesley brothers were willing to call for a truce. They would adopt a posture of public silence concerning the controversial teachings if other teachers would as well. With John away from the festering issues in Bristol, Charles was left to quell a growing insurrection at Kingswood led by teacher John Cennick. When Cennick refused to enter the truce, John decided to return to Bristol to tend to the matter himself.

"I went to Kingswood," John records in his journal, "intending, if it should please God, to spend some time there, if haply I might be an instrument in his hand of repairing the breaches which had been made."

But "repairing the breaches" would take more than love feasts and the overlooking of differences. It would require some direct confrontation and lead to some awkward personal interactions, but all with the hope that "we might again with one heart and one mouth glorify the Father of our Lord Jesus Christ."

When Wesley met Cennick, he found him "cold" and resistant to sorting out differences. Still, over the next several days, he pursued Cennick to identify the source of the tension. Finally, the recalcitrant Kingswood teacher laid it out plainly and simply: "You do not preach truth."

At the turn of the new year, as sides were clearly being drawn, Wesley observed that many in the society "had no ears to hear, having *disputed away* both their faith and their love."

As these disputes roiled on in Bristol, Whitefield was preparing to return from his journey to America. He put the finishing touches on an open letter in response to Wesley's sermon on free grace, which had been published more than a year earlier. Whitefield's letter was completed on December 24, 1740, but wasn't published until the following March. Its publication violated his promise not to oppose his beloved friend, and its contents threatened to destroy their relationship permanently.

Before his return to England, Whitefield sent a lengthy letter to Wesley, critiquing his doctrine. Though private, the letter was intercepted by zealous Calvinist supporters, who published it in February without

Whitefield's knowledge or approval. When it was distributed outside the Foundery in London, Wesley gathered up a copy, stood before the gathering with the letter in hand, and declared, "I will do just what I believe Mr. Whitefield would, were he here himself." He then led the congregation in tearing the private letter into pieces.

His stated reason for the tearing up the letter in public was simple. Private letters were meant to be private. But some Whitefield supporters believed it was a public attack on Whitefield himself, not the honorable act of an affronted preacher.

Meanwhile, the festering strife and division were once again boiling over in the societies in Bristol and Kingswood. Wesley returned in late February to put a stop to it. He met with the bands of the society, ascertained where the root of the division lay, and met with his chief opponent, John Cennick.

Examination and confrontation were becoming standard practices for Wesley. He was beginning to keep a tight rein on the organization of the societies and schools that he oversaw. It was becoming clear that without strong supervision, issues, divisions, and disputes overtook the progress that the Gospel was making. Cutting these issues at the root was paramount to his philosophy of a vibrant, long-term ministry.

The issues that John Cennick had with Wesley were theological—a concern with enthusiastic phenomena, Christian perfection, election, and preaching up *"man's* faithfulness," not the faithfulness of God. For Wesley, however, the theological disputes were secondary—at least according to his public statements. He was more concerned with Cennick's insubordination and the division caused by "bigots" for predestination.

"You should have told me of this before," Wesley charged Cennick, "and not have supplanted me in my own house, stealing the hearts of the people, and by private accusations separating very friends." When Cennick denied the accusation, Wesley showed him a letter that Cennick had written to George Whitefield that proved he was stirring up opposition.

After a thorough examination of the issues and face-to-face meetings with his opponents, Wesley decided there was just one thing to do—disband those who would not repent. On February 28, 1741, after offering every opportunity for his opponents to repent from evil speaking and prejudicing others against him and Charles, he stood before the society and disbanded John Cennick and a few of his staunchest followers. Standing before the gathering, he read the following:

> *Therefore, not for their opinions, nor for any of them (whether they be right or wrong), but for the causes above mentioned, viz., for their scoffing at the Word and ministers of God, for their tale bearing, backbiting, and evil-speaking, for their dissembling, lying, and slandering, I, John Wesley, by the consent and approbation of the band society in Kingswood, do declare the persons above mentioned to be no longer members thereof. Neither will they be so accounted until they shall openly confess their fault, and thereby do what in them lies to remove the scandal they have given.*

With that, the rupture throughout the united societies in Bristol and Kingswood was made complete.

When George Whitefield arrived in England in March 1741 after eighteen months in America, he was even more entrenched in his convictions. Upon his return, he published his open letter to Wesley, critiquing and directly opposing his friend and the sermon "Free Grace."

The accidental publication in February of his private letter of rebuke to Wesley—which the recipient had publicly torn up—though painful, was excusable. All of their private correspondence was very honest, confrontational, and often heated. But the deliberate publication of a direct critique hurt Wesley deeply.

"If you had disliked my sermon," he wrote to Whitefield in a long letter in April, "you might have printed another on the same text, and have answered my proofs without mentioning my name: this had been fair and friendly. Whereas to proceed as you have done is so far from friendship that it is not moral honesty." Furthermore, Wesley felt the critique dealt with only a small portion of his arguments and critiqued "all the wrong expressions."

But none of this argument cut as deeply as the fact that Whitefield had publicly and purposefully revealed that Wesley had cast lots when deciding whether or not to preach his "Free Grace" sermon. He saw that disclosure as an attempt to discredit and therefore humiliate him. "Moral honesty does not allow of a treacherous wound or of the bewraying of secrets." Not that he would cease to cast lots to make decisions. Indeed, he even defended the practice throughout his life. But Whitefield's intentions were seen as harsh. "A Spaniard would have behaved more tenderly to his English prisoners," Wesley wrote in a final thrust of passion.

The open letter caused "an open and probably irreparable breach," which was never wider than in the spring of 1741.

If John Wesley was circumspect concerning Whitefield's desire for unity, his brother Charles was downright skeptical. Charles had invited Whitefield to preach in Bristol in March 1741, only to have Whitefield preach directly against the teachings of the Wesley brothers. Charles was furious.

"[Whitefield's] fair words are not to be trusted," he wrote to John. Whitefield's return to Bristol ignited a short-lived turf war over control of the societies and the Kingswood School, which Whitefield and John Wesley had organized together.

Just as Wesley had directly confronted Molther, Cennick, and others, he met directly with Whitefield "to hear him speak for himself, that I might know how to judge." Though Wesley was pleased with his friend's openness, their meetings—as well as a subsequent meeting six days later—resulted in no shift in thinking. Whitefield said that Wesley preached "two different gospels" (presumably *justification* and *perfection*). Therefore, Wesley concluded that his friend had "resolved publicly to preach against me and my brother wheresoever he preached at all."

To Wesley, this honest conversation was refreshing, and he greatly respected Whitefield for his straightforward criticism, even though the two would never agree. However, the face-to-face meetings had their intended result—expunging the rancor from their relationship. Wesley detailed his concerns in a lengthy letter to Whitefield in late April, and Whitefield responded in August with a letter demonstrating a thawing of the dispute, as he gave an "account of God's dealing with his soul."

In October, seven months after the publication of his open letter, Whitefield wrote a letter of apology to his wounded friend, expressing his contrition for having exposed the private matter of casting lots. "Though much may be said for my doing it," he wrote apologetically, "I am sorry now that any such thing dropped from my pen, and I humbly ask pardon." And, as if he missed a very dear friend, he added, "I find I love you as much as ever, and pray God, if it be his blessed will, that we may be all united together."

By late 1740 and into 1741, the ice between the two evangelists had melted. This is not to say they agreed on doctrine. Still, when Whitefield died in 1770, Wesley preached at his funeral and suggested they had come to an understanding. "There are many doctrines of a less essential nature," he said, "with regard to which even the sincere children of God (such is the present weakness of human understanding) are and have been divided for many ages. In these we may think and let think; we may 'agree to disagree.'"

Though their breach was in one sense healed, their ministries forever took different paths. In 1741, Whitefield and his followers built a preaching house in London a scant quarter mile from Wesley's Foundery. It was called the Tabernacle, expressing Whitefield's vision for a temporary structure for worship, taking his cue from the wandering Israelites. But if Whitefield hoped to build a temporary ministry, Wesley was laying the foundation for a permanent establishment and movement.

The two continued a lifelong theological and methodological division. But both remained ever hopeful of a heavenly reconciliation.

Shortly after Whitefield's death, one of Wesley's followers asked him whether they would see Whitefield in heaven—a question typically reserved for heretics. His answer demonstrates Wesley's undying love and respect for his longtime friend.

"No, madam," he replied, before explaining, "George Whitefield was so bright a star in the firmament of God's glory, and will stand so near the throne, that one like me, who am less than the least, will never catch a glimpse of him."

Chapter 10
Thou Art beside Thyself

*There is a better religion to be attained,
a religion worthy of the God that gave it.*

If critics hoped that controversy would stifle the growth of Wesley's popularity and following, they were severely disappointed. In fact, the opposite seemed to happen, with interest increasing in the thoughtful yet passionate controversialist.

Having established bases in London and Bristol, Wesley began a search in other parts of England and Wales for souls who had been overlooked and neglected by the Established Church—mainly the poor and laborers, such as coal miners, who were supporting the nation on the cusp of the Industrial Revolution. He traveled relentlessly on horseback in pursuit of these lost souls.

His greatest opportunity came in May 1742 at the invitation of Selina Hastings, the countess of Huntington, to visit the colliers of the north in Newcastle-upon-Tyne, nearly three hundred miles north of London. "I was surprised," Wesley wrote of his first impressions of the northern town. "[So] much drunkenness, cursing and swearing (even from the mouths of little children), do I never remember to have seen and heard before, in so small a compass of time. Surely this place is ripe for him who 'came not to call the righteous but sinners to repentance.'"

In Newcastle, he established another base of ministry, visiting some fifty times over the next half century. But it was not just Newcastle, Bristol, and London—cities that, on a map, form a triangle that spreads across England—that he would reach. He stopped in hundreds of towns, villages, and cities in between in order to share the good news about God and His grace.

Wesley's extensive reach also brought extensive criticism. And though much of the criticism was theological in nature, there was an unshakable practical critique that his ministry was irrational, ecstatic, and dangerous. Like St. Paul's opponent, Festus, Wesley's enemies claimed, "Thou art beside thyself." The charge that Wesley was an "enthusiast" was starting to stick, and it was quickly becoming clear that he would need to first define, and then defend, the Methodist movement he was forming.

For most, it was fanatical enough that Wesley and the other evangelical leaders preached their doctrines outside the church walls—in fields and society meetings. But adding to the perceptions, Wesley's ministry brought with it unusual phenomena, which cast him, in the eyes of his critics, as a lunatic at best or a charlatan at worst.

These phenomena began and centered in Bristol at the outset of his ministry, first in society meetings and private homes, and then at the outdoor preaching events. The first instance recorded in Wesley's journal is of a young woman at the Baldwin Street Society who "cried out aloud, with the utmost vehemence, even as in the agonies of death." This was immediately followed by two others who "were seized with strong pain and constrained to 'roar for true quietness of their heart.'"

A few days later, "a young man was suddenly seized with a violent trembling all over, and. . .sunk to the ground." Then, at Newgate Prison in London, many in the audience "dropped on every side as thunderstruck." Wherever Wesley went, in these early years especially, there were "groanings," cries, "violent agonies," and various other "outward signs which had so often accompanied the work of God."

Even though he uses his journals to defend his extraordinary ministry, there is a sense from his accounts that he is not entirely certain what to make of the occurrences, and that he is not exactly comfortable with them. He often prefaces reports of extraordinary events with a cushion of distance: "The fact I nakedly relate . . ." he writes, before describing an apparent exorcism of demons from a young woman. "And [I] leave every man to his own judgment of it."

"This fact, too, I will simply relate so far as I was an ear- or eye-witness of it," he writes at another time, as if to inform the reader that he himself is not sure what happened.

He was keenly aware of how unusual these things appeared to others. Many were "deeply offended" by the events, and at times Wesley "prayed that God would not suffer those who were weak to be offended."

These troubling events raised eyebrows and created some of Wesley's fiercest critics. But Wesley, who otherwise desired order and predictability in all aspects of his life, understood these uncontrollable physical demonstrations—the yelling, crying, agony, laughter, falling down as dead—as the work not of God, but of the devil, "who knew his kingdom shook" and was making his final defense for a soul nearing its Savior. It is no wonder then that when he relates these stories of chaotic phenomena, the individuals are relieved from their torment and find order through the controlled, but still emotional, praising of God.

Still, many—especially from the high church formalist tradition—could not see through the chaos to the fruit of Wesley's ministry. In May 1739, an unusual door to preach seemed to open to him in a small-town church outside of Bristol, but it shut suddenly when he received a note: "Sir, Our minister, having been informed you are beside yourself, does not care you should preach in any of his churches."

In the eyes of most, John Wesley was, in the vernacular of eighteenth-century England, what was termed "an enthusiast." His brother Samuel, who died tragically in 1739, was the first to warn about enthusiasms during John's evangelical conversion, when others were claiming dreams and visions.

To be labeled an enthusiast was a catch-all derogatory term for an unreasoning, emotional religious fanatic. Wesley noted the loose use of the term, claiming "it is a convenient word to be thrown out upon anything we do not like, because scarce one reader in a thousand has any idea of what it means." One of Wesley's early critics, a London vicar, defined the term to Wesley's general liking and eventual advantage: "Enthusiasm is a false persuasion of an extraordinary divine assistance, which leads men on to such conduct as is only to be justified by the supposition of such assistance." It is, more simply put, a person who believes that God is on his side, and therefore whatever he does—no matter how peculiar—is sanctioned by God.

In his sermon titled "The Nature of Enthusiasm," first published in 1750 (but likely in development as part of his preaching repertoire for years beforehand), Wesley refines this definition and turns his critic's conclusion on its head:

> *[Enthusiasm is] a religious madness arising from some falsely imagined influence or inspiration of God; at least, from imputing something to God which ought not to be imputed to Him, or expecting something from God which ought not to be expected from Him.*

Certainly Wesley affirms there are enthusiasts who base their lives on visions, dreams, and impressions. Wesley and his followers were not enthusiasts. They were merely receiving what they had been promised by scripture. The real enthusiasts, by this definition, were the nominal Christians, or those "who imagine themselves Christians and are not." They are the ones who were "expecting something from God which ought not be expected from Him"—namely, His favor.

This clever turn of argument notwithstanding, Wesley's critics charged him with claiming to be above authority, that he and his followers were driven by inward impressions of the Spirit of God instead of the Word of God, and that he thought himself above even the rebuke of reason or scripture. But Wesley rejected these charges, insisting that he was reasonable, scriptural, and correctable.

It was regarding these points that Wesley wished to distinguish himself from others. Many who were swept up in the revival were claiming visions, dreams, and "impressions" that were in fact directing their behavior and beliefs. Though Wesley himself showed some initial interest and acceptance of such ecstasies, it was a direction to which he quickly became resistant. When he encountered a group called the French Prophets, he "tested the spirits" of these seeming oracles who spoke in the first person voice of God. He also became exasperated by those who claimed that their impressions replaced, and even trumped, the written Word of God.

In a gathering outside Kingswood, he warned the people against being deceived by false teachers.

> *I told them they were not to judge of the Spirit whereby anyone spoke, either by appearances, or by common report, or by their own inward feelings. No, nor by any dreams, visions, or revelations supposed to be made to their souls, any more than by their tears, or any involuntary effects wrought upon their bodies. I warned them all these were in themselves of a doubtful, disputable nature; they might be from God and they might not, and were therefore not simply to be relied on (any more than simply to be condemned) but to be tried by a farther rule, to be brought to the only certain test, "the law and the testimony."*

Even after these warnings, he ironically records in his journal that, "while I was speaking, one before me dropped down as dead."

A critique of his ministry that bit deeper than these other episodes was the charge that Wesley and the Methodists were exceedingly prideful. His critics charged him with claiming extraordinary gifts of the Spirit of God and equating himself with the power and authority of the apostles. They questioned his accounts of miracles and his high view of his role within God's present work, and viewed him as a schismatic intent on destroying the church for his own advantage. Wesley, of course, denied the bulk of these charges, arguing that though he was indeed a part of an extraordinary and "great work of God," the miracles and access to the power of God were not unique to him, but were available to all of God's children.

Still, his published journal struck some readers as self-interested propaganda. They observed that Wesley almost always portrayed himself as a conquering hero endowed with God's special favor. His voice, in this respect, was one that never changed. But getting to the heart of his motives is an elusive task. Some are convinced of his authenticity—others are not.

In Wesley's voluminous response to his critics, one thing becomes clear: He did not want his ministry to be judged by his extraordinarily controversial methods and practices. Rather, he wanted his methods and practices to be judged in light of their fruit. "Consider now," he wrote to one critic in defense of his ministry, "the habitual drunkard that was, is now temperate in all things. The whoremonger now flees fornication. He that stole, steals no more, but works with his hands. He that cursed or swore, perhaps at every sentence, has now learned to serve the Lord with fear, and rejoice unto him with reverence. Those formerly enslaved to various habits of sin are now brought to uniform habits of holiness."

Lives were being transformed as a result of this unusual ministry. And for Wesley, this fact was enough to justify even some of the controversial episodes.

Beginning in 1742, Wesley began to define and defend his brand of Methodism through writing and publishing long tracts and small books. Previously, he had published sermons, his journals, and multiple extracts from other authors. But now the growth of his movement and influence necessitated a robust explanation of what he was—and was not—leading.

That year, he published the third installment of his journal, which includes the outbreak of these "enthusiastic" episodes. He printed the journal with the express purpose "to declare to all mankind what it is that the Methodists (so called) have done and are doing now—or rather, what it is that God hath done and is still doing in our land." This was quickly followed by *The Character of a Methodist*, in which he attempts to place the Methodist family within historical, orthodox Christianity. Aside from his sermons, it is the first public biblical defense of his doctrine of Christian perfection—though he never uses the term. Then, in response to the Reverend Josiah Tucker's attack on Methodism, he published *The Principals of a Methodist*. This tract centers on defending his doctrines, particularly on justification and perfection.

The Character of a Methodist and *The Principles of a Methodist* were essentially defensive in tone. But in 1743, he published what is perhaps his most positive, successful, and lyrical vision of Christianity in *An Earnest Appeal to Men of Reason and Religion*. Previous attacks on his theology and burning criticism of his supposed enthusiasm could not grasp the heart of his teaching that true religion is seated "in the heart, in the inmost soul, but ever showing itself by its fruits, continually springing forth. . .spreading virtue and happiness all around it." This appeal puts forth a vision of a revolutionary Gospel that contrasts with a world without that good news:

We see—and who does not?—the numberless follies and miseries of our fellow creatures. We see on every side either men of no religion at all or men of a lifeless, formal religion. We are grieved at the sight, and should greatly rejoice if by any means we might convince some that there is a better religion to be attained, a religion worthy of the God that gave it.

Then he continues to express this hope more positively:

And this we conceive to be no other than love: the love of God and of all mankind; the loving God with all our heart and souls and strength, as having first loved us, as the fountain of all the good we have received, and of all we ever hope to enjoy; and the loving every soul which God hath made, every man on earth, as our own soul.

This, says Wesley, is "the medicine of life, the never-failing remedy, for all the evils of a disordered world, for all the miseries of men."

Inward transformation by the love of God, he believed, would lead to the transformation of society and the world. It was a vision by which he appealed to reasonable and religious men—many of whom were his critics—to come and join in the work.

The publication of these works, while effective in consolidating the Methodist movement, also gave ammunition to a new wave of critics. Wesley's journals in particular, though winsome, entertaining, and informative—instant classics—revealed concrete anecdotes of miraculous events, mixed with unusual and strange phenomena. The journals therefore caused great discomfort among most religious leaders who wished Wesley would just go away. It was becoming clear that he would not.

Opposition grew from many quarters, and publications against him were becoming common. But as the criticism grew, so did Wesley's response. His first *Appeal* did much to win over some of his more charitable critics, but it did not defend against each and every attack. So he wrote a much longer three-part defense, titled *A Farther Appeal to Men of Reason and Religion*, published in stages spanning the years of 1745 and 1746. This work is much more defensive and less organized than the first *Appeal*, though it does reveal important retorts to charges of his critics. But the length and disorganization blunts its effectiveness. Perhaps this writing was in part responsible for his self-critical evaluation in a letter to a friend: "I scarce ever yet repented of saying too little, but frequently of saying too much."

Though Wesley understood that his day and his ministry were a unique and "great work of God," he was also intent on demonstrating that there were other reasonable ministries in the Bible, in history, and at present that validated his own work. In 1744, he abridged and published two works by the New England revivalist Jonathan Edwards: *Distinguishing Marks of a Work of the Spirit of God* and *A Narrative of the Late Work of God at and near Northampton.* These works represent a thoughtful contemporary defense of accounts and episodes similar to those of Wesley's ministry—groanings, screamings, and people falling in public meetings. These publications added a level of authority to the events that occurred during his own work.

All the while, writings against Wesley's Methodism were becoming voluminous. What struck him most deeply were critiques from clergy and bishops in the Established Church, which forced him to respond and comprise many of his early works. *Principles of a Methodist* (1742) was a response to a Bristol minister; *A Farther Appeal* was largely in response to London bishop Edmund Gibson's anonymous critique; and in 1745, Wesley responded publicly to a London vicar's attack that lambasted his journals as proof that he was "guilty of enthusiasm to the highest degree" in his *Answer to Mr. Church.* His 1746 work titled *Principles of a Methodist Further Explained* was another defense against attacks by the same London pastor, whom Wesley regarded with esteem and care, calling him afterward "a gentleman, a scholar, and a Christian."

Wesley hesitated to enter into controversies with individuals, but when he did, he exhibited remarkable grace and restrained himself from entering into personal attacks. He usually viewed his opponent not as an enemy to be vanquished, but as a potential colaborer. When the aging Bishop Gibson revealed—what was apparently an open secret—that he was the author of an anonymous 1745 critique of Wesley, the Methodist leader took the critique seriously. But he closed his response with a stinging rebuke, followed by an invitation.

> *Your Lordship has, without doubt, had some success in opposing this doctrine. Very many have, by your Lordship's unwearied endeavours, been deterred from hearing at all; and have thereby probably escaped the being seduced into holiness, have lived and died in their sins.*

It was a harsh, but ringing reproach. But he continued with an invitation:

My Lord, the time is short. I am past the noon of life, and my remaining years flee away as a shadow. Your Lordship is old and full of days, having past the usual age of man. It cannot, therefore, be long before we shall both drop this house of earth, and stand naked before God: No, nor before we shall see the great white throne coming down from heaven, and Him that sitteth thereon. On his left hand shall be those who are shortly to dwell in everlasting fire, prepared for the devil and his angels. In that number will be all who died in their sins; and, among the rest, those whom you preserved from repentance. Will you then rejoice in your success? The Lord God grant it may not be said in that hour, "These have perished in their iniquity; but their blood I require at thy hands!"

This rebuke and invitation apparently had a profound impact on the aging bishop, as "a vulgar report got abroad that the Bishop of London had turned Methodist!"

Wesley's ability to joust with opponents both small and great is remarkable. But after ten years of nonstop controversy and the publication of his most lucid and intense writings, he was becoming weary. Responding to the Reverend Conyers Middleton's rebuttal of miracles in 1749, Wesley wrote in his journal: "[I] spent almost twenty days in that unpleasant employment" of responding to critiques.

From 1750 to 1751, he entered into a three-part verbal battle with George Lavington, bishop of Exeter, who had compared the enthusiasm of the Methodists with that of the "papists," a derogatory term for Roman Catholics.

Wesley's lengthy response, *A Letter to the Author of the Enthusiasm of Methodists and Papists Compared*, was his most substantive open letter, and it took a toll on him. "Heavy work, such as I should never choose," he wrote in his journal regarding his response to Lavington, "but sometimes it must be done. Well might the ancient say, 'God made practical divinity necessary; the devil, controversial.' But it is necessary. We must 'resist the devil,' or he will not 'flee from us.'"

This decade of ministry laid a vision and a defense of Wesley's ministry to which he would refer again and again. But as time moved on, he simply could not dedicate his time and energy to his critics. He had a growing number of souls under his care who needed his attention and organizational wisdom.

Chapter 11
Method to the Madness

Preaching like an apostle, without joining together those that
are awakened and training them up in the ways of God,
is only begetting children for the murderer.

I go away, God willing, next Monday," George Whitefield wrote to Wesley from Bristol in 1739, at the advent of the revival. "If you were here, before my departure, it might be best. Many are ripe for bands. I leave that entirely to you."

With thousands coming to hear Whitefield, Wesley, and others, it was becoming evident to all that preaching alone had a limited impact on the people. In the preaching, people got a taste of the Gospel, but there needed to be a way to teach them how to live in the transformation of the Gospel, lest the hearing of it be followed by a return to their former ways of life.

The solution to this conundrum, at least at first, was to organize the people into bands—groups of five or six people ordered by gender and marital status—who collectively formed the society. George Whitefield had little appetite for such an organizational task and was opposed to leading a party with his name attached—for fear of pride. God had gifted him with oratorical brilliance, coupled with the clear, loud, pleasing preaching voice that drew great multitudes in England and America; Wesley's gifts centered on organizing souls with the goal of fostering the deep spiritual growth that leads to lives of service.

"I am but a novice," Whitefield wrote to his friend regarding organizing the people into bands. "You are acquainted with the great things of God."

Since his days in the Holy Club at Oxford, Wesley had demonstrated an unusual knack for leading small groups of people to pursue a godly life. His time in Georgia challenged that ability, but even then his philosophy of bands, and organization in general, was dramatically shaped by the structure of the Moravians.

When he looked at the Church of England—the church he loved and to which he was committed—he saw what he believed to be, in general, a deficiency in its inability to connect believers together in a meaningful way in order to pursue godly living. The Church, to his mind, was failing to pass on its fundamental teachings and practices as laid out in the *Articles of Religion* and *The Homilies*. It was his lifelong conviction that Methodism was the answer to this deficiency, and that one could not, and should not, exist without the other.

As a leader, he held together the tenuous relationship between Methodism and the church as the decades passed. Many within his movement put immense pressure on him to leave the national church, form Methodism into its own entity, and thus cut ties entirely. These ideas were in line with the strategies of the Dissenters and Nonconformists, who had been prominent in controversies during his parents' generation. There were others, however, such as his brother Charles, who were uneasy about the independent nature of Methodism and wished for it to come further under the authority of the Church of England.

Wesley was accused of being a schismatic—one who was "destroying Christian fellowship." This was a charge to which he was sensitive. He believed, or at least hoped, that he was giving the church a much-needed boost, and that the true schismatics and dissenters against the church were those *within* the church—"unholy men of all kinds," those who "deny the Scriptures of truth," and ministers who administer the Lord's Supper to those who have "neither the form nor the power of godliness."

He believed the attacks against him for being a dissenter and a schismatic should be turned aside. He was intent on restoring the Church's true faith, and argued that the church should turn its attention inward to its own deficiencies, rather than attack him. To his mind, he was not "destroying Christian fellowship" within the church; true Christian fellowship was virtually nonexistent. In churches all over England, people were not following scriptural commands by "watching over each other's souls," or "bearing one another's burdens." All of this failure to connect the people of God together in a meaningful way caused him to ask a friendly critic: "Are not the bulk of the parishioners a mere rope of sand?" His vision was to bind these believers together in love, in keeping with Colossians 2:2.

In late 1738, Wesley drew up *Rules of the Band Societies* as a guide for the growing network of bands established first in Bristol and then spreading to London, Newcastle, and throughout England. More than rules to be followed, these were guidelines that explained the purpose and practice of the bands, whose leaders were chosen from within—rather than appointed by Wesley or some other delegate.

To become a member of a band, one would have to be able to claim "the forgiveness of sins" and "peace with God." The bands were exclusively for justified Christians who were pursuing holiness. But the *Rules* also made clear that, by joining a band, a member subjected himself or herself to the honest assessment of "faults" from other members, and had to commit "to be on this and all other occasions entirely open, so as to speak everything that is on your heart, without exception, without disguise, and without reserve." For Wesley, complete transparency was tantamount to true Christian fellowship.

The Rules of the Bands also included five questions to be read at weekly meetings, which served as a spiritual assessment of the prior week and fulfilled the purpose of the bands to "confess your faults one to another, and pray for one another, that ye may be healed." These were intensely intimate groups.

John Wesley quickly found that confession of sin and the pursuit of holiness in the groups were incredibly messy endeavors, given human sinfulness and the constant attacks of the devil. But he was up to the task and relentlessly pursued purity within the bands in his societies.

The messiness of sin immediately raised an important question: What would he do with those members of the society who fell back into active sinful waywardness? Wesley knew that continuing in sin was damaging for both the sinning member and the society as a whole; therefore, it must be diligently confronted. So he began the practice of regularly "examining" the bands to purge them of "disorderly walkers."

This method of examination began in Bristol in 1741 and continued throughout Wesley's ministry. He—or, later, one of his appointed assistants—personally met with any member of a band of whom "any reasonable objection was made" to their faithfulness to the *Rules*. But he also met "face to face with their accusers" because he understood that false accusations and misunderstandings could happen. He recognized that these "disorderly walkers" failed to represent the Gospel in its fullness to a watching world, thus hurting the society as well as their own souls.

After meeting with both the accuser and accused, Wesley or his assistants would take one of three approaches to resolution, depending on the severity of the sin and the repentance of the sinner. The first approach was for the accused to remain in the society in good standing. This was the case when someone was found to be misunderstood or falsely accused. It was also the prescribed course of action when the accused openly confessed and "promised a better behavior."

A second approach was to put members on trial for three months. This was done when there was some doubt—but no proof—as to how forthcoming the accused member had been, or if the offense was not so grievous as to require expulsion. After the three-month trial, an assessment was made, and a member could then be fully reinstated or entirely expelled.

The final approach was to expel unrepentant rule breakers, with the hope of restoration in the future.

To help those who had grown slack, Wesley experimented with the formation of distinct bands, sometimes called penitent bands, filled exclusively with similarly struggling souls. Though the practice did not take hold on a larger scale, a similar practice of ordering more mature transgressors into select bands did.

To make clear who was—and who wasn't—a member of the society, Wesley began giving members "tickets," simple sheets of paper that were proof that one was entitled to the privileges of membership. These tickets were distributed—or taken away—quarterly during the year. Wesley anchored the novel concept of tickets to the biblical practice of sending "commendatory letters." He viewed this task as essential to the health of the societies, later defending the practice of expulsion to a clerical critic:

> *When any members of these or of the United Society are proved*
> *to live in known sin, we then mark and avoid them; we separate*
> *ourselves from every one that walks disorderly. Sometimes, if the case*
> *be judged infectious [to the Society at large] (though rarely), this is*
> *openly declared.*

Wesley's ultimate goal was straightforward. He was driving people toward his view of total holiness—Christian perfection. Ironically, however, perfection is not what he expected. Rather, he demanded genuine repentance and spiritual growth from his followers, and there was no better place in his system to fulfill this desire and hope for perfection than in the bands.

The bands served a crucial purpose in Wesley's system. But a system built on a series of societies held together by intense small groups of the most committed believers could not reach the mass of people. Through field preaching, many were captivated by the Gospel but were not ready or possessing enough understanding of the implications of the Gospel to join such a committed band of brothers or sisters. A mature Methodist system would have to account for the various spiritual stages of individuals, and it would later come in the form of *classes*—larger groups of about a dozen people under the direction of an appointed leader who could walk with members and teach them how to walk in holiness. It was the classes, rather than the bands, that became the heartbeat of Methodism.

Though the classes developed accidentally, they ended up meeting an indispensable need for an organization dedicated to holiness. The fortuitous discovery happened in February 1742 while Wesley was discussing with some members of the Bristol society how they might pay debts related to their property. They decided that the most effective way was to collect a penny a week from each of the members. Not only would this give people virtual ownership of the society—real ownership would remain in the hands of Wesley and his trustees—but it would instill in them a giving spirit in line with scriptural mandates.

The plan raised practical questions that would ultimately be answered by the forming of classes. How would the money be collected? What if a member could not pay? Should the poor be compelled to give, or be expelled if they do not? To answer these issues, the societies decided to appoint leaders to visit groups of about a dozen people at their homes to collect the penny every week. This allowed the leaders to quietly discern a member's ability to pay the penny. If the member could not, the leader would supply the amount from his or her own pocket.

The result of this practice unexpectedly opened the door to a wealth of opportunities to meet the spiritual needs of the society. Wesley explains the development as the leaders shifted from penny collectors to spiritual leaders:

> *In a while, some of these informed me, they found such and such an one did not live as he ought. It struck me immediately, "This is the thing; the very thing we have wanted so long." I called together all the Leaders of the Classes (so we used to term them and their companies), and desired that each would make a particular inquiry into the behaviour of those whom he saw weekly. They did so. Many disorderly walkers were detected. Some turned from the evil of their ways. Some were put away from us. Many saw it with fear, and rejoiced unto God with reverence.*

As a result, the leaders of the classes became unofficial pastors to their classes. The role of leader continued to develop as they were required to meet with each member of the class once a week, "in order to inquire how their souls prosper; to advise, reprove, comfort or exhort," and report their findings to the minister and steward of the society.

As exciting as this development was, it quickly became clear that though there were advantages to having leaders visit their class members at their homes, there were even greater disadvantages. Issues of time, privacy, and housing made it more practical for the classes to come together weekly in one place—a home, the society building, or elsewhere. What grew out of this gathering was often deep fellowship, as members cared for one another and their needs and found pastoral counsel from their leaders.

Once this new system was established in 1743, one could not be a member of the society without being an active member of a class. There was just one requirement for admission: "a desire to flee from the wrath to come, to be saved from their sins." According to this lofty but indiscriminate requirement, one could come to the society (at first) as "the vilest offender" or as a saint in the world's eyes. Attendance and participation, therefore, were open to those educated in the faith, as well as to those uneducated—to the justified and the unjustified alike.

But members could not, and would not, be able to remain in the status of "vile offender" for long. Whether they truly desired to flee from the wrath of God's judgment, Wesley believed, "will be shown by [their] fruits." Therefore, before admittance, prospective members of the society had to agree to three general rules, with specific subsets:

- "Avoiding evil of every kind," such as taking the name of the Lord in vain, drunkenness, fighting or quarreling, unprofitable speech, and the like.
- "Doing good of every possible sort and as far as possible to all men."
- "Attending upon all the ordinances of God," which included attending public worship, partaking of the Lord's Supper, family and private prayer, searching the scriptures, and fasting.

To the best of his ability, Wesley held his members to these rules.

I had been often told it was impossible for me to distinguish the precious from the vile without the miraculous discernment of spirits. But I now saw, more clearly than ever, that this might be done and without much difficulty, supposing only two things: first, courage and steadiness in the examiner; secondly, common sense and common honesty in the Leader of each Class. . . . The question is not concerning the heart, but the life. And the general tenor of this I do not say cannot be known, but cannot be hid, without a miracle.

Classes were organized in a variety of ways, and each retained a unique character. Some were composed solely of men; some were a mixture of men and women; and still others were composed of only women. Men-only and mixed classes were led by men; women-only classes were led by women. Though the order of class meetings varied based on the gifting and personality of the leader and its members, the meetings generally began with a hymn or a prayer, followed by the leader describing the state of his or her soul, including struggles and joys. After the leader's confession, the other members were asked one by one to give an account of their spiritual journey for the week. This gave them an opportunity to examine their own hearts more carefully, and also gave the body of believers—and the leader, first and foremost—an opportunity to offer feedback, rebukes, insight, and wisdom.

As such, the classes had a practical teaching element not found in the more egalitarian bands. Larger society gatherings in the preaching houses focused on doctrinal teaching; in the classes, the focus was on spiritual instruction; and the bands focused on putting these elements into practice through confession and prayer.

The classes, then, became the main mechanism by which souls could be nurtured on their spiritual journey toward Wesley's hope for perfection. For the final phase in their pursuit of perfection, the more zealous and mature class members entered into bands with like-minded members to spur one another on.

There was also more to the organization that separated classes from bands. In order for the society to function as an effective spiritual organism, it also needed to function practically. Thus, each society was overseen by a steward—a person competent in temporal matters, who could oversee the building facilities as well as manage people, including preachers, class and band leaders, housekeepers, visitors of the sick, and general members. And though it was not required for a steward to have any teaching or preaching gifts, he was responsible for the doctrine taught by anyone who preached at society gatherings. As a result, the stewards had doctrinal authority over local and itinerant preachers, as well as over the assistants who reported directly to Wesley.

At its healthiest, a society reached out to the community and gave opportunities for the pursuit of deep spiritual maturity.

As Methodism continued to grow and spread to dozens of cities, towns, and villages throughout England, it became evident that it needed an overarching structure to maintain the various societies. Wesley could not personally oversee all the societies at once. He needed help.

He began organizing the societies into geographical regions, called *circuits*, and appointed helpers as assistants over these circuits. These assistants became Wesley's chief inner circle who would implement his vision. They were called to a demanding role as they oversaw every aspect of the societies within their appointed circuits—the leaders, the classes, and the bands—and were expected to preach morning and evening wherever they were.

By 1746, England and Wales were divided into seven circuits, overseen by twelve assistants. The abundance of leaders paved the way for rapid growth; by 1748, there were nine circuits; and by 1749, England, Wales, and Ireland were divided into twelve circuits: London, Bristol, Wiltshire, Cornwall, Staffordshire, Cheshire, Leeds, Haworth, Lincolnshire, Newcastle, Wales, and Ireland.

Though the assistants were given much authority and responsibility, it was clear to all that John Wesley was in charge. He held his assistants, circuits, and societies together with an iron fist, into what he called a "connexion." All of the moving parts—the bands, classes, societies, and circuits—were cogs in a finely tuned machine that imposed order onto a fast-moving and very often chaotic revival.

The importance of structure became clear as a result of experimenting with a lack of organization. At the 1745 conference, Wesley and his assistants decided to "make a trial" of preaching in two areas, Wales and Cornwall, without establishing societies there. This would allow for more preaching, to more people, in more cities, without the encumbrance and the slow, hard work of developing an organization.

Three years later, Wesley and his assistants assessed the practice at the 1748 conference. According to the conference minutes, "almost all the seed has fallen by the wayside. There is scarce any fruit remaining." Wesley listed the causes of the failure:

> *1. The Preacher cannot give proper exhortations and instructions to those who are convinced of sin, unless he has opportunities of meeting them apart from the mixed, unawakened multitude. 2. They cannot watch over one another in love, unless they are thus united together. Nor, 3. Can the believers build up one another, and bear one another's burdens.*

This experiment of preaching without ordering a society was a trial that Wesley would not dare repeat. In later years, he grew even more resistant to such disorganized ministry. In his 1763 journal, he warns that even "preaching like an apostle, without joining together those that are awakened and training them up in the ways of God, is only begetting children for the murderer." In 1766, he told his company of preachers, "It is far easier to preach a good sermon than to instruct the ignorant in the principles of religion." Wesley's system provided both.

Wesley's organizational structure set Methodism on a sure footing, and the movement continued to grow and spread, eventually affecting the entire world. It was, however, a messy work that would "try the parts and spirits" of all who labored. But more so than even his preaching, teaching, and writing, it was Wesley's organizational ability that made his ministry so successful.

By contrast, though George Whitefield was extraordinarily gifted in preaching, and was the greatest evangelist of his generation, he was much less interested in creating an organization, even decrying the practice as a prideful desire to found a party. But in retrospect, the winsome evangelist apparently regretted his failure to adequately organize the fruit of his ministry. Shortly before his death, he lamented: "My brother Wesley acted wisely. The souls that were awakened under his ministry he joined in Class, and thus preserved the fruit of his labor. This I neglected, and my people are a rope of sand."

Whitefield's self-deprecating assessment of his indisputably effective ministry may not be entirely fair. Wesley's organization had issues of its own that haunted him throughout his life. He knew he had to fight doctrinally and practically to keep Methodism pure, leaders spiritually vital, and his societies faithful. But just as Whitefield had his regrets and fears, so also Wesley, at the end of his life, had his. In 1786, he wrote, "I am not afraid that the people called Methodists should never cease to exist either in Europe or America. But I am afraid lest they should only exist as a dead sect, having the form of religion without the power. And this undoubtedly will be the case unless they hold fast both the doctrine, spirit, and discipline with which they first set out."

The system that Wesley put in place was highly effective and helped retain the fruit of his labors and that of his helpers. With his methods, he brought order to chaos.

Part III

Opportunities in Crisis

Chapter 12
Love Lost

*Hardly has such a case been from
the beginning of the world.*

Since 1729, when John and Charles Wesley reconnected at Oxford in the Holy Club, the two were the closest of brothers. When John ventured to Georgia, Charles went with him. When John returned to England, the brothers had evangelical conversions within days of one another and worked in close concert in the great evangelical revival. In the 1740s, they were viewed by the public as two heads of the same Methodist movement. They were inseparable colaborers in the vineyard, coadvisors, close confidants, and friends.

Both were bachelors into the second half of the 1740s, and this status gave them the freedom and ability to dedicate all their time and energy to their grueling schedule with its incessant travels and ministry obligations. This was purposeful. Marriage, John believed, had the real possibility of hindering his call to itinerate ministry. But more than that, basing his conviction on his understanding of St. Paul's teaching on marriage and some early church fathers, he wrote in *Thoughts on Marriage and a Single Life* (1743) that one who married would necessarily suffer loss to his soul. He had been influenced by Christian mystics who believed that marriage was the "less perfect state." As a result, John publically declared that he had "no design" to marry. In so doing, he painted himself into a corner.

After John's disastrous relationship with Sophy Hopkey in Georgia, he and Charles pledged to each other that neither would marry, nor take any steps toward marriage, without the other's knowledge and consent. The pledge went untested over the next decade, but by 1748 both brothers had grown restless in their singleness and in their failure to conquer their "unholy desires and inordinate affections." They were becoming convinced, in part by objections to John's 1743 tract, that marriage was a legitimate, and even necessary, solution to the problem. But the results of their shift toward marriage led to a great strain on their relationship, altered the makeup of the Methodist movement, and led to a blemish on John Wesley's reputation—if not his very character—that could never be erased.

On his way through Wales on a ministry tour to Ireland in August 1747, Charles Wesley rested at the home of the Welsh magistrate, Marmaduke Gwynne, who was a convert of Howell Harris, a Welsh Calvinist Methodist. A friend of the Wesleys, Gwynne attended the second Methodist conference in Bristol in 1745, and thereafter Charles had found him a kind and generous supporter of his work.

On this particular trip, one of Gwynne's daughters, twenty-one-year-old Sarah (or Sally, as she was called) caught the attention of the traveling preacher—so much so that when he met John in Ireland a few weeks later, Charles told him of his "embryo intentions" of marriage. Charles found John to be indifferent, later writing in his journal that his elder brother "neither opposed, nor much encouraged" the idea.

These "embryo intentions" continued to develop rapidly over the next year. When Charles returned to Garth seven months later suffering from a severe toothache, the Gwynne family nursed him to health. Then, in June 1748, Marmaduke brought Sally to meet Charles in Bristol, where they began a tour of England to oversee the work of the ministry. The trio parted when Charles left the Gwynnes in Wales and continued on to Ireland. By then, however, he had resolved to marry Sally.

At the same time, John had found a potential mate in a young widow named Grace Murray. Wesley's junior by a dozen years, Murray had first been moved by the ministry and preaching of George Whitefield, but she had found forgiveness of sins while listening to a woman read the fifth chapter of Romans. She lost her husband, an often-absent sailor who resisted her newfound faith, when he drowned on a transatlantic journey in 1742. Though her husband had insisted that she keep her "madness" of religion to herself, her conversion gave her "an insatiable thirst for the salvation of all men," which compelled her to offer this salvation to the worst of sinners.

After her husband's tragic death, Grace moved to her hometown of Newcastle, where she became a leader of several female Methodist classes, ministered to women throughout the surrounding region, and brought many to "the remission of sins." John took her (in the company of others) on ministry journeys, and she became part of the Wesley family as a servant of the orphanage in Newcastle. There, John could carefully observe her over several years, until he felt as if knew her "inside and out."

In August 1748, when Grace nursed John back to health after an illness, he "observed her more narrowly than before. . .[and] esteemed and loved her more and more." When they began "sliding" into discussions about marriage, she seemed pleased. According to his unpublished account of her comments, she said, "This is all I could have wished for under heaven."

When John recovered from his illness and was again ready to depart, he told Grace, "I am convinced God has called you to be my fellow-laborer in the Gospel." He told her he would return in the spring to take her to minister with him in Ireland, and that "if we meet again, I trust we should part no more."

"Rejoicing," he left her, believing he had found his mate. But there was one major problem. He needed the approval of his brother and his assistants, all of whom had promised to take "no step" toward marriage without consulting one another. This effort would take months, and it was clearly not his priority. Furthermore, Grace would have to remain silent about the arrangement until these consultations were completed. John's dithering and Grace's silence proved fatal for their star-crossed romance.

Over the next several months, John and Charles took diverging paths concerning marriage. When Charles returned from his ministry in Ireland in the autumn of 1748, he rested in Garth and there proposed marriage to Sarah Gwynne. According to his private journal from that time, he and John had "consulted about every particular and were of one heart and mind in all things." The following April on a cloudless day, John performed the service of the wedding.

"My brother seemed," Charles later reflected, "the happiest person among us."

It was the beginning of a lifelong happy marriage for Charles and Sally.

When John left Newcastle in September 1748, he unwittingly left Grace Murray to another suitor: one of his assistants, John Bennett. Bennett moved quickly to woo Grace, whose affections were divided between the two men. Just one day after Wesley left town believing his status with Grace was secure, she entered into an understanding with Bennett that they would marry after he secured the necessary approvals. Consequently, the next few months would prove to be the most confusing, intriguing, and ultimately sad period in the life of John Wesley—and the second time his heart was broken by a woman he professed to love.

By the time Wesley returned to Newcastle in the spring of 1749, Grace told him that her agreement with John Bennett had fizzled, leading Wesley to believe that "the affair between [her and Bennett] was as if it had never been."

During the subsequent tour of Ireland with Grace, Wesley was deeply impressed with her effectiveness as they visited the societies. "I saw the work of God prosper in her hands," he wrote.

> *She lightened my burden more than can be expressed. She ex-*
> *amined all the women in the smaller Societies and the believers*
> *in every place. She settled all the women Bands; visited the sick;*
> *prayed with the mourners; more and more of them received remis-*
> *sion of sins during her conversation and prayer. Meantime she was*
> *to me both a servant and a friend, as well as a fellow-labourer in*
> *the gospel.*

In Grace Murray, John found a woman he deemed "the most useful woman in the kingdom," well fit to be the wife of the leader of Methodism. Before they returned from Ireland, they entered into a contract *de praesenti* for marriage—a legally binding agreement that represented "a mutual promise or contract of present matrimony," though not always consummated. The contractual binding, however, did not have the force of a de facto reality. The arrangement had only the strength of commitment between the two parties. And Grace Murray's commitment was weak.

Fuel was added to the uncertain fire when the pair came to Bristol, where Grace heard rumors that there was another woman in John's life. Feeling betrayed and jealous, she sent off an affectionate letter to John Bennett, renewing his passions for her. When Wesley and his company went to London, a woman there gave Grace a taste of the nastiness and intrigue that likely awaited her as the wife of such a prominent leader. "The people would not suffer you," the woman told Grace privately. "You would be miserable all your life. And that would make him miserable, too. So that, instead of strengthening, you would weaken his hands." She ended her "counsel" with a parting shot: "If you love yourself, or if you love him, never think of it more."

These two events were enough to cause Grace to reconsider marriage to Wesley, but when they returned to Newcastle in early September, she found John Bennett eager to make good on his promise of marriage from the previous year. He was willing to claim his right to her over her commitment to John Wesley, setting the stage for an ugly confrontation.

Wesley's tendency in such instances was to withdraw his interest and revert to the mind-set of a metaphorical martyr. Believing that Grace's affections lay with Bennett, Wesley wrote her a note saying that he "thought it was not proper that she and I should converse any more together." He had decided that fighting over her would only hurt her. When Grace received the note, she wavered once again and convinced Wesley that she was committed to him. Truth was, she was not ready to part with either man, but neither man could continue to wait.

On September 6, having finally tired of her waffling, Wesley demanded a decision. "Which will you choose?" he asked. "I am determined by conscience, as well as inclination, to live and die with you," she replied. Her answer gave him the confidence to finally fight for her.

With renewed resolve, he penned a letter to John Bennett, charging the young assistant with failing to inform Wesley of intentions of such importance (for indeed Bennett had broken one of the *Rules of a Helper*). Further, Wesley accused Bennett of betrayal for attempting to steal Grace away and argued that, by law, he had a prior right to her because she had first been engaged to him, which negated any later arrangement between her and Bennett.

Wesley mailed a copy of the letter, dated September 7, to Charles for review and sent another copy to Bennett. Neither missive hit its intended mark. The copy to Bennett was never delivered. The one to Charles had the effect of setting him in motion to intervene against John's seemingly rash and unwise steps.

While John waited for events to unfold, Grace made "repeated requests" to him to "marry immediately." But he insisted that he must first satisfy John Bennett's claim, speak to his brother and to all of his assistants and to each society throughout England—a truly monumental task. Neither time nor circumstances would permit this mission to be accomplished. However, Wesley and Grace renewed their marital contract, the *de praesenti*, on September 21, this time in the presence of witnesses.

When Charles received his copy of John's September 7 letter to Bennett, he immediately set out on a mission to put a stop to the mess his brother was making. The choice of a wife for John put the entire Methodist movement at stake—the societies, the preachers, and the people. No one was more keenly aware and protective of this reality than Charles.

Charles objected to John's engagement to Grace Murray on several counts. First, she was "low born," a "servant," of a lower class and level than John. As such, John's marriage to her had the potential to "break up all our Societies, and put a stop to the whole work of God."

Charles also objected because he believed that Grace was prev ously engaged to John Bennett, a misconception confirmed by Bennett's friends.

Furthermore, he believed that John was being driven by "inordinate affections."

Sensing an impending disaster, Charles hatched a conniving plan to deliver his brother from what he viewed as a grand mistake. His first step was to meet with Grace to convince her that marriage to John would be a scandal that would harm the Gospel. He put a letter in her hands that would have caused any soul to step back. Out of his belief that Grace had first been engaged to Bennett, Charles put the weight of the matter on her to see that John was not just any man, but "one of such importance, that his doing so dishonest an action would destroy both himself, and me, and the whole work of God." Charles argued that the weight of the entire Gospel hinged on Grace's decision. "Had not the Lord restrained you, what a scandal had you brought upon the gospel; nay, and you would have left your name as a curse upon God's people."

As if this letter were not enough of a betrayal of his brother, Charles deceived Grace by telling her that "Mr. Wesley will have nothing to say to you." He led her to believe that it was John's will for her to marry Bennett—and to do so immediately. In so doing, he believed he was saving his brother, saving Methodism, and saving the work of God in England.

All the while, John knew that something was afoot, and it is possible he could have fought to win Grace's affections, convince Charles, and send Bennett away. But he refused to change his ministry schedule. As a result, Charles took Grace to marry John Bennett on October 3. This act crushed John Wesley. Whether Grace Murray could ever have lived up to his idealized view or matched his unrealistic expectations of a wife, John saw in her a perfect match that was snatched away.

Throwing salt on a very open wound, Charles insisted that John meet with the newly married couple, "that I might acknowledge my sin" before them all. But when they met, it soon became

ᴢh much too late—that whatever legitimate objections
⌄ have had, he was mistaken concerning some of the
ᵤ. After the meeting, John lamented the sad reality: "I should see her face no more."

John, the thwarted lover and betrayed brother, reflected on these events as if he were the protagonist of a sinister Greek or Shakespearean tragedy: "If these things are so, hardly has such a case been from the beginning of the world!"

Not only had he lost his love, but he had lost her at the hands of his beloved brother.

Following the Grace Murray affair, John Wesley, most often an unflappable, emotionally stable individual, began to suffer a profound depression, which led to irrational and destructive decisions. According to Charles, John was so distraught over the affair that within weeks he was going throughout England looking for a wife, proposing to some, and no longer receiving the advice of others. "I am no longer of his council," Charles wrote to mutual friend Ed Perronet.

By intervening in the Grace Murray affair, Charles believed he had fulfilled a "ministry" of "deliverance." John, on the other hand, thought that Charles had ruined his chance at happiness. So fractured was their relationship at this point that for the first time in their lives, separation seemed possible—even likely. After an understandably intense and emotional meeting between the two brothers shortly after the "whirlwind," Charles wrote to Ed Perronet, "If I must break with him, [I] would retreat gradually and hide it from the world." This, in essence, is what he did over the course of the next few years—skipping the 1751 Methodist conference and trimming his preaching schedule and travel itinerary. When Charles ruefully spoke to his brother about the possibility of separation, John "seemed pleased with the thought of parting."

Eight months later, John had his eyes set on a new potential mate: a widow named Mary Vazeille, also known as Molly. If Charles had thought that Grace Murray was beneath his brother's dignity, John's new belle was even worse. Upon meeting her, before he was even aware of a potential relationship, Charles described her in his journal as "a woman of a sorrowful spirit." He must have been surprised when he learned of John's interest; but even if he was opposed, there was nothing he could do about it.

John saw Mary in a different light—as a potential partner in ministry. The oldest recovered letter he wrote to her gives insight into his hopeful expectation of a worthy spouse. He encourages her as she is about to embark on a journey through parts of England, saying, "I believe riding, so far as your strength will allow, will much confirm your bodily health. And the conversing with those in various parts who know and love God will greatly strengthen your soul. Perhaps. . .[God] too may make you useful to some of them."

Despite his hopes for a partner who would travel and minister in a similar fashion to his own—riding hundreds of miles on horseback, visiting people incessantly—his vision did not match the reality of Mary's passion or ability. Blinded by his hope, he pressed on with his expectations.

The contrast between how Charles and John measured others was summed up by Charles years later: "Our different judgment of persons was owing to our different tempers: his all hopes and mine all fears." In this instance, John's optimism could have been tempered by the pessimism of his younger brother.

When Wesley met her, Mary Vazeille was a forty-year-old widow with grown children, the youngest of whom was in her mid- to late teens. Mary and her former husband were Huguenots—a persecuted French Protestant group—who lived in London, where her husband had amassed a small fortune as a successful merchant before he died in 1747.

John courted her in private, and little is known of his deliberation of the matter. After his experience in the Grace Murray affair, it's hard to blame him for keeping the relationship private, especially from Charles. But keeping the relationship private from virtually every other counselor as well proved unwise and hurtful to his cause. Furthermore, it broke his promise to Charles not to take any steps toward marriage without consultation.

In February 1751, eighteen months after losing Grace Murray, John was "resolved to marry" and informed Charles.

"I was thunderstruck," Charles writes in his journal.

John did not seek permission or counsel, nor did he inform his brother about whom he would marry. He and Mary were wed in late February, in a ceremony with few witnesses and no extant records. Not only did Charles not attend, but he learned the name of the bride-to-be from a friend. "Several days afterward," he wrote, "[I] was one of the last to hear of that unhappy marriage."

For John, the marriage began happily enough. "O how can we praise God enough," he wrote a month into their marriage, "for making us helps meet for each other!" But even in this letter there is a sense that he needed to assuage his wife's insecurities, coupled with his own inability to express his love to her. "You have surely a right to every proof of love I can give."

When Wesley married Mary Vazeille, he wanted a partner in ministry—someone who would and could travel with him, who could lead other women, and who could fulfill administrative tasks. He entered the marriage on the condition that he "should not preach one sermon, or travel one mile the less" on account of the marriage. She, on the other hand, wanted a lover—one who would stay by her side and devote himself to her. Both would be disappointed.

By April 1752, Wesley was writing to London banker Ebenezer Blackwell, an important friend and confidant, concerning Mary's desire to travel: "The more she travels, the better she bears it. It gives us yet another proof that whatever God calls us to He will fit us for." But his optimism could not mask a growing realization that the hectic life of an itinerant ministry did not suit her.

In fairness, he could not have been an easy husband to have. He was away more often than he was at home, investing his energy, time, and emotions on thousands of souls while neglecting the one soul for whom he had promised to forsake all. Mary could not have felt cherished, judging by an early letter in which John writes in a valiant tone, "Oh what mystery is this! That I am enabled to give you up to God without one murmuring or uneasy thought!" One can imagine any newlywed wife hoping for a little more "murmuring" from a distant lover.

Though no woman could have tamed Wesley's all-consuming passion to spread his gospel, there is reason to believe that an all-consuming jealousy pushed him further away. John soon found that Mary had an explosive temper that he could in no way tame, which must have come as a shock to one who was deliberate, and often dispassionate, in everything he said. These issues would remain for the duration of their tumultuous, thirty-year marriage.

John was not the first Wesley to have marital problems. Financial troubles for his parents, Samuel and Susanna, brought inevitable stress and became the source of intense conflict. In 1725, when John was twenty-one, his mother wrote to him that "it is an unhappiness almost peculiar to our family, that your father and I seldom think alike."

During that same period, his older sister Emilia wrote to him, encouraging him to put his "worldly affairs" in order before entering into an unhappy marriage. For John, finances would never be a major issue, though the debts he personally incurred for preaching houses to support his ministry surely put pressure on him. His frugality and financial wisdom set most of the financial stress out of his life. But his sister continued to warn him with words that have the eerie ring of prophecy: "Believe me, if you ever come to suffer the torment of a hopeless love, all other afflictions will seem small in comparison of this."

Within a few years, John's marriage was slowly crumbling. Adding to the torment of his unhappy home life was the affliction of his fractured relationship with Charles. Because each brother felt betrayed by the other—John by Charles's role in the ending of his relationship with Grace Murray, and Charles by John's subsequent marriage to Mary Vazeille—their bond was preserved only by tattered strands of brotherly obligation and their dutiful commitment to a common cause in the Gospel.

Moreover, Charles had begun to take an increasingly critical view of his brother's leadership of Methodism. He ridiculed, though privately, John's defense of his marriage to the societies and thought that when John directed the society's meetings, he "misspent his strength in trifles."

Charles's antipathy for Mary Wesley would prove to be deepseated and lifelong. And she reciprocated the sentiments. Charles and Sally avoided meeting with Mary, and she with them, for most of the rest of their lives. When they did meet, it strengthened their desire and resolve never to meet again. Charles sardonically referred to Mary as "my very best friend," because, as good friends do, she told him all his faults—and then some. This toxic relationship further drove the brothers apart.

Another issue developed between the brothers in the mid-1750s that tore them even further apart, and it was related to the direction of Methodism. The Methodist movement always had a tenuous relationship with the Church of England. Though John saw the movement as an extension of the church, the church tended to see Methodism as a subversion. Many within the movement wanted it to be completely separate from the church—that is, to be a dissenting church on its own.

Charles had grown increasingly uncomfortable with the movement's anti-church stance, which was prevalent among many of its assistants, and wanted to put the genie back in the bottle. While John was committed to remaining in the Church of England, he felt he was holding together a fragile alliance between those who wanted to leave and those who, like Charles, wanted a closer association with the church.

These tensions, along with a growing desire to stay at home with his wife and children, led Charles to become more detached. Not only did he skip the 1751 conference, but he also stopped coordinating his preaching circuits with John and quietly refused to obey his brother's directives about when and where to preach. Things finally came to a head in July 1755 when Charles ignored John's request that he minister in Cornwall, "which," in John's words, "might save my time and strength." John concluded his letter tersely, writing, "Then I will go to Cornwall myself; that is all." But that was not all. In cryptic shorthand, John added, "For a wife and a partner I may challenge the world! But love is rot. Adieu." This letter was likely the last one the brothers exchanged for the next five years.

In late 1757, against the wishes and advice of friends, John Wesley appointed Sarah Ryan as housekeeper of the New Room in Bristol. The housekeeper was entrusted with enormous responsibility in keeping the society building running both physically and spiritually.

Mrs. Ryan, a woman in her early thirties, was estranged from her husband as a result of learning that he was already married to someone else. She had been growing by leaps and bounds ever since her life was captured by the Gospel, delivering her from a past of promiscuity. Such testimonies of redemption and transformation invigorated Wesley, and he was eager to watch these redeemed souls grow in grace.

Sarah Ryan's promiscuous past raised alarm bells in Mary Wesley, who from the outset of her marriage to John had been exceedingly insecure and jealous. John's interest in Sarah's testimony and spiritual life gave Mary further concern, and by 1758, it seems she may have had reason for concern.

John used letters to counsel, encourage, and generally pastor hundreds of correspondents. His correspondence was often very warm, affectionate, and effusive—to men and women alike. His letters to Sarah Ryan were no different in this regard. When his critics—including his wife—questioned his appointment of Sarah Ryan to the housekeeper's position, John wrote to Sarah, promising to stand with and support her. But he clearly saw in her something he did not readily find in his own wife—the spiritual vitality of one who desired to learn from him. This was the greatest danger to him, and it threatened his fragile marriage and growing ministry.

On January 20, 1758, John again wrote to Sarah Ryan, encouraging her to endure the trials in her new controversial role without "stirring of resentment" and to gain "a deeper knowledge of yourself and God, of His power to save, and of the salvation He hath wrought in you."

But the content and tone of his letter became inappropriate when he wrote, "The conversing with you, either by speaking or writing, is an unspeakable blessing to me. I cannot think of you without thinking of God. Others often lead me to Him; but it is, as it were, going round about: you bring me straight into His presence." He signed and folded the letter, and placed it in his coat pocket without sealing it.

When he went to preach that evening and took off his coat, his wife went through his pockets, read the letter, and according to Wesley, came into "such a temper as I had not seen her in for several years."

Rather than apologize or repent, he doubled down, arguing that there was nothing inappropriate in what he had said. In a subsequent letter to Sarah Ryan, he wrote, "After many severe words, my wife left me, vowing she would see me no more."

To the end of his life, John Wesley adamantly maintained that he was innocent of the charge of adultery, but his wife continued to accuse him throughout their marriage. He denied he had written anything inappropriate in his letters—either out of an unbelievable and insensitive relational naïveté, or out of a cynical self-deception. But though he may not have committed adultery, he allowed other women dangerously close to his heart while in the midst of a broken marriage.

After a period of separation, Mary returned at his invitation, but their marriage would always be marked with suspicion, distrust, arguments, frequent separations, accusations, and backbiting.

While the two most important relationships in Wesley's life were in jeopardy—with his brother and with his wife—he had no truer friend than London banker Ebenezer Blackwell. Successful in business, Blackwell was not intimidated by John, Charles, or Mary Wesley, nor was he unfamiliar with conflict. Committed to the cause of Methodism, he could see through and confront the leaders with utmost discretion. He proved a much-needed glue for these fragmented relationships, serving as a peacemaker between John and Charles, and between John and Mary, beginning in the 1750s and extending into the early 1760s.

When Mary Wesley tried to control her husband's confidants and contacts, it caused John to feel imprisoned in his own home. This included her attempts to control John's visits with Charles and Sally, both of whom found Mary unbearable. Seeing how Mary was driving a wedge between John and Charles, Ebenezer Blackwell invited Charles and John to visit him at his spacious estate in Lewisham, outside of London, where John had often gone for writing and respite. Blackwell hoped that the two brothers could spend a week or two attempting a reconciliation.

In explaining his intentions to Charles, Blackwell said that "from henceforth you may go on with that love and harmony which is and must be expected of any persons so engaged and so united as you two are." When Charles rebuffed the offer, Blackwell wrote to him that he was "vastly disappointed," knowing that "a true Christian harmony. . . can never be perfected without both yourself and Mrs. Wesley [coming] to town." Blackwell maintained that he had "nothing to do in this affair but to make, and if possible [keep], peace between you all, which by the grace of God I would most willingly do." But the tensions between the brothers would continue for nearly another decade.

While Blackwell tried to broker peace between Charles and John, he also intervened between John and Mary. No person who loved John spoke more truthfully to him throughout the first decade of his troubled marriage. He was indeed, according to John, one of his "best friends." When the Sarah Ryan incident led Mary Wesley to leave John, Blackwell once again stepped in, rebuking Wesley for receiving "improper" letters from women who were complaining about his wife, and for not being "cautious enough" in his letters to women.

When John wrote in defense of himself and his letters, Blackwell pushed back.

"When I have spoken to you, it has been without reserve; and if at any time I have expressed myself a little freer than many others would dare to do...it has constantly been with a view if possible to have established peace between yourself and Mrs. W[esley]." The London banker then conceded the difficulty of dealing with Mary, saying, "[I] would even then be glad to be excused [of the] honour [of meeting with her] if it was not out of civility to yourself."

For decades, John and Mary's marriage would need an unending supply of patches to keep it together, until she finally left him for good in 1774. But during the crucial decade when Wesley lost the love of his brother and the love of his wife, he found love from Ebenezer Blackwell. In a world where men of prominence are often surrounded by unctuous people pleasers and hateful enemies, Wesley was well served by Blackwell, who sternly, yet lovingly, rebuked him as a true friend.

By 1760, the Wesleys' marriage was in tatters. John had stopped writing and speaking to Sarah Ryan to try to appease his wife, but jealousy continued to drive Mary. She tracked her husband throughout England, sometimes traveling great distances to take note of who was with him in his chaise. After finding that Mary's fears could not be assuaged, and finding his ministry hindered, John began to assert what he believed to be his right to meet and correspond with whomever he chose—though he did, in accordance with Blackwell's rebuke, become more cautious in his letters.

Perhaps most importantly in 1760, John reached out once more to his brother Charles. "Where you are I know not, and how you are I know not," he wrote, breaking a five-year silence in their known correspondence. "I hope the best."

The relationship had changed. Though Charles would never again be as active in the work, he and John were drawn back together to once again forge an unbroken bond. While intimately acquainted with the other's faults, they were diligent to protect each other from outside attacks.

By then, John believed that Mary had succumbed to "diabolical lunacy." In a letter to a friend, he said he did not think his life was safe with her. Another friend once walked into a room to find Mary in a rage, holding locks of her husband's hair in her hand after dragging him by it across the floor. Still, their marriage had seasons of peace over the next decade and a half. "My wife gains ground," he wrote to Charles in 1763; and in 1766, he noted that she "continues in an amazing temper. Miracles are not ceased." But the peace did not last. Mary proved a "cross" to him and was almost universally disliked by everyone close to him. "[H]is singular forbearance towards the worst of wives," Wesley's nephew later wrote, "was apparent to all."

Two recurring issues in the marriage finally came to a head in the early 1770s. First, Mary would regularly break into John's wardrobe to steal his papers, letters, and journals. This only enraged the man who had made his livelihood in large part through his writing. Second, in order to defend her own reputation, Mary often shared John's faults, "real or supposed," along with a mixture of lies and innuendo, with "not one or two intimates only" but with all who would listen.

Mary had become so embittered against her husband that she allied herself with some of his enemies—a new generation of Calvinists intent on quashing Wesley's teachings on grace. To get back at him for perceived hurts, Mary Wesley released some of John's papers for publication by his enemies. Charles was deeply concerned about this and implored his brother to do everything in his power to stop these scurrilous publications. But John was done fighting with Mary and kept his focus on the continuation of his itinerant ministry.

John had plans to travel to Canterbury and Dover, taking with him his sixteen-year-old niece, Sarah (Charles's daughter, who was named after her mother), with whom he had grown especially close. Concerned that the entire ministry was potentially at risk, Charles tried to convince John to cancel the trip and stay home to defend himself against the negative publicity. Young Sarah was crushed at the thought of not going with her uncle on this journey, but was greatly relieved by her father's report when he returned from a meeting with John:

> *My brother is indeed an extraordinary man. I placed before him the importance of the character of the minister; the evil consequences which might result from his indifference to it; the cause of religion; stumbling blocks cast in the way of the weak and urged upon him by every relative and public motive, to answer for himself, and stop the publication. His reply was, "My brother, when I devoted to God my ease, my time, my life, did I except my reputation? No."*

As if to underscore his resolve, John said, "Tell Sarah I will take her to Canterbury tomorrow." Despite his failure to fight the accusations against him, the papers were never published.

After accusing John of adultery for twenty years—a charge he insisted was false and unfair—Mary finally left him for the final time in 1774. In 1778, having attempted to work through at least four separations and reconciliations, and having suffered through immeasurable public humiliation and countless character assassinations, John wrote a final letter to his wife, which he claimed was written "without either anger or bitterness."

If you were to live a thousand years, you could not undo the mischief that you have done. And till you have done all you can towards it, I bid you farewell.

When Mary Wesley died in October 1781, John did not learn of it until two or three days after her burial—a sad ending to the saddest chapter in his life story.

Chapter 13
Love Your Enemies

It being my rule, confirmed by long experience,
always to look a mob in the face.

The summer of 1741 presented the leaders of the revival with their first real organized resistance. At least implicitly, the revival was a denunciation of the status quo and a rebuke of the church's effectiveness. Further, it was an admonition against the religious apathy of the general masses, many of whom claimed Christianity as their faith. This was true in America as well as in England.

On July 8, 1741, pastor and theologian Jonathan Edwards entered a church in Enfield, Connecticut, that was resistant to the Great Awakening that had been under way for years in other areas. His sermon, titled "Sinners in the Hands of an Angry God," was not typical of his usual preaching. Rather, it was a last ditch effort to warn the stubborn parishioners of God's promised coming judgment. The message portrayed a stark, biblical, and poetic vision of the "slender thread" preventing unrepentant sinners from receiving God's fierce, miserable, and eternal wrath in hell. The sermon's vivid depictions of hell had their desired effect. Edwards, a careful, intellectual preacher, was interrupted several times by the congregation, some of whom wept or cried out, "What should I do to be saved?" Edwards's answer was in his message: "Now you have the extraordinary opportunity, a day wherein Christ has thrown the door of mercy wide open, and stands in calling and crying with a loud voice to poor sinners."

The effectiveness of the Great Awakening had given Edwards and other revivalists the confidence to preach boldly. That summer, Wesley prepared a message of his own with similar sentiments for a similarly resistant audience at Oxford University, where he remained a fellow—albeit an absent one. The academic community by then already viewed him as "a little crack brained."

Wesley spent more than a month preparing for his July 25 sermon, drafting both a Latin and an English version, which apparently was part of his continuing professional development. The title of the sermon was provocative enough—"Hypocrisy in Oxford"—as was the scripture passage on which the sermon was based: "How is the faithful city become an harlot!"

The manuscript denounced Oxford for failing to heed its own statutes, as demonstrated in (1) doctrine taught against the Christian faith, and (2) the general sinful practices of the bulk of the university community. Wesley believed that preaching this message was his duty and "an instance of love to our neighbor." But the caustic tone could do little more than incite his audience, especially when Wesley capped his introduction with a resounding rebuke: "How faithful [Oxford] once was to her Lord. . . . But how is she now become an harlot! How has she departed from her Lord! How has she denied him and listened to the voice of strangers!"

On June 18, more than a month before he was to preach, Wesley told former Holy Club friend John Gambold the intentions of his message. Scandalized, Gambold told him he thought it would be ineffective, as "all here are so prejudiced that they will mind nothing you say." Even so, Wesley felt that "whether they will hear or whether they will forbear," he must "deliver [his] own soul."

During the next month, his mind was changed. Some have suggested that a late night meeting with Lady Huntington on June 28 persuaded him to change course. But whether it was due to the counsel of others or some internal misgivings, Wesley set aside the manuscripts for the sermon. He kept them in his files but apparently never preached the sermon in English or in Latin. Instead, he preached what became a classic sermon, "Almost Christian," based on Acts 26:28. The newer sermon made a positive case for Wesley's evangelical convictions and used his own testimony and spiritual journey of failure, rather than the failings of the Oxford community, for his approach to show what an "almost Christian" is in contrast to an "altogether Christian." Finally, he invited his audience to "experience what it is to be not almost only, but altogether Christian!" This was a remarkably altered tone from "Hypocrisy in Oxford."

Still, it seems as if Wesley felt he had failed to fulfill his duty—to "deliver" his own soul. Three years later, he returned to Oxford for what would be his final invitation to preach to his beloved school. This time, he returned to a confrontational tone, though the edges were dulled from his intended "Hypocrisy in Oxford" sermon. The sermon he preached, titled "Scriptural Christianity," became another classic in his corpus of sermons.

In the message, from Acts 4:31—"They were all filled with the Holy Ghost"—he first explains true, biblical Christianity and suggests that it is missing at Oxford, offering his own testimony of failure as humble proof. He finished his discourse with a flourish, once again turning prophet by suggesting that "so many of you are *triflers*; triflers with God, with one another, and with your own souls." Finally, very much as Jonathan Edwards had done in his famous sermon, Wesley warned that if the people would not heed God's message and his messengers, God would send "the last messengers of God to a guilty land [of] famine, the pestilence. . .or the sword" in a final judgment.

When the message caused more offense than conviction, Wesley knew he would no longer be welcome there. "I preached, I suppose, the last time" at Oxford, he wrote in his journal. But he never regretted the message. "I am now clear of the blood of these men," he continued. "I have fully delivered my soul."

Like Jonathan Edwards, Wesley did not relish condemnatory messages. But also like Edwards, he knew the truth that there was judgment coming and made it necessary for him to declare, as an act of love, even this severe truth to the enemies of God.

Wesley's enemies at Oxford may have been many, but the greatest harm they would do was to neglect and ignore him. Other enemies, however, were intent on doing him physical harm—adversaries who came in the form of mobs he encountered in towns and villages throughout England, Wales, and Ireland, particularly during the turbulent 1740s.

These ruffians were what Wesley once called "the scum of Cornwall, the rabble of Bilston and Darlaston, the wild beasts of Walsall, and the turnkeys of Newgate."

Throughout Wesley's ministry, some would come to his unconventional preaching venues merely to cause a disturbance. His journal entries of these events offer some of his more humorous insights: odd anecdotes peppered with ironic observations.

In 1742, in a field outside of Pensford, the "rabble" tried to lead a reluctant bull into the crowd. As Wesley later reported in his journal:

The beast was wiser than his drivers and continually ran either on one side of us or the other, while we quietly sang praise to God and prayed for about an hour. The poor wretches, finding themselves disappointed, at length seized upon the bull, now weak and tired after having been so long torn and beaten both by dogs and men, and by main strength partly dragged and partly thrust him in among the people. When they had forced their way to the little table on which I stood, they strove several times to throw it down, by thrusting the helpless beast against it, who of himself stirred no more than a log of wood. I once or twice put aside his head with my hand, that the blood might not drop upon my clothes; intending to go on as soon as the hurry should be a little over. But the table falling down, some of our friends caught me in their arms and carried me right away on their shoulders; while the rabble wreaked their vengeance on the table, which they tore bit from bit. We went a little way off, where I finished my discourse without any noise or interruption.

Wesley was able to quell the rioters and continue preaching. At other times, his preaching was drowned out and he was forced to withdraw to another location to preach, and sometimes he was prevented from preaching at all. Some rabble-rousers "came in among us as lions," he explained, and "in a short space became as lambs; the tears trickling apace down their cheeks, who at first most loudly contradicted and blasphemed." Still, he saw this opposition and persecution as a cosmic battle. "I wonder if the devil has not wisdom enough," he reflected, "to discern that he is destroying his own kingdom. I believe he has never yet, any one time, caused this open opposition to the truth of God without losing one or more of his servants, who were found of God while they sought him not."

The angry mobs could often be vicious, chasing Wesley and his companions with clubs, cleavers, or any other potentially deadly instrument at hand. He was often pelted with stones, smeared with dirt, grabbed by his "soft hair"—as one of the rabble once noted in surprise—and chased into houses, which they threatened to burn or tear down.

Wesley's accounts of the persecution rarely offer reasons for the gathering of angry mobs and riots, but generally he believed they were mistaken about him and that reason would ultimately prevail. Some rioters believed he was a political dissident. Others thought he was trying to destroy the national church. Still others believed he was a "papist," a derogatory term for a Roman Catholic. Finally, others—perhaps even the majority—were merely drunken gangs looking for entertainment or sport by disturbing the meetings of this prudish Methodist preacher who was trying to reform the manners of the town.

Still, Wesley believed that the mobs were thirsty for blood. Indeed, in 1740, preacher William Seward encountered an aggressive mob, who stoned him, causing his death a few days later and making him the first Methodist martyr.

Wesley's accounts of these fast-moving disturbances read almost in slow motion, with vivid details of various members of the mob, what they did, and how he responded. The descriptions have inspired hundreds of mob-scene paintings as a result. But by and large, he viewed these opponents as potential followers. It was his "rule, confirmed by long experience, to always look a mob in the face." That is, rather than following the instinct to run from a mob, he turned toward them and spoke to them—often preaching to them. He was overwhelmed, not with hatred, but with his heart "filled with love, [his] eyes with tears, and [his] mouth with arguments."

This approach proved effective in Wednesbury in 1743, when Wesley faced one of his most thoroughly documented mob scenes, due in part to accusations by magistrates that he was inciting mobs and could be prosecuted for breaking the royal edicts. Throughout his journeys, what he said to the mobs differed with each circumstance. At times, he began with "softer" words; on other occasions, he escalated to the posture he assumed at Oxford when he warned of impending judgment. But whatever the message—severe or gentle—he was a man whose character was remarkably lacking in spite.

Certainly his enemies could be deluded, spiteful, and dangerous, but Wesley believed they could also be reasoned with, convinced, and shown the transforming power of God's love. In the summer of 1745, he came to Cornwall—a county on the southwest peninsula of England where he had faced significant opposition—ready to meet the resistance and encourage his followers with some words from Jesus' command in Matthew 5:44 to "love your enemies." Though the content of these messages was never recorded, one aspect of the message was likely an encouragement to his supporters to love those enemies who persecuted them. It was, therefore, a call for his followers to stay above the fray.

We get a glimpse of how Wesley loved his enemies in a sermon titled "A Catholic Spirit," published in 1750, which was a direct message to his opponents, and particularly those who held "a difference in opinions or modes of worship," but who in "general" believed the same "main branches of Christian doctrine."

The message is a biblical call to "universal" or "catholic" love for one another despite differences in particulars of conviction and forms of worship. The heart of the sermon is a series of probing questions: "Do you 'love your enemies'? Is your soul full of goodwill, of tender affection toward them? Do you love even the enemies of God? The unthankful and unholy? Do your bowels yearn over them?" These rhetorical questions are powerful in their own right, but for Wesley they seemed overly abstract.

To solidify the application, he included a totally unexpected solicitation to his opponents and adversaries: "Love me." This line he movingly repeated six times, calling on his Christian opponents to move from the abstract to the real, and each time showing more particularly the nature of biblical love for other Christians.

Love me, with a very tender affection, as a friend that is closer than a brother; as a brother in Christ, a fellow citizen of the New Jerusalem, a fellow soldier engaged in the same warfare, under the same Captain of our salvation. Love me as a companion in the kingdom and patience of Jesus, and a joint heir of his glory.

The love to which he called both his followers and his opponents is an active love. It is a love that prays for enemies; a love that "provokes to love and good works"; and a love that "so far as in conscience" allows, will "join with me in the work of God."

He applied this, however imperfectly, both publicly and privately, attempting to set aside differences of opinion—to "think and let think," as he would say about Methodists. But he often encountered people of a different temperament and conviction. In his journal, he relates one such incident of an encounter with an ardent Calvinist while on a horseback journey in 1742:

I overtook a serious man, with whom I immediately fell into conversation. He presently gave me to know what his opinions were; therefore I said nothing to contradict them. But that did not content him. He was quite uneasy to know whether I held the doctrine of the decrees as he did. But I told him over and over, "We had better keep to practical things, lest we should be angry at one another." And so we did for two miles, till he caught me unawares and dragged me into the dispute before I knew where I was. He then grew warmer and warmer, told me I was rotten at heart, and supposed I was one of John Wesley's followers. I told him, "No; I am John Wesley himself."

The man, of course, was surprised—"as one who had happened upon a snake," Wesley wryly notes in Latin—but the traveling preacher did not give up on him. As Wesley continues his story, he suggests that the stranger would gladly have run away outright. "But being the better mounted of the two, I kept close to his side and endeavoured to show him his heart, till we came into the street of Northampton."

This was his general way of loving his enemies.

John Wesley did not see attacks on him as personal attacks. He saw them as part of a cosmic war on God. Therefore, he was able to see his opponents not as personal enemies, but as enemies of God. But just because they were enemies of God did not mean they were evil per se. They were captives of the devil to be rescued, rather than enemies to be vanquished.

And he also saw his treatment of his enemies in light of how God Himself has treated His enemies. Writing to a Cambridge fellow who had attacked the foundations of miracles in the early church, Wesley observes:

> *His love resembles that of him whose mercy is over all his works.*
> *It soars above all these scanty bounds, embracing neighbours and*
> *strangers, friends and enemies: yea, not only the good and gentle, but*
> *also the froward, the evil, and unthankful. For he loves every soul*
> *that God has made; every child of man, of whatever place or nation.*

This noble and dispassionate view of his enemies, however, had a dangerous and tragic flip side. It is one thing to deflect personal attacks as impersonal cosmic battles in order to view one's opponents as ministry targets. It is another thing entirely to refuse to heed personal opposition or concerns—legitimate or not—because the opposition is against God instead of against oneself. With Wesley, this can be seen particularly in relation to his wife, whom he viewed as an impediment to his work in ministry; though, even in this tragic relationship, he showed a remarkable level of forgiveness and grace.

If he never clearly crossed the line, he teetered on it, obtuse to accusations, criticisms, and concerns, which could become abusive in personal relationships and with those who reported to him. In short, as admirable as this trait was in Wesley, it did not come without its drawbacks and failures.

There were no greater or more powerful enemies of Wesley's work than some of the bishops of the church who wrote against him and his ministry. In 1745, he reflected that "several of the bishops began to speak against us, either in conversation or in public. On this encouragement several of the clergy stirred up the people to treat us as outlaws or mad dogs. The people did so, both in Staffordshire, Cornwall, and many other places." How he handled these leaders is instructive of how he treated his enemies.

The first bishop he engaged publicly in debate was Edmund Gibson, who was bishop of London until his death in 1748. Gibson had written an anonymous critique of Methodism in 1744, which spurred Wesley to write *Appeals to Men of Reason and Religion.* When Gibson finally attached his name (and thus authority) to a treatise belittling the Methodists, Wesley responded in an open letter that is both respectful and courteous. He wrote it "in such a manner as I ought and as I desire to do" to a man in such authority. This response is remarkable, as has been earlier noted, in how he invites his opponent to join him in the work, for "the time is short."

The bishop's death a year later did not remove his critique from Wesley's memory. He would never forget Gibson's claim that there was at the time no "great work of God." But as harmful as these critiques were, Wesley did not relegate the bishop to an apostate class destined for hell. Nearly thirty years after Bishop Gibson's death, Wesley called him "a great man, indeed, who I trust is in a better world."

Another bishop with whom he entered a public debate was George Lavington, bishop of Exeter, who in 1749 and 1751 compared the enthusiasm of the Methodists with that of the Catholics. Wesley's reply to Lavington caused him to lament the "heavy work" of controversial writings. His direct and courteous replies to the bishops stand on their own as samples of charitable argumentation. But just as he had with the London bishop, he longed for unity with the bishop of Exeter.

A picture of this unity came in 1762 at the Exeter Cathedral, just fifteen days before Bishop Lavington's death. Even though the two men never came to terms regarding their differences, Wesley's journal for August 29 records the encounter and the spirit in which he had approached it: "I was well pleased to partake of the Lord's Supper with my old opponent, Bishop Lavington. O may we sit down together in the kingdom of our Father!"

Wesley treated with grace even his most acerbic and stalwart critic, Bishop William Warburton of Gloucester, who attacked Wesley in 1762 as a fanatic and a charlatan. Wesley's response shows signs of one who is clearly frustrated by years of unfair criticism, which he had already addressed multiple times, both orally and in writing. Even so, his sharpest words to Warburton are a simple request:

> *If your Lordship should think it worth your while to spend any more words on me, may I presume to request one thing of your lordship— to be more serious? It cannot injure your lordship's character or your cause. Truth is great, and will prevail.*

His public response to Warburton avoided his harshest thoughts. To Charles, he privately bemoaned: "I was a little surprised to find Bishop Warburton so entirely unacquainted with the New Testament; and notwithstanding all his parade of learning, I believe he is no critic of Greek." Wesley kept this low assessment out of the public fray; and however nasty Warburton's charges were, Wesley believed he would see him in heaven.

From bishops of the church to academics at Oxford, to commoners intent on doing him physical harm, to strangers on the way, John Wesley encountered his enemies with a deep and long-standing conviction that his enemies were in desperate need of God's love and Wesley's intercession. It was his lifelong pursuit to love and pray for his enemies.

Chapter 14
Least of These

I bear the rich, and love the poor.

From the beginning, the Methodist movement was led by "outcasts of men" to outcasts of society. It was a ministry based on the impulse of Christ to "seek and to save that which was lost." Wesley wrote defiantly to the general critics of the legitimacy of his ministry:

> *The rich, the honourable, the great, we are thoroughly willing (if it be the will of the Lord) to leave to you. Only let us alone with the poor, the vulgar, the base, the outcasts of men.*

Gathering these outcasts together into his societies, however, presented issues that he turned into opportunities. Always a student of the early church, and one who sought to restore the practice and teachings of it, Wesley found a model and obligation from Acts 4, where the early Jerusalem church provided for those who lacked out of the surplus of others. Some even sold their homes and properties and shared the money with the apostles to distribute to the needy. Wesley implemented a similar, though perhaps less radical, system within his societies. The more affluent of the societies were taught to give more to the society; and like the apostles in Acts 4, the stewards of the society distributed the money to those who were in need as they saw fit.

Wesley believed that if this plan were duly enacted, none of the poor in the societies would lack in any of the "necessities of life." The system was never implemented perfectly, to Wesley's great regret. Nevertheless, it was a system that alleviated many of the needs of multitudes of impoverished members of his societies.

In order to achieve his aim of meeting all the needs of the poor in their midst, Wesley needed to convince his followers of his vision for how Christians were to view money. A failure to approach money rightly, he taught, was detrimental not just for meeting the needs of the poor, but also for the spiritual state of the financially stable. The Methodists' very souls were at stake.

In a sermon on Luke 19:6 preached at least twenty-seven times between 1741 and 1758 in various locales throughout the British Isles and printed in 1760, Wesley sets forth his teaching on "The Use of Money." In the sermon, he lays out three simple yet demanding rules for how Christians should pursue and use money: gain all you can, save all you can, and give all you can. This easy-to-remember triad of diligence, frugality, and generosity was the foundation of every Christian's obligation.

First, he encouraged his people to work diligently to make money, so long as it didn't hurt anyone—either themselves or their neighbors—in mind, body, or soul, and to continue to improve the task by "experience, reading, and reflection" to gain even more.

Second, once the money was gained, he called on them to save. "Do not throw it away in idle expenses," he warned, "which is just the same as throwing it into the sea." In particular, he cautioned against using money to indulge the desires of the flesh, gratify the desires of the eye, or gain the praise of men "by superfluous or expensive furniture" and the like.

These first two rules, of gaining and saving all possible resources, were simple enough and fell well within the tradition of the Protestant work ethic that drove the development of so much industry in the Western world. But Wesley went further. There must be a "farther end" in the use of money than self-preservation and promotion. This farther end, for Wesley, was the honorable preservation of God's resources.

When the Possessor of heaven and earth brought you into being, and placed you in this world, he placed you here not as a proprietor, but a steward: As such he entrusted you, for a season, with goods of various kinds; but the sole property of these still rests in Him, nor can be alienated from Him. As you yourself are not your own, but His, such is, likewise, all that you enjoy. Such is your soul and your body, not your own, but God's.

Since all that we possess has been entrusted to us from God, we are to render unto Him "not a tenth, not a third, not a half, but all that is God's, be it more or less."

Wesley was so convinced of this system of rules that he held to them throughout his long life. When his income increased through book royalties, which were entirely unexpected, his cost of living remained largely the same, but his giving increased. "I look upon all this revenue," he once explained, "as sacred to God and the poor."

Many of his critics suspected him of attempting to make a fortune through ministry, but nothing could be further from the truth. In 1745, he wrote: "If I leave behind me ten pounds [when I die], you and all mankind bear witness against me that 'I lived and died a thief and a robber.'"

He demanded these rules of himself, as well as those in his connexion.

The foundation of John Wesley's view of the poor comes from Matthew 25:40: "Inasmuch as ye have done it unto one of the least of these my brethren, ye have done it unto me." He took these words literally, believing that Jesus Christ was present and dwelling in the poor—a teaching he acquired from the French philanthropist Gaston Jean Baptiste de Renty. The poor, according to Wesley, were the very embodiment of Christ. To ignore them was to ignore Jesus; to serve them was to serve Jesus Himself. In a sermon summing up the foundation of serving all men, Wesley declared:

A poor wretch cries to me for an alms. I look and see him covered with dirt and rags. But through these I see one that has an immortal spirit, made to know and love and dwell with God to eternity.

I honour him for his Creator's sake. Lo, I see through all these rags that he is purpled over with the blood of Christ. I love him for the sake of his Redeemer. The courtesy, therefore, which I feel and show toward him is a mixture of the honour and love which I bear to the offspring of God; the purchase of his Son's blood, and the candidate for immortality. This courtesy let us feel and show toward all men.

These lofty and idealized sentiments sound as if they were written by a young man about to embark on a mission to reach the poor, only to be disappointed and disillusioned later to find the harsh realities of the messiness of human nature. Instead, this sermon was preached by a man who, by 1787, had spent fifty years serving the poor. He knew their limitations, their failures, the ungratefulness of some, and the general difficulties of working among them. He had entered the dirtiest and darkest of homes, buildings, and alleys in order to reach the needy, and he had contracted "the itch," lice or fleas, more than one hundred times. Even so, the filth of eighteenth-century poverty was not a deterrent. The poor, according to his reading of the Bible, are where Jesus is.

As such, he did all he could for the poor. Not only did he organize his societies to care for the less fortunate, but he relentlessly gave to beggars and the needy from his own pocket, most often discreetly, neither to be noticed by men nor to be disrespectful of their honor. He often went door to door, seeking contributions for the poor. Out of his own money, most of which came from his publishing royalties, he told a confidant in 1787 that he never gave away less than £1,000 per year—a staggering amount considering that many laborers at the time earned only £20 or £30 per year.

This was the vision he wished to instill in his people: "Let those animating words be written on your hearts, and sounding in your ears," he implored in a sermon from 1777. "Inasmuch as ye have done it unto one of the least of these, ye have done it unto me."

Wesley organized his societies in such a way as to help the needy among them in various ways. He had long been convinced of the importance of visiting people in prison—especially those condemned to die. But he found no shortage of other opportunities for ministry to the overlooked of society.

The Kingswood School, which he had established with George Whitefield at the beginning of the revival, became a lifelong project that he implemented to protect a handful of poor, wild children from idleness and from other corrupting educational systems. It was a school that alternately encouraged and greatly discouraged him and tested his resolve. He gave a tremendous amount of time and energy to making the school successful, especially in the late 1740s and into the early 1750s, by developing a curriculum and writing grammars in English, Greek, Latin, Hebrew, and French, and abridging dozens of classic works for their study.

Always an innovator, he was willing to experiment with different ways to help those in need. In late 1740, he employed twelve of the poorest who were out of work. The trial task for these dozen was the "carding and spinning of cotton" in the society room for four months during winter. It helped provide for their needs and also gave them meaningful activity. Despite the promising start, this practice did not take hold on a larger scale.

Seeing that many of the poor were being taken advantage of by the high interest rates of pawn brokers, he decided to raise funds at the Foundery for the stewards to give out small loans—a lending stock. The no-interest loans would be repaid in weekly payments, and finally paid off in three months. In 1746, its first year, 250 borrowers were "relieved" with the service, and thousands more were helped through-out Wesley's lifetime.

Another way of providing for the needy was in the provision for widows. Rather than assume the costly task of helping poor widows at their own residences, he gathered them together to live in houses that his trustees purchased, which they called the Poorhouse. These women were gathered into a community where they lived and ate together and where traveling preachers could also come to lodge. The preachers ate the same food at the same table with the women, "as a comfortable earnest of our eating bread together in our Father's Kingdom."

This practice of dining together cut across class lines and is reminiscent of another practice of the early Methodists—the love feast. Wesley had been introduced to the custom of the love feast by the Moravians, who in the 1720s attempted to restore the *agape* feast from Acts 2:42, 1 Corinthians 11, and Jude 12—a communal meal reminiscent of the Lord's Supper. At this table, which consisted of bread and water, the poor and the rich came together with the recognition that there is no distinction between them, but "Christ is all and in all."

"I bear the rich," John Wesley wrote to a friend in 1764, "and love the poor. Therefore, I spend almost all my time with them!" But, over time, his efforts to instill in his people a love for the poor seemed to be a losing battle. He convinced people of his first two rules: gain all you can and save all you can, but he lamented the results. "Diligence and frugality must produce riches," he observed in 1790, but as the riches increased, "nine in ten of these decreased in grace, in the same proportion as they increased in wealth."

He constantly warned of the corrupting influence of the love of money and riches. He wrote to one "possessing everything" that "the dangers of prosperity are great. . . . If poverty contracts and depresses the mind, riches sap its fortitude, destroy its vigour, and nourish its caprices."

The sum of the issue, he believed, was that increased riches competed with our love for God. Riches have the tendency to "beget and to increase" the desire of "happiness out[side] of God. . . 'loving the creature more than the Creator.'"

Because of this great danger, Wesley did all he could to rid himself of excess money. He wrote in response to one who mistakenly questioned his acceptance of a large sum, saying, "Money never stays with me; it would burn me if it did. I throw it out of my hands as soon as possible, lest it should find a way into my heart."

The final decade of his life was filled with a great concern for wealth's impact on the spirituality of the Methodists. In addition to dozens of cautions about the corrupting nature of riches sprinkled throughout many sermons, he published "The Danger of Riches" in his newly founded periodical, *The Arminian Magazine*, in 1781. In 1788, he followed that with "On Riches" in his eighth volume of *Sermons on Several Occasions*, and in 1790 suggested that the love of money is the primary cause of the "inefficacy of Christianity" to "restore" the "spiritual health of mankind." This concern remained vibrant to his dying day, as his final published sermon, shortly after his death in 1792, was "The Danger of Increasing Riches."

Sadly, the message fell largely on deaf ears. His people had gained all they could and saved all they could, but to his great disappointment, most still failed to give all they could.

In 1776, Wesley received a letter from the House of Lords, demanding an accounting of his silver and gold plate, or utensils, for possible taxes that may be levied. The letter read accusingly,

> *Reverend Sir,*
> *As the Commissioners cannot doubt but you have plate for which you have hitherto neglected to make entry, they have directed me to inform you that they expect you forthwith to make due entry of all your plate. . . .*

If he had refused, it would have signified to the authorities his "refusal to their Lordships."

But just as his critics had no basis for accusation, neither did the government. His response was short and honest:

> *Sir,*
> *I have two silver teaspoons at London, and two at Bristol. This is all the plate which I have at present; and I shall not buy any more while so many round me want bread.*

I am, sir,

Your most humble servant.
John Wesley

In regard to the use of money, John Wesley practiced what he preached. In the final year of his life, with a shaky, eighty-seven-year-old hand, he wrote his final entry in his exacting cash book:

For upwards of eighty-six years, I have kept my accounts exactly; I will not attempt it any longer, being satisfied with the continual conviction, that I save all I can, and give all I can; that is, all I have.

Chapter 15
Sovereign Remedy

The love of God. . .is the sovereign remedy of all miseries.

Eighteenth-century England saw a great influx of people move from a rural, agricultural life into cities such as London, Bristol, and Newcastle. This opened up opportunities for the evangelicals to minister to the masses, but it also intensified the great problems of city life—filth, poverty, and disease. Illness was so prevalent that, in a twelve-month span between 1747 and 1748, "the poor hospitals" treated more than 32,500 patients. "I saw the poor people pining away," John Wesley wrote, reflecting on hospital care for the poor, "and several families ruined, and that without remedy."

The poor and the sick needed help. They needed an advocate, an adviser, and someone to care for them. Wesley viewed the situation as a "desperate expedient" and was intent on providing that help.

His compassion was rooted in Jesus' commands to care for the needy, but it was not a short-lived compassion. He had served the poor and the sick since his days at Oxford, and he would continue until his death. While on his journey to America, he had begun reading medical literature in his free time, preparing himself as best he could, knowing that medical services would be greatly needed among the colonists and the Indians.

His Georgia journal for September 8, 1736, records the fruit of visiting the sick.

I had often observed that I scarce ever visited any persons, in health or sickness, but they attended public prayer for sometime after. As a result, this increased my desire of seeing not only those who were sick, but also all my parishioners.

As a parish priest—even if a failed one—Wesley had recognized early on that once people felt a preacher's loving concern, it often unlocked a door into their soul. He used this knowledge throughout his ministry to spread his message, and encouraged others to do likewise.

When he returned to London in 1741, he was overwhelmed by the enormity of the task of visiting and caring for London's sick and poor. He began "settling a regular method of visiting the sick" by mobilizing his religious society. First, he reminded the members that "many of our brethren and sisters had not needful food; many were destitute of convenient clothing; many were out of business, and that without their own fault; and many sick and ready to perish: that I had done what in me lay to feed the hungry, to clothe the naked, to employ the poor, and to visit the sick, but was not alone sufficient for these things." The result of this urgent plea was the institution of a new office in the society—the visitor of the sick—who joined the other officers: the assistants, ministers, stewards, schoolmasters, housekeepers, and leaders of the bands and classes. This new office could be held by multiple people, depending on the size of the city and society. Just as Wesley divided England into circuits, he also organized his city ministries into divisions and assigned to the visitors of the sick the responsibility for visiting each sick society member three times a week. Later, he further enumerated the role of these officers:

> *To inquire into the state of their souls, and to advise them as occasion may require. To inquire into their disorders, and procure advice for them. To relieve them, if they are in want. To do anything for them which he (or she) can do.*

Wesley's call to visit the sick was rooted in the same conviction that lay behind his care for the poor—that to visit the sick was to visit Jesus. It was therefore a task, not merely of society officers, but of all true Christians. In a 1786 sermon, published four decades after he first organized the visitors of the sick, Wesley explained that while visiting the sick imparted grace to the ill, it was also a means of grace for the visitor. Therefore, a Christian's neglect of visiting the sick was detrimental to the soul and a cause of "spiritual weakness."

Wesley's system continued to develop beyond visitation and offering spiritual counsel and medical advice. "I thought out of the desperate expedient," he explained, "I will prepare and give them [medicine] myself." This step was not unique in the history of the church. There had long been an association between the parish priests and the practice of medicine. But by Wesley's day, specialization within both medicine and religion had made the crossover between the two fields increasingly rare. Wesley wanted to recapture medicine—or *physic* as it was called in his day—as a spiritual discipline; medicine was by its nature a spiritual exercise—an attempt to restore what had been lost because of our sinfulness at the Fall. Dividing physical and spiritual health into separate fields was tantamount to dividing a person into separate entities—a body and a soul. Reuniting the fields preserved a view of humanity as a body united with a soul, as God intended. Wesley therefore dedicated a tremendous amount of resources to medicine.

John Wesley was concerned with the plight of the sick, and he was irate about the system of medical care in his day. Physicians, he believed, were far too theoretical and distant from patient care—they rarely even visited the sick. The work of treatment was done foremost by apothecaries and surgeons, who were called on as needed. The problem with this system was that apothecaries, who distributed medicine, were also the ones who prescribed the remedies. Such a system lent itself to avarice, as greedy apothecaries took advantage of the sick by prescribing unnecessary and expensive concoctions.

Wesley approached the problem by hiring a specifically Christian apothecary and surgeon for the Foundery, and in 1746, he opened a dispensary—a free clinic that dispensed reasonably priced medicine. His intent was to strip away the incentives for apothecaries to oversell medicine for their own profit.

In 1747, Wesley gathered 725 recipes of medications to treat various illnesses—from the minor to the deadly—and assembled them into a book titled *Primitive Physick; or an easy and natural method of curing most diseases.* According to the book's preface, Wesley "hoped to soften the evils of life, and prevent, in part, the sickness and pain to which we are continually exposed." The book caught on with the general public, going through twenty-three editions during Wesley's lifetime and several more editions after his death. It was a grand attempt at putting medicine into the hands of the people.

Simply treating illnesses as they arose was not sufficient for Wesley. He was intent on preventing illnesses by healthy living—diet and exercise practices into which he put a great deal of thought throughout his lifetime. He carefully observed the short- and long-term effects of foods, sleep patterns, and exercise, and he used these observations to counsel anyone who would listen—friends, correspondents, the anxious, the depressed, the spiritually lethargic, and the chronically ill.

He observed how "animal food" gave him headaches and various other ailments, and he went back and forth between a "vegetable diet" and one that included animal flesh, while carefully observing how his diet affected his "soul and body." He noticed the harmful effects of tea and coffee, warned against the "poison" of hard liquor—though he was no teetotaler—and believed that early to bed and early to rise was one of the secrets of longevity.

None of this seems revolutionary to modern readers; but in Wesley's day, basic health education was essential to many who would otherwise waste their bodies away on ignorant, unhealthy living. Furthermore, Wesley encouraged the poor and the sick to pursue a life of cleanliness and industry, which prevented further health issues.

He rigorously applied these same principles to his own life and advocated for them incessantly. But his applications were often quirky. He saw exercise as "one grand preventative of pain and sickness," and duly prescribed walking. During the winter months, he often paced back and forth in his room for exercise, and the acquired a "chamber-horse"—a device with an accordion spring and a seat that simulated horseback riding—so he could remain fit for riding.

Viewing the sedentary lifestyle common to academics, writers, and preachers as particularly dangerous to their health, he adopted the practice of reading and writing while standing or leaning at his standing desk, and he was adamant that other writers and preachers do the same.

But his greatest quirk came in his fascination with the new technology that accompanied advances in electricity—a field that he believed held the greatest and least expensive promise of a universal medicine.

The eighteenth century was an age of wonder regarding electricity, as scientists and inventors of the likes of Benjamin Franklin in America made important discoveries about the nature of this strangely contained "fire." Harnessing the power of fire for humanity's betterment intrigued Wesley's generation. In October 1747, Wesley went with friends to see "electrical experiments," and he was flabbergasted by the "mystery" as he observed "how fire lives in water and passes through it more freely than air."

But more than the wonder and conveniences that electricity offered, Wesley was fascinated by its potential to cure diseases. By 1753, he had heard reports of two people cured of chronic pain through low-voltage electric shocks. This led him to advise a woman "troubled many years with [a] stubborn paralytic disorder" to try this "new remedy." With this treatment, she found "immediate help." But even if the therapeutic use of electricity showed promise, Wesley lamented that the medical community—the physicians and apothecaries—would "decry of medicine so shockingly cheap and easy."

If the medical establishment would not entertain these new remedies, then Wesley would. Around 1754, he got an apparatus of his own and advised many ill to "try the virtue of this surprising medicine." He soon had so many patients that he divided London into four areas with four treatment locations, at which some "found an immediate, some a gradual cure."

Wesley became obsessed with this new science and its potential for curative powers. Reading the works of the leading thinkers on electricity of his day—Benjamin Franklin, Benjamin Hoadley, Benjamin Wilson, Richard Lovett, and others—he sifted through their theories and sought to make practical use of these developments in order to help the sick. Believing that electricity was a "liquid" so fine that it penetrated the tiniest nerves, he compiled a list of diseases—mostly nervous disorders— that he thought could be cured with electric shock. He also gathered 120 testimonies of cures, which he published anonymously in 1759 in a book called *The Desideratum; or Electricity Made Plain and Useful*. "How much sickness and pain may be prevented or removed," he surmised, "and how many lives saved by this unparalleled remedy."

The Desideratum (Latin for "desired thing") was his best attempt at trying to convince a reluctant medical establishment that they should at least experiment with and investigate the promise of this new technology—which he viewed as "the general and rarely failing remedy" for various specific illnesses. Perhaps after a fair trial and experimentation, he believed, the medical community would find it to be "the noblest medicine yet known in the world."

Despite Wesley's lifelong practice of electrocuting himself and others to treat various ailments, neither the medical community nor his followers shared his exuberant and eccentric hope for the therapeutic use of electricity. When he wrote to his ailing brother Charles in 1761, he encouraged him to try "electrifying" as a remedy. "Never start at its being a quack medicine," he wrote, seemingly sensitive to a charge that would begin to stick to him regarding his incursion into the medical field. But even though Wesley had reason to question both the ethics and practices of eighteenth-century medicine, most of his contemporaries found his solutions to be no better. His zeal to be on the cutting edge of alleviating human pain was met with his own limitations and those of his era.

Whether there is any merit to electrotherapy, as he insisted, his *Primitive Physick* is filled with remedies in which a reader would be hard pressed to find much value. For example, to remedy baldness, he offered the following prescription: "Rub the part, morning and evening, with onions, till it is red, and rub it afterwards with honey." Other remedies were indeed effective, even if they were as simple as rubbing the head to alleviate a headache.

A glaring mistake that ran through more than twenty editions of the book caught the eye of a critical reader in 1775, sparking criticism of the book when he wrote to the editor of several periodicals. The mistake, in a remedy for "one poisoned," read: "Give one or two drams of distilled verdigris." The intended effect was to induce vomiting by ingesting a poisonous copper compound. But as the critical reader noted, two *drams* of verdigris had the potential to kill not only one person, but twenty or thirty. When this was brought to light in anonymous letters to the editor of several London newspapers, Wesley replied by nonchalantly blaming a printing error: He had intended to prescribe one or two *grains* instead of drams of verdigris—which amounted to one-sixtieth the dose.

What followed was a monthlong barrage of attacks against Wesley, charging him with being "an unfeeling quack, regardless of, and sporting with the health and lives of his fellow creatures."

The affronted would-be physician finally replied with a mixture of defensive posturing and a call to "calm, dispassionate" criticism. Somewhat chastened, he closed his defense with these words: "Fifty years ago, I imagined I knew a great deal. Now I am convinced I know exceedingly little. And the voice of my heart, both to God and man, is, 'What I know not, teach thou me.'"

If his reply won over any critics, he lost them a few days later by boasting in another paper that the controversy "makes many inquire concerning [*Primitive Physick*], and so disperses it more and more." The criticism struck a nerve in Wesley, who desired nothing more than to make effective medicine more accessible.

Shortly after the newspaper attacks, a blistering critique of *Primitive Physick* was printed by apothecary William Hawes, "shewing that a great number of the prescriptions therein contained are founded on ignorance of the medical art." Furthermore, Hawes asserted, it is a publication calculated to do essential injury to those who may place their confidence in it." As a result, Wesley carefully reworked the next edition, published in 1780, reducing the number of remedies by almost two hundred. In any case, the book remained in print long after his death in 1791.

At the conclusion of his preface to *Primitive Physick*, Wesley writes:

The love of God, as it is the sovereign remedy of all miseries, effectually prevents all the bodily disorders the passions introduce, by keeping the passions themselves within due bounds; and by the unspeakable joy and perfect calm serenity and tranquility it gives the mind, it becomes the most powerful of all the means of health and long life.

Because sickness and disease are rooted in humanity's rebellion, no remedy is complete apart from a restored relationship with God. For this reason, Wesley advised his followers to seek treatment only from a physician who "fears God."

His view of the unified body and soul led him to care for the needs of the body, but even more so to care for the needs of the soul, "which are of infinitely greater importance." In a sermon about visiting the sick, he told his audience that it was not enough to send a doctor to care for their bodies, if that doctor was unlikely to tend to the "higher end" of "saving their souls from death." Such care was simply an incomplete remedy.

Wesley always pursued the health of both the body and the soul, and though he faced severe criticism for stepping outside the bounds of his educational training, he never gave up on his vision to care for both. In this great human crisis, he saw an open door to minister to the souls of the afflicted.

Part IV

Transformational Gospel

Chapter 16
Perfect Love

I tell you flat,
I have not attained the character I draw.

On New Year's Day, 1762, John Wesley recorded the following report in his journal:

We had, I believe, pretty near 2,000 of the Society at Spitalfields in the evening. . . . And we found God was in the midst, while we devoted ourselves to Him in the most solemn and explicit manner.

Thus began a most remarkable year in Wesley's life and ministry—so remarkable, in fact, that it reminded him of words his brother Charles "frequently" said during the early days of the revival:

Your day of Pentecost is not fully come. But I doubt not it will, and you will then hear of persons sanctified as frequently as you do now of persons justified.

Wesley attached this quote and reflection to the end of the twelfth installment of his published journal, which covers up to late October 1762, and finished with this conclusion: "Any unprejudiced reader may observe that it was now fully come."

But if his "day of Pentecost" indeed came in 1762, it was spawned by his most controversial teaching—Christian perfection—and brought with it some of the severest criticism, difficulties, and afflictions he would face. By the end of the year, he was able to write: "I now stood and looked back on the past year—a year of uncommon trials and uncommon blessings." Before entering into the new year, he resigned himself into God's hands. "What the end will be I know not," he wrote, still in the midst of unresolved conflict, "but it is enough that God knoweth."

John Wesley began his quest for sanctification at Oxford in 1725, but it took more than a decade for him to realize that his pursuit of holiness in his own power was misguided. But when his heart was "strangely warmed" at Aldersgate in 1738, he accepted and began to declare the doctrine of salvation by faith alone. Initially, he believed that he could receive this holiness *in toto*, as well—victory over the guilt, the power, and the existence of sin in his life. So he was greatly disillusioned when he continued to struggle with sin and doubt. This conflict set him on the long journey of trying to pinpoint his doctrine of sanctification. The journey was filled with ambiguities, developments, and changes over the three decades from 1740 to 1770, and these differences have served to confuse even his most careful followers—inspiring some and enraging others.

Though, after Aldersgate, Wesley knew he was justified, he still maintained that there was more to the Christian life than simply being absolved of the punishment for sin, and that there remained more scriptural promises of blessings to be fulfilled in this life. God's grace, he believed, is a transforming grace. He took the name for his doctrine of sanctification—*Christian perfection*—most likely from one of his early mentors, William Law, who published *A Practical Treatise upon Christian Perfection* in 1726. This phrase caused more perplexity than Wesley intended, and he had to defend the term regularly. He often pointed to the places in the Bible where, according to the translation authorized by King James in 1611, it speaks of the *perfection* of believers:

- "Be ye therefore perfect, even as your Father which is in heaven is perfect."
- "Herein is our love made perfect. . ."
- "Not as though I had already attained, either were already

perfect.... Let us therefore, as many as be perfect, be thus minded..."

- "That ye may stand perfect and complete in all the will of God."

In his first defense of his earliest sermon on "Christian Perfection" in 1741, Wesley says that "seeing they are the words of God, and not of man...we may not, therefore, lay these expressions aside."

By "perfection," he did not mean perfection in knowledge, free from mistake, free from infirmities, or free from temptation. In later years, he denied the possibility of "Adamic," "angelic," "absolute," "infallible," or "sinless" perfection. But he did teach that it is the privilege of the children of God to be "made free from outward sin." As his doctrine developed, he taught that those who have matured from children, to young men and women, and finally to "perfected" mature adults, have dominion over sin.

His teaching met with immediate resistance and further alienated him from the Calvinists—and from George Whitefield in particular—with whom he was already in dispute over the doctrine of election. Whitefield wrote that it is "a fond conceit...to cry up perfection and yet cry down the doctrine of final perseverance."

In the midst of such opposition from friend and foe alike, Wesley declared that, "even though all men should be offended," he would not lay aside what he believed to be the scriptural teaching on perfection. But perhaps because this teaching was not his only focus—or even his primary focus—the controversy simmered in the background for nearly twenty years before making a resurgence in the late 1750s.

Though at first he taught something of a progressive growth in sanctification, by 1758 he had begun teaching that perfection—much like justification—is gained by faith in an instant and can also be lost. In 1759, he began to explicitly distinguish between "voluntary" and "involuntary" sin, arguing that believers, in their corrupted, post-Fall bodies, can have freedom from all "voluntary transgressions of a known law" of God, or sin "properly so-called."

Both voluntary and involuntary transgressions need the atoning blood of Christ, and thus believers must continue to rely on Jesus and

His righteousness. This definition and view of sin would be Wesley's working definition for the rest of his life.

The subtleties of Wesley's teaching were missed by most Methodists—lay members as well as preachers. Still, a wave of members claiming to have reached the higher state of perfection brought Wesley great trials and blessings during the late 1750s and into the 1760s, and set the stage for what many have described as "the heaviest trial" of his life.

Thomas Maxfield was Wesley's very first lay preacher. For twenty years, he was one of the Methodist leader's most faithful, dependable, and effective colaborers. Converted at a Wesley-led meeting in Bristol in 1739, Maxfield grew rapidly in his faith. When Wesley left the Foundery society in 1741, Maxfield stepped forward.

When Wesley subsequently heard reports about the preaching of this young, unordained convert, he returned to Bristol to put a stop to it. However, his mother, Susanna, convinced him to hear Maxfield's extraordinary gift before acting; and when he did, he claimed Maxfield as his very first "son in the gospel" and delegated increased authority to him.

In the early 1760s, Wesley appointed Maxfield as the leader of a select band in London—a small group of like-minded believers who "seem to have tasted of the same blessing" of sanctification. Under Maxfield's leadership, members of the group began placing a high value on dreams, visions, feelings, and inward impressions as signs of their entire sanctification. This is not likely to have been enough to raise Wesley's concern, as he was open to occasional supernatural phenomena. But Maxfield and his followers soon began looking down on others, particularly those preachers who spoke against them.

When Maxfield began teaching a "higher" view of Christian perfection than Wesley taught—proclaiming that one could be "perfect as an angel"—and began telling others that Wesley's view was too low, he formed a faction against the leader. When Wesley caught wind of this in late 1761, he sought to meet with all the involved parties, in accordance with his standard practice for verifying reports of unbecoming behavior. He invited his assistant to meet with some of the accusers, in order to "remove any misunderstandings," but Maxfield refused to meet.

The issues were set on the back burner as Wesley spent five months in 1762 touring the work in Ireland, where he found dozens of "witnesses of the great salvation" of the second blessing, but the result was "more pure," lacking the extravagances, and with "none who dreamed of being immortal or infallibly incapable of temptation."

Wesley then returned to England for three months of visiting the English societies, during which time he and Charles met with Thomas Maxfield and told him all the things they "disliked." The brothers were satisfied to learn that some of the charges were misrepresentations, and on others Maxfield was willing to change. But the satisfaction would not last for long.

Despite Maxfield's assurances, unsettling rumors continued to reach Wesley. When he ended his tour in late October, he took a few days to collect his thoughts before writing a long letter to his wayward assistant, expressing in more exacting detail the things he disliked. What is striking about this letter is that it charges Maxfield with violating two character traits essential to Wesley's doctrine of perfection. Wesley told Maxfield that he saw in his behavior a "littleness of love" and the "appearance of pride."

The issues with Maxfield were compounded by problems with one of his associates, George Bell, who was a former corporal in the Life Guard—a senior regiment in the British Army. Converted in 1758, Bell claimed to be entirely, infallibly sanctified in 1761, whereupon he began claiming that he could heal people. Like Maxfield, Bell had gained a strong following by leading ecstatic meetings.

When Wesley heard rumors about these meetings, he decided to covertly observe for himself. He later reported in a letter to Charles that one of the meetings was like a "bear-garden," which may describe the sound made by Bell's followers, who were screaming "unscriptural, enthusiastic expressions," and the roaring of Bell's opponents. In an effort to "mend them or end them," Wesley moved the ecstatic meetings to the Foundery, where he hoped to bring order to the group. "The reproach of Christ I am willing to bear," he recorded in his journal, "but not the reproach of enthusiasm."

At another meeting, when Bell began speaking "as from God, what I knew God had not spoken," Wesley had had enough. Before banning Bell from the society, Wesley met with him to attempt to "convince him of his mistakes." But Bell was "as unmoved as a rock." Shortly thereafter, Maxfield broke with Wesley, and together with Bell took about one-fifth of the London society with him.

If there was one saving grace for Wesley, it was this: In early 1763, George Bell prophesied that the world would come to an end on February 28. Wesley publicly distanced himself from Bell, writing to inform the newspapers of his displeasure, and insisting that he and Bell were no longer in "connexion" with each other.

When the predicted day came, many were in an uproar, awaiting what they believed to be the Second Coming of Christ. As people gathered to watch the end of the world, George Bell was arrested for disturbing the peace.

That evening, John Wesley preached to the remaining members of the society on Amos 4:12—"prepare to meet thy God"—and "the utter absurdity" of Bell's claims that the world would end that evening. Afterward, in his journal, he wryly noted that, after taking a short look at the multitude awaiting the world's end, "I went to bed at my usual time and was fast asleep about ten o'clock."

The result of the tumult was more than just personal for Wesley. He found his people "confused and distressed by a thousand misrepresentations." Despite the discouragements and the evil that had been spoken against him, he had to press on. "My point was still," the indefatigable leader reflected in his journal, "to go straightforward in the work whereto I am I called."

A great part of this work was to rehabilitate his damaged ministry and bring clarity to his teaching on sanctification. In early 1763, he published a reply to Bishop Warburton, who had accused him of "laying claim to almost every apostolic gift." Wesley also published "A Discourse on Sin in Believers" in which he insisted that, though by God's grace a believer need not yield to sin, "sin remains [in believers] still, and often struggles to break from the cross" on which it was previously crucified. Therefore, he taught, believers must "watch against the flesh, as well as the world and the devil."

The crises of the previous year prompted Wesley to work through issues in his theology, and over the next several years a shift became evident in his writing. Whereas many of his earlier discussions on Christian perfection centered on sin, his letters and tracts now presented a more positive declaration of sanctification. Finally, in 1766, he published his full teaching on sanctification in a book called *A Plain Account of Christian Perfection*. This Christian perfection is the pure love of God and neighbor. Furthermore, the main way to discern its presence is not in knowledge, ecstatic experiences, or even spiritual gifts, but in the "always abiding" presence of the fruit of the Spirit, as delineated in Galatians 5. Christian perfection is marked not by confidence and pride, but by meekness and humility.

It is perfect love.

During the decade of the 1760s, Wesley was battered and beset by trials. Friends betrayed him, and fellow Christian leaders decried his teaching—including George Whitefield, who criticized "that *monstrous doctrine of sinless perfection* [that] for a while turns some of its deluded votaries into temporary monsters." Though Wesley was willing to accept hundreds of accounts—"witnesses"—of others receiving this sanctifying grace, oddly, he never openly declared the same for himself. Indeed, it is hard to see how one so filled with introspection, high moral standards, and self-doubt could think he was a specimen of Christian perfection.

Even if he had received sanctifying grace, in public he rarely spoke about the state of his own soul—though he encouraged it among others. Doctrinal truths, he believed, and rectitude of character have no "necessary correlation."

In his voluminous public writings, he makes no claim to have received this second work of God. There are, however, private revelations, particularly to his brother Charles, that demonstrate a surprising level of private self-doubt for a leader so seemingly self-assured.

John wrote a series of letters to his brother between 1766 and 1767, trying to rally Charles to join him in fulfilling their roles as "chief conductors" of the work—John as the "head" and Charles as the "heart"—to "be all devoted to God!" In another letter, he wonders why the work of God "has spread so far, and it has spread no further," and then answers his own question, saying that the chief reason is his and Charles's lack of personal holiness. "If we were more holy in heart and life, and more thoroughly devoted to God," he claims, "would not all the preachers catch our spirit and carry it throughout the land?"

However, if a letter to Charles dated June 27, 1766, is taken at face value, Wesley contradicts and confuses every other evidence of his spiritual life and journey. Much of the letter is written in shorthand to thwart prying eyes, but the words are shocking.

> *I do not love God. I never did. Therefore I never believed in the Christian sense of the word. Therefore I am only an honest heathen, a proselyte of the Temple. . .and yet to be so employed of God! And so hedged in that I can neither get forward nor backward! Surely there was never such an instance before, from the beginning of the world! If I ever had that faith, it would not be so strange. But I never had any other [evidence] of the eternal or invisible world that I have now; and that is none at all, unless such as fairly shines from reason's glimmering ray. I have no direct witness, I do not say that I am a child of God, but of anything invisible or eternal.*

Though difficult to believe in light of the testimony of his lifelong ministry, it is a letter that calls into question the very limits of his experiential, subjective religion. Still, he insists on teaching the doctrines he gleaned, rightly or wrongly, from scripture. "I find rather an increase than a decrease for the whole work of God and every part of it."

This very private revelation to his most trusted confidant is shocking for a man so dedicated to God and His work. But he also made a more public declaration in a letter dated March 5, 1767, to the editor of *Lloyd's Evening Post*. In defense of an early sketch of a perfect Christian in a tract called *The Character of a Methodist* (1742), Wesley makes it clear that his life has fallen short of his doctrine.

> *I have told all the world I am not perfect; and yet you allow me to be a Methodist. I tell you flat I have not attained the character I draw.*

Even though he never made any truly discernible claim to have received the blessing of Christian perfection, and though he faced stiff resistance, he continued to teach about perfect love throughout his ministry. He was convinced not so much of his own infallibility or sinlessness, but of what he believed to be the biblical truth of Christian perfection.

Chapter 17
A Thousand Tongues

What is of infinitely more moment than the spirit
of poetry is the spirit of piety.

When John and Charles Wesley received their spiritual awakening in May 1738, they found such a radical transformation in their own lives that they would spend the next five decades seeking to bring the same to all who would listen. This transformation was not just an external change, as the two had been living distinct from the world and in the pursuit of holiness for more than a decade. But the change for them was also internal—it was a radical transformation of the heart.

The two brothers expressed this change in different ways. John was methodical, plain, and clear in his language. He wrote in prose, influencing others with his treatises, his descriptive and voluminous journals, his sermons, and his *Notes upon the Bible*—the latter two representing the standards for what Methodists believed. Charles expressed himself to greatest effect in poetry. John could say descriptively and emotionally concerning his transformation, "I felt my heart strangely warmed." But Charles's words could fly off the page and resonate with all Christians, with his experience becoming a part of their own: "My chains fell off, my heart was free."

Even in the midst of their personal strife, John and Charles, each with his own giftedness and temperament, would "challenge the world together" and bring a religion of the heart to multitudes of hungry souls.

When Charles was awakened on May 21, 1738, he immediately put his experience into verse. Within days of his conversion, he wrote "Where Shall My Wandering Soul Begin?" and "And Can It Be?"— two hymns that still express the heart of Methodists in particular and Christians in general. For Charles, it was the beginning of expressing his heart and exalting God through upward of nine thousand hymns, which he wrote until his death in 1788.

Without John and the growth of his Methodist organizational structure, this beautifully important body of work would likely have become a lost treasure. Likewise, without Charles's verse, John's success and the import of his organization, which some said was "born in song," would have been greatly diminished.

John Wesley was fascinated by hymns, even though he knew that his own poetry wasn't of a caliber worthy of public display. Early in the eighteenth century, hymns in English were something of a novelty, until Isaac Watts, a nonconformist leader, began to buck a long-standing tradition of singing or chanting only explicitly biblical poetry by publishing original verses of his own to be sung in his dissenting services, thus paving the way for hymnody in the English world. The Wesley brothers' familiarity with Watts's hymnody intensified while they were in Georgia in the 1730s, where they also encountered Moravian hymns. John translated some of the German hymns, compiled them with some Isaac Watts hymns, and published one of the earliest hymnals produced in North America, *Collection of Psalms and Hymns* (1737).

The return of the Wesley brothers to England from their failed mission to Georgia, followed by their spiritual awakening, gave them new material for hymnals—their own experiences written in verse by Charles. In 1738, John published a volume in London that was similar to what he had published in America; and in 1739, he published *Hymns and Sacred Songs*, which put the hymns of Charles Wesley into print for the first time.

Herein lies the essence of what John Wesley so relentlessly advocated during his long ministry. "A man may be orthodox in every point," he declared in a 1742 sermon, "and yet it is possible he may have no religion at all. . . . He may be almost as orthodox—as the devil. . .and may, all the while be as great a stranger as he to the heart of religion."

In a letter defending his approach to working with Christians of other "opinions," he wrote, "Orthodoxy, or right opinion, is but a slender part of religion at best." He was further convinced, echoing the apostle Paul's words to Timothy, that one could retain "a form of godliness" but not have its power.

The singing of hymns privately or in the company of others in bands, classes, or society meetings was John Wesley's most practical method for capturing the heart as well as the head with the truths of the Gospel.

John Wesley claimed to be "*homo unius libri*"— a man of one book, the Bible. It is the book to which he turned "to find the way to heaven," and therefore the book he used to point others to heaven. This is not to say he didn't read other books. He read prolifically from books of a wide variety of fields. But he read them through the standard of the Bible. It is difficult to overestimate how deeply the scriptures penetrated his thinking. While his sermons were not verse-by-verse expositions of the text, his quotations and allusions to texts of scripture through all his writings—his sermons, treatises, journals, and letters—demonstrate a man well versed in even the most obscure passages of the Bible.

His niece, Sarah Wesley, once asked him how she might know God more intimately. Part of his prescription was "to spend at least an hour a day reading and meditating on the Bible." This recommendation is one that he likely held at a minimum for himself throughout his life, along with his regular times of morning and evening prayer.

Charles's approach to the Bible was similar. Among his thousands of hymns are verse-by-verse reflections on biblical texts and paraphrases, in line with the hymns of Isaac Watts, who led England in a transition from singing exclusively biblical texts in worship to hymnody with more of a subjective dependence on the Bible. But even in Charles Wesley's hymns, one can scarcely find a line of verse that is not a quote, allusion, or image from the Bible. Furthermore, in line with Watts, Charles viewed the pages of the Old Testament through New Testament lenses. Seeing how the Old Covenant foreshadowed Christ implicitly, Charles wrote explicitly that Jesus is the promised Messiah, "Israel's strength and consolation."

Charles Wesley gave us some of the most cherished hymns in the English language: "And Can It Be?" "Love Divine, All Loves Excelling," "Come, Thou Long-Expected Jesus," "Hark! the Herald Angels

Sing," "Arise, My Soul, Arise," "Christ the Lord Is Risen Today," "Lo, He Comes with Clouds Descending," "A Charge to Keep I Have," and "Jesus, Lover of My Soul," among others. But more than these cherished hymns, Charles Wesley introduced an appeal to subjective experience, which fits within Wesleyan theology.

It is often suggested that Isaac Watts wrote with an eye more toward objective theology—the grandeur and sovereignty of God. Watts did, however, venture into the subjective, with hymns such as "When I Survey the Wondrous Cross." In his hymnody, Charles draws on the subjective emotions of humanity in our encounter with an exceedingly gracious and loving God. This approach would affect worship in the English-speaking world from then on.

John was particularly excited about this change. Years after Charles began hymn writing, John observed that, though his brother's poetry and verse were indeed inspired, "what is of infinitely more moment than the spirit of poetry is the spirit of piety."

John Wesley's practical theology can be seen in the contrast between an objective reflection on God and the subjective experience of Him. When a schoolteacher inquired about John's thoughts about a book on the doctrine of the Trinity by the Reverend William Jones, Wesley revealed his approach to speculative theology:

> *Mr. Jones's book on the Trinity is both more clear and more strong than any I ever saw on that subject. If anything is wanting, it is the application, lest it should appear to be a merely speculative doctrine, which has no influence on our hearts or lives; but this is abundantly supplied by my brother's hymns.*

Very early in his ministry, John Wesley experimented with printing hymnbooks to spread the hymns of the Moravians, Isaac Watts, his brother Charles, and others—a practice he continued for the length of his ministry. Though he was skeptical of speculative theology and cold orthodoxy, he found in the hymns an ideal platform from which to teach doctrine and set a balance against the opposite extreme of a merely subjective approach to God.

John himself was not a writer of hymns, but he was a translator, compiler, editor, and distributor of hymns. This work was essential for the publication of Charles's hymns, as Charles was far more of a private person who needed the help of his brother to promote his brilliant gift.

In 1742, the brothers published *A Collection of Tunes Set to Music, as They Are Commonly Sung at the Foundery*, their first hymnal to include the tunes, much like modern hymnals. But this volume did not catch on. It was their earlier *Collection of Psalms and Hymns*, published in 1741, that would generally be used for the next decade among the Methodists. In 1749, Charles published two volumes of his own hymns; but they were sold by subscription only, thus limiting their influence. They were also produced without John's knowledge, and he later said that he did not approve of all the hymns.

In 1753, John made another bold attempt at publishing a hymnbook for general use. It was titled *Hymns and Spiritual Songs Intended for the Use of Real Christians of All Denominations* and was often simply referred to as *Spiritual Hymns*. As the full title shows, this hymnbook was a cry for "a spirit of universal love," despite the diversity of opinions and modes of worship. It included a preface that expressed Wesley's hope for this unity.

Spiritual Hymns became the standard for Methodist worship for the next three decades. Following its publication in 1753, John Wesley stepped away from his hymnbook publishing ventures. It is likely no coincidence that his break from these pursuits occurred during the great rupture in his relationship with his hymn-writing brother. During this dispute, Charles continued to write hymns, and he published five short volumes between 1756 and 1759: *Hymns for the Year 1756*, *Hymns for Intercession for All Mankind* (1758), *Funeral Hymns* (1759), *Hymns on the Expected Invasion* (1759), and *Hymns to Be Used on the Thanksgiving Day* (1759).

The strain on the brothers' relationship, it seems, crippled them both in this most vital work. But as they began to reconcile in 1760, their interest in musical collaboration was renewed as well. In 1761, they published *Select Hymns; with Tunes Annexed*, which once again showed the hand of John's careful editorial work and purpose for the project. As John's interest increased, so also did Charles's genius. The years between 1762 and 1766 proved to be his most productive hymn-writing period, as he crafted more than 6,200 scriptural hymns in just four years, an astonishing average of 1,230 hymns per year. Though both brothers had gifts that were amazing in themselves, to be at their most effective they needed each other.

John Wesley recognized the unique capacity of hymns to connect one's heart to a very personal God. He was also keenly aware that one could draw near with his lips while his heart remained far from God. It was a topic of significant concern, and it was a regular topic of discussion at the annual Methodist conferences. At the 1746 conference, John asked, "How shall we guard more effectually against formality in public singing?" The answers to this question are simple. Make "careful choice of hymns"; choose "hymns of praise or prayer, rather than descriptive" ones; do not sing "too much"; choose tunes suitable for the words; and be sure the people understand the words they are singing. For John, the very method of singing, and not merely the words or choice of songs, was important.

The issue was revisited at the 1768 conference, with a warning against "those complex tunes which it is scarce possible to sing with devotion" and the "long quavering" hallelujahs sung in some hymns, and "vain repetitions" of verses. Finally, he warned against singing "too slow." In 1780, he added another concern: "Exhort every one in the congregation to sing, not one in ten only."

The publication of *Select Hymns* in 1761 also included seven "Directions for Singing," in order that "this part of divine worship may be more acceptable to God, as well as the more profitable to himself and others." The directions are largely practical. "Learn the tunes," "sing all," "sing lustily," "sing modestly," and "sing in time." But the import of his direction is summed up in the seventh and final one: "Above all, sing spiritually. . . . Aim at pleasing Him more than yourself or any other creature."

Wesley tried his best to navigate the Methodists around pitfalls he had seen and experienced in his five decades in ministry, in addition to publishing and providing in his hymnbooks what he viewed as the greatest "variety" of hymns the world had to offer.

Though the *Select Hymns* volume was important in many ways for the Wesleys, as they continued to develop new ways of worship, it was the older *Spiritual Hymns* from 1753 that continued as the Methodist standard for worship. But John was still not satisfied. By 1780, he had collected and ordered a new standard hymnal called *A Collection of Hymns for the Use of the People Called Methodists*. It was more than five hundred pages long, divided into five parts, ordered thematically, and comprised 525 hymns. Perhaps the most significant editorial touch found in the hymnal is the choice of the opening hymn:

> *O for a thousand tongues to sing,*
> *My great Redeemer's praise,*
> *The glories of my God and King,*
> *The triumphs of His grace!*

This hymn written by Charles Wesley on May 21, 1739, the first anniversary of his conversion, would serve as the opening hymn throughout all Methodist hymnbooks for generations. The opening line was inspired by the Moravian leader Peter Böhler, who once told Charles Wesley, "Had I a thousand tongues, I would praise Him with them all."

"O for a Thousand Tongues to Sing" was initially intended as a very individualistic hymn, but the work of the Wesleys turned this phrase on its head. Through Charles's verse and John's compilations, editorial work, and distribution of these magnificent works, the two were able to give voice to thousands of tongues—indeed even millions—over the next three centuries, offering Christians everywhere the ability to express the feelings of a heart set free by an ever gracious God.

Directions for Singing (1761)

I. Learn these tunes before you learn any others; afterwards learn as many as you please.

II. Sing them exactly as they are printed here, without altering or mending them at all; and if you have learned to sing them otherwise, unlearn it as soon as you can.

III. Sing all. See that you join with the congregation as frequently as you can. Let not a slight degree of weakness or weariness hinder you. If it is a cross to you, take it up, and you will find it a blessing.

IV. Sing lustily and with a good courage. Beware of singing as if you were half dead, or half asleep; but lift up your voice with strength. Be no more afraid of your voice now, nor more ashamed of its being heard, than when you sang the songs of Satan.

V. Sing modestly. Do not bawl, so as to be heard above or distinct from the rest of the congregation, that you may not destroy the harmony; but strive to unite your voices together, so as to make one clear melodious sound.

VI. Sing in time. Whatever time is sung, be sure to keep with it. Do not run before nor stay behind it; but attend close to the leading voices, and move therewith as exactly as you can; and take care not to sing too slowly. This drawling way naturally steals on all who are lazy; and it is high time to drive it out from us, and sing all our tunes just as quickly as we did at first.

VII. Above all, sing spiritually. Have an eye toward God in every word you sing. Aim at pleasing Him more than yourself, or any other creature. In order to do this, attend strictly to the sense of what you sing, and see that your heart is not carried away with the sound, but offered to God continually; so shall your singing be such as the Lord will approve here, and reward you when he cometh in the clouds of heaven.

Chapter 18
Shaking Hell's Gates

I did not seek any part of this power.
It came upon me unawares.

T he work to which John Wesley was called was too great to do
alone—even for a relentless, purposeful, nonstop traveling evangelist who met with and ministered to more souls during his lifetime
than most would reach in five lifetimes. Whether he had a grand scale in
view from the beginning is debatable, but by at least 1763 he noted that
God had raised him and the Methodists for an extraordinary task—"to
reform the nation, and in particular, the Church, to spread scriptural
holiness over the land." To even approach such a goal, he needed many
others to come alongside him. He needed what he called helpers, out of
which came a select group of assistants, who were preachers in "connexion" with him to bring about this reformation.

Early on it seemed that a partnership with George Whitefield or
the Moravians would be a natural fit, but their differing theological and
practical views set them on separate, even if parallel, courses of ministry.
John desperately wanted to be part of a movement *within* the Church
of England, and he sought the support of the ordained clergy of local
parishes. But he was ultimately pushed out.

By 1744, there were four clergy members who professed alignment
with Wesley's Methodism. Desiring nothing but to "save their own
souls, and those that hear them," they met together at the Foundery for
the first conference of Methodism. This gathering, as with all annual
conferences to follow, was held at the pleasure and invitation of John
and Charles Wesley, with humbly stated intentions:

That all things be considered as in the immediate presence of God;

That we may meet with a single eye, and as little children who have
    everything to learn;
That every point may be examined from the foundation;
That every person may speak freely what is in his heart; and
That every question proposed may be fully debated, and "bolted to the bran."

At these conferences, decisions were made centrally—though John very often had decided beforehand—concerning doctrinal beliefs, discipline, practices, and organization.

In addition to the four ordained clergy members, John invited four others of a more controversial nature to be in connexion with him. These were four unordained lay preachers who desired to be among his assistants. At the beginning of the meeting, they stood outside the door while the ordained members, as a first order of business, agreed to let them in.

Such a decision did not come lightly for Wesley, who only a few years earlier would have decried any such repudiation of the customs of the Church. Indeed, it was his own mother who had convinced him that one of the lay preachers, Thomas Maxfield, was a gifted orator used of God and should be given a chance to preach. But just as he had wrestled with the appropriateness of field preaching, Wesley also wrestled with appointing lay preachers. At this first conference, the question was posed: "Are lay assistants allowable?" The answer was one that determined many of Wesley's decisions concerning how ministry practice was set forth: Lay preachers were allowed "only in cases of necessity."

Such a determination opened the door for some of Wesley's most powerful opportunities to transform a nation, but also some of his greatest perils and disappointments. Still, he viewed this as an age of "necessity" and deemed it most expedient to go forward, not merely with the few properly ordained and trained who would join him, but also with the many untrained but zealous lay preachers who would learn from him and go forth to a world in desperate need of the Gospel.

Out of his voluminous defenses of this practice, one of his most convincing is found in a 1748 letter to a critic of the use of lay preachers, later published as *A Letter to a Clergyman*. The letter presents an analogy between physicians and preachers.

"Seeing life and health are things of so great importance," he begins, "it is without question highly expedient that physicians should have all possible advantages of learning and education," and be tested by "competent judges before they practice publicly." He then leads the analogy to several suppositions. "Suppose," Wesley argues, "[a physician] bred at the University of Dublin" settles in a location "for some years [and] makes no cures at all. . . . Will you condemn a man who having some little skill in physic and a tender compassion for those who are sick and dying all around him, cures many of those, without fee or reward, whom the doctor could not [or would not] cure?" Wesley then patiently applies the analogy point by point to the authority of preachers.

"Seeing life everlasting and holiness, or health of soul, are things of great importance," he continues, "it was highly expedient that ministers, being physicians of the soul, should have all advantages of education and learning," and be, like physicians, tested by "competent judges, before they enter in the public exercise of their office, the saving of souls from death."

Here, Wesley inserts a hypothetical trained minister who "saves no sinners from their sins," and then introduces a layman who does the work of the minister. "Will you condemn such a preacher," he asks, "because he has not learning [or authority]?" He then comes to the ultimate conclusion and defense of his practice, "that every Christian, if he is able to do it, has authority to save a dying soul."

For Wesley, the value of expediency determined his controversial decision.

The training and instruction of Wesley's assistants and helpers began immediately. Concerned that his preachers would fare no better than those he critiqued, he crafted an enduring list of *Twelve Rules of an Assistant* (later "assistant" was replaced with "helper" to apply to the larger group).

The first two rules deal with the helper's demeanor: "Be diligent" and

"Be serious." Next are two rules concerning relationships with women, advising caution and requiring advice before entering into marriage—the rule that John Bennett broke in proposing to Grace Murray right under Wesley's nose. Rules 5 through 7 deal with confronting sin in others, followed by two rules calling on the preacher "of the gospel [to be] the servant of all" and not to "affect the gentleman" by dress or deportment. The initial list, drafted in 1744, included rules 10 through 12, regarding the use of money, debts, and time, but these rules about money were later removed from the list and replaced by a general rule of obedience to execute all the Methodist rules as "a son in the Gospel."

The rules were stringent, and Wesley held the initial eight assistants to a very high standard. But he also had a significant amount of work to do himself in nurturing and educating these men. Some were ordained and needed to learn this evangelical doctrine; but even more of the helpers were not ordained and had little or no theological education.

Wesley expected his helpers to be "learners rather than teachers." He gave them a steady diet of books to read, such as Henry Scougal's *The Life of God in the Soul of Man*; Thomas à Kempis's *The Christian Pattern*; John Bunyan's *The Pilgrim's Progress*; William Law's *Tracts*; Bishop Beveridge's *Private Thoughts*; John Heylin's *Devotional Tracts*, Thomas Halyburton's *The Life of Mr. Halyburton*; and John Baptiste Saint-Jure's *The Holy Life of M. De Renty*; as well as collections of sermons.

This ultimately led to a monumental editorial task "to provide a complete library for those that fear God" filled with abridgments of all the "most valuable" books on practical divinity "in the English tongue." This fifty-volume project became *The Christian Library*, published between 1749 and 1755. These volumes were to be kept at all the larger societies for the use of the helpers and for public readings of the books by society members.

Not only were the expectations of learning and educational growth high for these helpers and assistants, but their roles were even more demanding:

(1) To expound every morning and evening. (2) To meet the United Society, the Bands, the Select Society, and the penitents once a week.

(3) To visit the Classes once a quarter. (4) To hear and decide all differences. (5) To put the disorderly back on trial, and to receive on trial for the Bands or Society. (6) To see that the Stewards, the Leaders, and the Schoolmasters faithfully discharge their several offices. (7) To meet the Leaders of the Bands and Classes weekly, and the Stewards, and to overlook their accounts.

Wesley oversaw the assistants and helpers under him and taught them how to counsel souls, visit the sick, and remove unruly members and officers. But perhaps most pressing of all, if his publishing history and the conference minutes are any indication, he trained these men to be more effective preachers by teaching them doctrine and general methods of preaching. Many of these helpers were rough, uneducated, uncouth—but zealous—men.

In 1749, presumably responding to the rise of distracting preaching habits over the previous five years, Wesley published a tract called *Directions Concerning Annunciation and Gesture*, in which he instructs preachers to use a clear, "pleasing" voice with variation in tone, along with gestures and posture to match—and not distract from—the message.

By putting all this organizational structure together and overseeing these preachers, John Wesley came to command an army of laborers—and by the mid-1750s, close to fifty preachers had joined him. The *Twelve Rules of the Helper* was first introduced in 1744. By 1745, he had amended them to include this final and most important rule:

You have nothing to do but to save souls. Therefore spend and be spent in this work. And go always, not only to those who want you, but to those who want you most.

Wesley's organization had dozens of assistants, helpers, class leaders, and stewards, some of whom were remarkably gifted. And though they lacked proper training, "it is plain God has blessed their labour." Even so, Wesley explained that if a leader is "remarkably wanting in gifts or grace, he is soon taken notice of and removed."

Removal for such insufficiency did indeed occur regularly. Wesley, though patient and gracious in allowing growth in his preachers and leaders, was also discerning enough to know that some could never measure up to the task. More concerning than lack of gifting, however, were those helpers who needed to be removed for indiscretions or divisions.

Because Wesley's ministry was so expansive and lengthy, he was often plagued by issues among his preachers. The first major crisis was with John Bennett, who married Wesley's early love, Grace Murray. Wesley continued to invite Bennett to labor with him, though their relationship was forever breached, and separation was inevitable by the early 1750s. But another preacher, James Wheatley, who had been with Wesley since 1742, was accused of immorality with several women. Though confronted, Wheatley was not repentant, and thus was removed from the connexion in 1752.

Though such instances were not pervasive, how John dealt with these preachers often caused friction between Charles and him. True to their natural temperaments, John was apt to "prefer grace before gifts" in his preachers, and he focused on the immense need for the quantity of preachers throughout the societies. Charles, on the other hand, sought for purity within the movement, preferring to "purge. . .the laborers" who were lacking in either grace or gifts.

The removals, and John's nonstop supervision, correction, placement of preachers, directions in preaching, and rules for every aspect of his connexion led many to charge John with one of the greatest challenges to his leadership. This was summed up by Charles, who wrote to John in 1751, "I am told from Bristol you 'rule the preachers with a rod of iron;' they complain of it all over England."

These critiques from Charles came at the rockiest time in the brothers' complex relationship, so these comments must be read in that context. In a letter to Lady Huntingdon, Charles expressed his desire to purge the preachers in order to "break [John's] power. . .and reduce his authority within due bounds." The letter was intercepted and given to John, who wrote to his brother with remarkable restraint. Concerning his power, he wrote, "I am quite ready to part with the whole or any part of it. It is no pleasure to me, nor ever was." The issue of John's use of power was an ongoing criticism that he could never shake, nor did he ever really try to.

His most spirited defense of his power came after several challenges to his authority a decade and a half later, when he spoke to the 1766 conference. His lengthy statement begins with an explanation of the history of the movement—that it was not *his* desire to have assistants, but the desire of others to come alongside of him in a voluntary and mutual desire to work together. Either he or an assistant could end their relationship at any time, but the authority rested with Wesley. In 1744, when he convened his first conference, he explained that he desired "their advice concerning the best method of carrying on the work of God" and that "I sent for them to *advise*, not *govern* me."

Wesley held on to this power with a firm fist but describes it as a great burden. "I did not seek any part of this power," he explained. "It came upon me unawares. But when it was come, not daring to bury that talent, I used it to the best of my judgment."

"Give me one hundred preachers who fear nothing but sin and desire nothing but God," John Wesley wrote to one of his choice successors, Alexander Mather, "and I care not whether they be clergymen or laymen, they alone will shake the gates of Hell and set up the kingdom of Heaven upon Earth."

For forty-five years, John Wesley had seen how God used Wesley's helpers in his absence as he delegated great responsibilities to others. He also saw how destructive some preachers could be. He was ever mindful of his possible death and its consequences for Methodism, but by 1784, at eighty years of age, he needed a concrete plan to keep the connexion from splintering into hundreds of disconnected groups.

He had long considered handing off his authority to a single individual. But one of his potential choice successors, John Fletcher, a Methodist theologian of great piety and devotion, was often in poor health and spent long periods convalescing. It became clear, not only to the aging leader but also to the preachers, that the organization needed a plurality of successors instead of a single leader like Wesley had been. This was confirmed by the fact that many grew tired of what they viewed as Wesley's "tyrannical" and "despotic" rule.

At the 1784 conference, Wesley set forth a plan called *The Deed of Declaration* to keep the connexion together. It was a legal document defining the *Conference of the People Called Methodists*—the deliberative body of the movement that decided doctrine, discipline, and preacher locations—as one hundred preachers who were to meet yearly, decide by majority vote, elect a president and secretary yearly, and retained all the powers of admitting, expelling, and stationing preachers that Wesley claimed until his death.

There was swift resistance to the plan at the conference. This was due in large part to the naming in the *Deed* of the one hundred preachers, all of whom were chosen by Wesley. The list excluded ninety-one others, some of whom were longtime Methodist preachers. Some of the affronted preachers were enraged by their exclusion from the list. Wesley replied that he had not "thought as well of them as they thought of themselves." To add to the tension, some of the preachers misunderstood the *Deed*, believing that those not listed as the "legal hundred" were being expelled from the connexion altogether, which was not the case.

Perhaps looking to the future had blinded Wesley to the present dynamics of the movement, but he was blindsided by the opposition. An appeal was presented to the conference, and bitter debate ensued, with several preachers threatening to leave the connexion. Though only five preachers ultimately departed as a result, the tensions were in part relieved by John Fletcher, who made an impassioned and tearful plea to both Wesley and his opposition by reminding them of their "work in which they were unitedly engaged," followed by "many sobbing aloud."

Though the *Deed* was not technically adjusted over the next year to account for the murmurings, Wesley understood the concerns of those in the conference who had raised objections. In a letter written to the conference less than a year after the 1784 gathering—but intended to be read after Wesley's death—he seems to have acquiesced to the concerns of the conference, imploring his successors never to "assume any superiority over your brethren." So even though the "legal hundred" remained in effect for nearly 150 years, all of the preachers in the connexion were invited to meet and participate in the conference.

Within a year of the controversial 1784 conference, Wesley defended his *Deed of Declaration* from the residual complaints it had created by finally expressing the vision and concern he wished to cast long past his death:

> *You see then in all the pains I have taken about this absolutely necessary [Deed of Declaration], I have been labouring, not for myself, (I have no interest therein), but for the whole body of Methodists; in order to fix them upon such a foundation as is likely to stand as long as the sun and moon endure. That is, if they continue to walk by faith, and to show forth their faith by their works; otherwise, I pray God to root out the memorial of them from the earth.*

Twelve Rules of a Helper

1. Be diligent. Never be unemployed. Never be triflingly employed. Never while away time, nor spend more time at any place than is strictly necessary.
2. Be serious. Let your motto be, "Holiness to the Lord." Avoid all lightness, jesting, and foolish talking.
3. Converse sparingly and cautiously with women, particularly with young women.
4. Take no step towards marriage without solemn prayer to God and consulting with your brethren.
5. Believe evil of no one unless fully proved; take heed how you credit it. Put the best construction you can on everything. You know the judge is always supposed to be on the prisoner's side.
6. Speak evil of no one, else your word, especially, would eat as doth a canker; keep your thoughts within your own breast till you come to the person concerned.
7. Tell every one what you think wrong in him, lovingly and plainly, and as soon as may be, else it will fester in your own heart. Make all haste to cast the fire out of your bosom.
8. Do not affect the gentleman. A preacher of the gospel is the servant of all.
9. Be ashamed of nothing but sin; no, not of cleaning your own shoes when necessary.
10. Be punctual. Do everything exactly at the time. And do not mend our rules, but keep them, and that for conscience' sake.
11. You have nothing to do but to save souls. Therefore spend and be spent in this work. And go always, not only to those who want you, but to those who want you most.
12. Act in all things, not according to your own will, but as a son in the gospel, and in union with your brethren. As such, it is your part to employ your time as our rules direct: partly in preaching and visiting from house to house, partly in reading, meditation, and prayer. Above all, if you labour with us in our

Lord's vineyard, it is needful you should do that part of the work which the Conference shall advise, at those times and places which they shall judge most for His glory.

Observe, it is not your business to preach so many times, and to take care merely of this or that Society, but to save as many souls as you can, to bring as many sinners as you possibly can to repentance, and, with all your power, to build them up in that holiness without which they cannot see the Lord. And, remember, a Methodist preacher is to mind every point, great and small, in the Methodist discipline. Therefore you will need all the grace and sense you have, and to have all your wits about you.

Chapter 19
Setting Up the Kingdom

When shall the Sun of Righteousness arise on these outcasts of men,
with healing in his wings!

John Wesley's gospel was one of transformation. He believed that Jesus came to transform hearts, and the Methodist movement existed based on this very premise. But the implications of the transformed heart went far beyond private expressions of piety. Wesley believed that the Gospel of Jesus Christ changes not just hearts, but conditions, too—bringing people out of poverty and poor health, and freeing them from oppression. As a result, the Gospel transforms society. With his marching army of preachers and society members—130,000 strong at his death in 1791—Wesley aimed not just to "shake the gates of hell" but also to "set up the kingdom of heaven on earth."

Very early in the evangelical revival, Wesley cast his transformational vision at Oxford in 1744 in a sermon he delivered called "Scriptural Christianity." His vision was that Christianity starts with individuals and spreads to others—and, as a result, will eventually cover the entire earth. This line of thinking is consistent throughout his corpus. In his 1746 sermon "The Way to the Kingdom," based on Mark 1:15, where Jesus asserts that "the kingdom of God is at hand," Wesley argues that when the Son of God took on flesh, He began to "set up His Kingdom among men and [reign] in the hearts of His people."

[When] God takes unto Himself His mighty power, and sets up His throne in our hearts, [we] are instantly filled with "righteousness, and peace, and joy in the Holy Ghost" (Romans 14:17). It is called "the Kingdom of Heaven" because it is (in a degree) heaven opened in the soul.

This kingdom, however, is not merely demonstrated in peace, joy, and a love for God, but also in righteousness and love toward "thy neighbor":

> *Not only thy friend, thy kinsman, or thy acquaintance; not only the*
> *virtuous, the friendly, him that loves thee, that prevents or returns*
> *thy kindness; but every child of man, every human creature, every*
> *soul which God hath made; not excepting him whom thou never hast*
> *seen in the flesh, whom thou knowest not, either by face or name; not*
> *excepting him whom thou knowest to be evil and unthankful, him*
> *that still despitefully uses and persecutes thee; him thou shalt love as*
> *thyself; with the same invariable thirst after his happiness in every*
> *kind; the same unwearied care to screen him from whatever might*
> *grieve or hurt either his soul or body.*

As a young man, Wesley had a tendency toward escaping from the world, influenced by what he would later call "the poisonous writers, the mystics." But he was deeply influenced by an elder who rebuked him as a young man at Oxford, when Wesley was seemingly intent on living the life of a hermit. The elder man told him, "Sir, you wish to serve God and go to heaven. Remember you cannot serve Him alone; you must therefore *find* companions, or *make* them; the Bible knows nothing of solitary religion." This exhortation set the stage not only for the Oxford clubs and the Methodist societies but also for a life of outward-focused ministry.

In his "Fourth Discourse on the Sermon on the Mount" in 1748, Wesley argues that "Christianity is essentially a social religion." This fact is made evident by Christ's commands to exhibit the intrinsically relational virtues of gentleness, mercifulness, and peacemaking, which "cannot possibly have a being. . .without an intercourse with other men."

Wesley long warned against an incomplete religion. While he recommended Henry Scougal's influential work, *The Life of God in the Soul of Man*, even going so far as to include it in his *Christian Library*, he warned against stopping at a privatized notion of Christianity. In this same sermon, he declares "it is true that the root of religion lies in the heart, in the inmost soul; that this is the union of the soul with God, the life of God and the soul of man. But if this root be really in the heart it cannot but put forth branches."

Throughout Wesley's ministry, he developed a practical Christian ethic that started with serving the weak, the poor, and the marginalized. Late in his ministry, this passion matured into activism, which helped to shape and inspire some of the greatest social reforms from the late eighteenth into the early nineteenth century.

In February 1772, the aging leader read what he called "a very different book" titled *Some Historical Account of Guinea* by Anthony Benezet, who, according to Wesley's estimation, was "an honest Quaker," living in Philadelphia. The book included details about the "rise and progress of the slave trade, its nature and contemptible effects." A sense of utter shock is evident in the journal entry he had written after he read the book, describing the slave trade as "that execrable sum of all villainies."

Reading Benezet was not Wesley's first exposure to American slavery. While living in Georgia, which at the time was a slave-free colony, he made frequent visits to the slave-holding colony of Carolina, where he observed the harsh treatment of African slaves. Reflecting on a conversation with one of the enslaved women, he wrote with an air of hopeful dreaming, "When shall the Sun of Righteousness arise on these outcasts of men, with healing in his wings!"

The British slave trade continued to grow commercially and cruelly throughout the eighteenth century, surviving with virtual impunity until voices began to cry out in the 1760s and 1770s. John Wesley's voice was but one in a growing chorus.

The result of the agitation of his soul over the slave trade was a pamphlet he wrote in 1774 titled *Thoughts upon Slavery*. The five-part tract was published first in England and then in America by Anthony Benezet, who was impressed by the tract's pathos.

The tract began dispassionately enough by defining slavery and giving a history of the modern slave trade. But Wesley's passion escalates throughout the treatise, describing the background and character of African slaves and giving an overly idealized picture of the people of the

African continent in an attempt to prove wrong those who defended the trade by suggesting that slaves were better off in America than in their native, "remarkably horrid, dreary, and barren land." Wesley showed that they were, in fact, far worse off.

He then educated uninformed readers about how slaves were captured and carried into captivity through fraud, deception, and wars, and told how they were crammed like animals into filthy ships and subjected to punishments and unjust laws, all of which would shock the sensibilities of an uninformed Englishman of the time. "Did the Creator intend," he asks, "that the noblest creatures in the visible world should live such a life as this?" If these men or women could be lashed, maimed, or killed by law for running away to freedom, Wesley said, "what punishment have these *Law-makers* to expect hereafter, on account of their own enormous offenses?"

While he takes jabs at the slave trade in the first three parts, they only set him up for his final assault on the horrendous practice in the final two parts. His argument in part four draws on points for a general audience, "setting the Bible out of the question," and showing that the practice cannot be "defended, on the principles of even heathen honesty." He then explains that because it cannot be defended by a common appeal to "natural justice" or mercy, proponents resort to an appeal to "absolute necessity" to uphold the economic system. He blasts this assertion, wondering how it can ever be necessary to enrich oneself at another's expense:

> *I deny that villainy is ever necessary. It is impossible that it should ever be necessary for any reasonable creature to violate all the laws of justice, mercy, and truth. No circumstances can make it necessary for a man to burst in sunder all the ties of humanity. It can never be necessary for a rational being to sink himself below a brute. A man can be under no necessity of degrading himself into a wolf. The absurdity of the supposition is so glaring, that one would wonder any one can help seeing it.*

His fifth and final section was an "application," speaking directly to the three components of the slave trade: the "captains" who captured slaves, the "merchants" who traded and transported them, and the "planters" who used the slaves on American plantations. Here he lays aside any dispassionate discourse, unleashing a fiery call for repentance.

To the captains employed in this trade. . .you have dragged [the African inhabitants] who had never done you any wrong, perhaps in chains, from their native shore. You have forced them into your ships like an herd of swine, them who had souls immortal as your own. . . . You have carried the survivors into the vilest slavery, never to end but with life.

He then drove home his point specifically to the captains, but surely intended for all those in the slave trade.

Is there a God? You know there is. . . . If you do not [relent from your sin], you must go on, till the measure of your iniquities is full. Then will the great God deal with you as you have dealt with them, and require all their blood at your hands.

Likewise, he turned to the merchants and asked, "Has gold entirely blinded your eyes, and stupefied your heart?" He then implored, "Be *you* a man? Not a wolf, a devourer of the human species."

Finally, he turned to the American "planters," "the spring that puts all the rest in motion."

O, whatever it costs, put a stop to [the cry of the blood of thy brother] before it is too late; instantly, at any price, were it the half of your goods, deliver thyself from blood-guiltiness!

After these direct appeals, he ends with a ringing declaration:

Liberty is the right of every human creature, as soon as he breathes the vital air; and no human law can deprive him of that right which he derives from the law of nature.

211

Thoughts upon Slavery was not the first, nor was it the most per-suasive, tract of the abolition movement; but it was early and it stirred others to action against this great injustice.

John Wesley was not the preeminent reformer of any social evil in his day, or after. But as a prominent leader of the evangelical movement, he was at the heart of many reforms, with fingers in a variety of causes with the intent of relieving the plight of the oppressed and disheartened. He therefore had a clearly visible hand in transforming society.

Wesley generally, but passionately, cared for the poor, teaching his followers to have a godly view of money and resources. He reached out to and gave his best resources to the sick. But the whole list of Wesley's pursuit of social change and the impact it had on a nation is long. He urged simplicity of dress among believers as a sign of equity among the rich and poor. He constantly warned of the dangers of the "poison" of hard liquors during the Gin Age, which lasted from 1721 to 1751, when alcohol consumption ravaged a generation. His passion to train and educate, including his oversight of the Kingswood School, paved the way for educational leaders such as Hannah More, Silas Told, Rob-ert Parkes, and the Sunday school movement, which taught the poor working children whose only day for education was Sunday.

As one who visited prisoners throughout his life, Wesley encouraged his army of preachers to do the same. He viewed eighteenth-century prisons as "a picture of hell on earth" and worked to improve prison con-ditions. When, for example, he saw the dire treatment of 1,100 French prisoners near Bristol in 1759, he raised funds to supply the prison-ers with the necessities of life—blankets, linens, and clothing—and he associated with and had mutual regard for the noted prison reformer John Howard.

When the American colonies were on the brink of revolution, he sought peace on the one hand by writing to the Americans *A Calm Address to Our American Colonies* (1775), calling on them to submit to the king. On the other hand, to those in his beloved country, he questioned the wisdom and justice of enforcing submission with bloodshed. "What an amazing way of deciding controversies!" he writes in *A Seasonable Address to the More Serious Part of the Inhabitants of Great Britain* (1776). He also wrote letters to the prime minister and others in authority. In a demonstration of the spirit with which he viewed the great issue of the day, he wrote to Charles, saying, "I am of neither side, and yet I am of both; on the side of New England and Old."

In all of these issues of poverty, alcoholism, education, prison, and war, John Wesley, along with other evangelicals, fought his own war against sin and Satan's destructive, disunifying kingdom, bringing in the light of the Kingdom of God.

In May 1787, twelve men gathered to form the Society for the Abolition of the Slave Trade. In August, they invited John Wesley to read a letter before the group. Wesley, then eighty-four years old, warned of the great opposition they would face, but encouraged them that if they persevered, they would ultimately be successful in abolishing this horrid trade. He promised his own support, including a new printing of his *Thoughts upon Slavery*.

That autumn, he wrote another letter to the society with growing interest in their cause. He advised the group to be careful and scrupulous in its methods, and also urged them to strike at the root of the slave trade, which he argued was not whether it was moral, but whether it was financially viable—the driving force of the trade. Moral arguments, he contended, would not win the day.

In March 1788, he advertised his intention to preach on slavery in Bristol, drawing a house "filled with high and low, rich and poor." While he preached, "a vehement noise arose, none could tell why." So great was the noise that it temporarily disrupted his message. His explanation of the disruption explains what he believed to be the cause of all the world's evil: It was, he said, "Satan [who] fought lest his kingdom be delivered up."

John Wesley lived eighty-seven years, most of which were devoted to bringing lost souls across the divide he himself had crossed by God's grace. This great spiritual abyss was and is also very real in the physical world of disease, oppression, and violence. He lived his life with a relentless passion to bring deliverance through the only One who could deliver—Jesus. He traveled thousands of miles a year; preached twice or more daily; wrote treatises, books, journals, and letters; conversed, counseled, and led. He relentlessly did whatever was in his power to bring lost souls to the Great Deliverer.

In 1789, late in his ministry, he observed that the fruit of his work had come full circle. In August, on one of his final tours through England, he found a change in the crowds from those he had faced early in his ministry—the great mass of mobs who threw rocks, rotten fruit, slurs, and insults his way. In the town of Falmouth in Cornwall, he was vividly reminded of the earlier days.

> *The first time I was here above forty years ago, I was taken prisoner by an immense mob, gaping and roaring like lions. But how is the tide turned; high and low now lined the street from one end of the town to the other out of stark love and kindness, gaping and staring as if the King were going by.*

Certainly, England had changed over the span of fifty years. But much of the change came as a result of Wesley's patient endurance of opposition. The transformation he had sought to bring to his world was by no means completed. But there were signs the transformation was indeed taking place, and that the Kingdom of God was being set up through Wesley and through other faithful believers in whom Christ reigned.

On February 24, 1791, John Wesley sat to write what would be his final letter. Burdened to the very point of death over slavery, he wrote to encourage Great Britain's greatest proponent of the abolition of slavery, William Wilberforce.

> *Dear Sir,*
>
> *Unless the divine power has raised you up to be as Athanasius contra mundum, I see not how you can go through your glorious enterprise in opposing that execrable villainy, which is the scandal of religion, of England, and of human nature. Unless God has raised you up for this very thing, you will be worn out by the opposition of men and devils. But if God be for you, who can be against you? Are all of them together stronger than God? O be not weary of well doing! Go on, in the name of God and in the power of His might, till even American slavery (the vilest that ever saw the sun) shall vanish away before it.*

Wesley died six days later, full of peace and rejoicing in the life he had lived and in the Savior to whom he had entrusted his soul. But the movement he had founded continued on. It was a transformational movement that spread across the sea, including to some of the "poor African" slaves, and it spread ultimately to every corner of the earth. More than two centuries later, John Wesley and his movement continue to have an impact on this broken world, as many continue to follow in the footsteps of a man who sought to bring lost, sinful, and needy men and women across the great divide to the Lover of their souls.

Notes on Sources

Unless otherwise noted, all original works of John Wesley cited in this book are from *The Bicentennial Edition of the Works of John Wesley (BWJW)*, which includes the most accurate, thorough, current, and annotated original works. At this time, only twenty-seven of the thirty-five volumes have been published. Instances where quotations come from other sources, are duly noted in the endnotes. Because Wesley's works are published in various popular volumes as well as online, we have chosen not to cite page numbers and volumes but rather to indicate sections and paragraph numbers—or dates, in the case of his journals and diaries—to assist the serious reader.

BWJW	*The Bicentennial Edition of the Works of John Wesley*. 27 vols. Nashville: Abingdon, 1976–.
JW	John Wesley as the author of a work. Unless otherwise noted in the citation, these works are in *BWJW* or in Thomas Jackson, ed., *The Works of John Wesley*, 3rd edition. London: Wesleyan Methodist Book Room, 1872. As Wesley's writings are in the public domain, many are readily available online, including early editions in Google Books.
JWD	John Wesley's Diary Unpublished during His Lifetime in *BWJW* vols. 18–24.
JWJ	John Wesley's Journals Published during His Lifetime in *BWJW* vols. 18–24.
JWJ MS	John Wesley's Manuscript Journals Unpublished during His Lifetime in *BWJW* vols. 18–24.
JWL	Letters from John Wesley, 1721–1739, from *BWJW* vol. 25; letters from 1740–1755 from *BWJW* vol. 26; letters from 1756-1765 from *BWJW* vol. 27. Because this edition is incomplete,

letters cited from after 1765 are from John Telford, ed., *The Letters of John Wesley*, 8 vols. London: Epworth Press, 1931. Also, unless otherwise noted, all letters to JW from others are quoted from these editions, including letters from George Whitefield and Charles Wesley.

JWS   John Wesley's Sermons in *BWJW* vols. 1–4. Because sermons are numbered differently based on editions, and because most sermons are now available online, citations are of the sermon title only and leave off any sermon numbering.

Conference Minutes   *Minutes of Some Late Conversations between the Rev. Mr. Wesleys and Others.* In *BWJW* vol. 10. These are also available in other editions, including digitally (without the critical comments). Like the sermons, they are cited here by year. If they are from the Large Minutes, it is noted in the citation.

CWJ   *The Manuscript Journal of the Reverend Charles Wesley, M.A.* Edited by Kenneth G. Newport Jr. and S. Kimbrough. 2 vols. Nashville: Kingswood Books, 2008.

WHS   *Proceedings of the Wesley Historical Society*

"Account of an Amour"   An extended memorandum, titled "An Account of an Amour," in JW's unpublished diary describing his love affair with Grace Murray, published in Augustin Léger, *Wesley's Last Love* (London: J. M. Dent and Sons, 1910), 1–105.

Notes

Introduction: Crossing the Divide
P. 9, "rage and bitterness": JWJ, October 18, 1749.
P. 9, "scarce ever saw before": Ibid.
P. 9, "terrors of the Lord": Ibid.
P. 9, "smoother and softer words": Ibid.
P. 10, "heart filled with love": Ibid.
P. 10, "amazed, they were ashamed": Ibid.
P. 10, "constrained to preach longer": JWJ, October 19, 1749.
P. 10, "All things are ready": JWJ, May 20, 1742.
P. 10, "a year of uncommon trials": JWJ, December 31, 1762.

Chapter 1: Controversial Fires
P. 16, Controversy was a familiar theme: There are several good early sources on the background and family history of the Wesleys. Among these are Luke Tyerman, *The Life and Times of the Rev. Samuel Wesley, M.A.* (London: Simpkin, Marshall, 1866); Adam Clarke, *Memoirs of the Wesley Family* (London: J. & T. Clarke, 1823); and John Kirk, *The Mother of the Wesleys: A Biography* (London: Henry James Tresidder, 1864).
P. 16, at which he proved inept: See Tyerman, *Life and Times of the Rev. Samuel Wesley*, 229. Both Susanna Wesley and her brother make note of Samuel's ineptitude in business dealings.
P. 17, "for ever": Parliament passed the Act of Settlement in 1701, which prohibited a Catholic from ascending to the throne "for ever," thus effectively ending the English Reformation.
P. 17, vandals in Epworth: Letter from Samuel Wesley to Archbishop Sharpe, September 12, 1705, in Clarke, *Memoirs of the Wesley Family*, 110.
P. 18, "Most of my friends": Ibid.

Chapter 2: Almost Christian
P. 19, "altogether Christian": JWS, "Almost Christian," I, para. 11–12.
P. 19, "I doubted not": JWJ, May 24, 1738.
P. 19, "to conquer their will": Susanna Wesley to JW, July 24, 1742; in JWJ, August 1, 1742.
P. 20, "discourse. . .on something": John Kirk, *The Mother of the*

Wesleys: A Biography (London: Henry James Tresidder, 1864), 156.

P. 20, corrected his heart: JWL to Susanna Wesley, February 28, 1732.

P. 20, "I do intend to be more": Susanna Wesley, May 17, 1711, in Kirk, *Mother of the Wesleys*, 282; John Telford, *Wesley Anecdotes* (London, 1885), 17 et al.

P. 20, "having been strictly educated": JWJ, May 24, 1738.

P. 20, "outward restraints being removed": Ibid.

P. 21, kindness for religion: Ibid.

P. 21, "notion of inward holiness": Ibid.

P. 21, "My dear Jacky": Susanna Wesley to JW, February 23, 1725, in JWL.

P. 21, "deserves great consideration": Ibid.

P. 22, "I think the sooner": Ibid.

P. 22, "seated in the heart": JWJ, May 24, 1738.

P. 22, "perpetually miserable": JWL to Susanna Wesley, May 28, 1725.

P. 22, "is extremely in the wrong": Susanna Wesley to JW, June 8, 1725, in JWL.

P. 22, Taylor's view of unattainable humility: JWL to Susanna Wesley, June 18, 1725.

P. 23, Hetty eloped with another man: Samuel Wesley to JW, August 2, 1725, in JWL.

P. 23, "inconceivably exasperated against her": JWL to Samuel Wesley Jr., December 5–6, 1726.

P. 23, "innocent enough": Ibid.

P. 23, struggle with young women: His entry in his diary for July 3, 1726, records in his cipher, "Never touch Kitty's hand again." On August 13 of the same year, he resolves never to touch a woman's breast again. Cited in V. H. H. Green, *The Young Mr. Wesley: A Study of John Wesley and Oxford* (New York: St. Martin's, 1961), 106.

P. 24, "You writ this sermon for Hetty": JWL to Samuel Wesley Jr., December 5–6, 1726.

P. 24, "One great reason for my writing": Ibid.

P. 24, she responded coldly: Susanna Wesley to JW, October 12, 1726, in JWL.

P. 24, some of the hostility waned over the years: See CW to JW, January, 20, 1728, in JWL.

P. 24, she could be reconciled to God: See "Hetty Wesley" in *WHS*, vol. 16, 88–94.

P. 25, "Christ Church is certainly the worst place": CW to JW, January 5, 1729, in JWL.

P. 25, books of a religious nature: JWL to Richard Morgan Sr., October 19, 1732.

P. 25, "ancient, if not apostolical": JWL to John Robson, September 30, 1735.

P. 25, "a constant ruling habit of soul": JWL to Richard Morgan Sr., January 15, 1734.

P. 26, "notions of religion": Richard Morgan Jr., to Richard Morgan Sr., January 14, 1734, in JWL.

P. 26, "I did go thus far for many years": JWS, "Almost Christian."

P. 27, holiness best achieved in Oxford: See JWL to Samuel Wesley Sr., November 15, 1734, and December 10, 1734.

P. 27, "according to their power": JWL to Samuel Wesley Sr., December 10, 1734.

P. 27, "The Christian faith will surely revive": Green, *Young Mr. Wesley*, 246, quoting a letter from CW to Samuel Wesley Jr.

P. 28, "[They] have no comments to construe": JWL to Rev. John Burton, October 10, 1735.

Chapter 3: Contrary Winds

P. 31, "better Christians": Benjamin Ingham, letter to his mother and family, May 1, 1736, in Richard P. Heitzenrater, ed., *The Elusive Mr. Wesley*, 2nd ed. (Nashville: Abingdon, 2003), 244.

P. 31, "dreaded and abhorred the sea": JWJ, February 3, 1738.

P. 31, the *Simmonds* encountered a rolling sea: See Francis Moore, *A Voyage to Georgia: Begun in the Year 1735* (London: Jacob Robinson, 1744), as well as JWJ, JWJ MS, and JWD.

P. 32, "The winds roared round about us": JWJ, January 25, 1736.

P. 32, "What if the Gospel be not true?": JWJ, January 24, 1738.

P. 32, "I can conceive no difference": JWJ, January 26, 1736.

P. 33, "before we could get one hundred yards": JWJ MS, February 7, 1736.

P. 33, "a sly hypocrite": JWJ MS, August 10, 1737.

P. 33, "the low watery, meadows": Wesley's description for the Georgia Trustees in JWJ, December 2, 1737.

P. 33, rainfall estimates: This rendering is based on modern-day calculations of rainfall estimates and assumes similar rainfall totals for the eighteenth century. Parts of England receive around thirty inches of rain per year, whereas Savannah typically receives just under fifty.

P. 33, "terrible" thunderstorms: Wesley's description for the Georgia Trustees in JWJ, December 2, 1737.

P. 34, "importunate" needs: JWJ, November 23, 1736.

P. 34, "a servant" rather than a "judge": JWJ MS, September 11, 1736.

P. 34, "who were well able to endure it": Ibid.

P. 35, minister in a nearby town to baptize: JWJ and JWD, May 5, 1736.

P. 35, "common fellow": *CWJ*, March 21, 1736.

P. 35, blame on Charles: See *CWJ*, March 21, 1736, and following entries.

P. 35, "kissed her a thousand times": *CWJ*, March 18, 1736.

P. 36, "could not be more trampled upon": *CWJ*, March 3, 1736.

P. 36, "spies and ruffians": *CWJ*, April 10, 1736.

P. 36, John's conference with the governor: JWJ MS, April 16, 1736.

P. 36, The plot against the Wesleys: *CWJ*, April 16, 1736.

P. 36, "utterly confounded": Ibid.

P. 36, "I was overjoyed at my deliverance": *CWJ*, May 11, 1736.

P. 37, none were beyond the reach of God: John Gambold writes of John Wesley: "In the spiritual care of his acquaintance, Mr. Wesley persisted amidst all discouragements; he overlooked not only one's absurd or disagreeable qualities, but even his coldness and neglect of him, if he thought it might be conquered." Quoted in Heitzenrater, *Elusive Mr. Wesley*, 240–41.

P. 37, "through the head": JWJ MS, August 22, 1736.

P. 37, "Villain, dog, let go my hands!": Ibid.

P. 37, "Blessed be God": Ibid.

P. 38, "more serious parishioners": JWJ, November 23, 1736.

P. 38, regular morning and evening prayers: See his letter to Thomas Bray quoted in JWJ, February 26, 1737.

P. 39, "to have no intimacy with any woman": JWJ MS, preface to the Georgia Journal, March 7, 1735–December 16, 1737.

Chapter 4: Georgia Storm
P. 41, "single eye": JWJ MS, preface to the Georgia Journal, March 7, 1735–December 16, 1737.

P. 41, "notorious villain": Ibid.

P. 41, "From this time": Ibid.

P. 42, "immediately condemned": JWJ MS, August 19, 1736.

P. 42, "There is no happiness but in holiness": Ibid.

P. 42, "none but the All-seeing Eye observed": JWJ MS, October 25, 1736.

P. 42, "the great offense": Ibid.

P. 43, "single eye": JWJ MS, November 1, 1736.

P. 43, resolution failed after ten days: JWJ MS, November 10 and 20, 1736.

P. 43, "beating the air": JWJ, January 26, 1737.

P. 43, "a very religious man": JWJ MS, January 5, 1737.

P. 43, "utter despair of doing good": JWJ, January 26, 1737.

P. 43, "the familiarities": JWJ MS, February 3, 1737.

P.43 , hinted at proposals of marriage: Ibid.

P. 44, "clergyman not to be encumbered": Ibid.

P. 44, "utterly disapproved": JWJ MS, February 5, 1737.

P. 44, "sincerity in religion": Ibid.

P. 44, "excellent natural temper": Ibid.

P. 44, "I find, Miss Sophy": JWJ MS, February 6, 1737.

P. 44, "obstruct the design": JWJ MS, February 8, 1737.

P. 44, "strong enough to bear": Ibid.

P. 45, "at least till": JWJ MS, February 14, 1737.

P. 45, "many tears"; "weigh thoroughly the whole affair": JWJ MS, March 3, 1737.

P. 45, "deep consideration": JWJ MS, March 4, 1737.

P. 45, "the goodness of God": Ibid.

P. 45, "What [God] required of me was a costly sacrifice": Ibid.

P. 46, "saw less and less reason to expect": JWJ MS, March 8, 1737.

P. 46, "who lay struggling in the net": Ibid.

P. 46, "Surely I am in a dream": JWJ MS, March 9, 1737.

P. 46, "not remarkable for handsomeness": JWJ MS, March 8, 1737.

P. 47, "bear with her": JWJ MS, May 7, 1737.

P. 47, he learned of. . .her previous "dissimulations": JWJ MS, June 4, 1737.

P. 47, "However, if she die in her iniquity": JWJ MS, July 4, 1737.

P. 47, "A new hindrance to admitting Mrs. Williamson": JWJ MS, June 25, 1737. Brackets in the original.

P. 48, "the slippery ground": JWJ MS, June 7, 1737.

P. 48, "Don't condemn me": JWJ MS, July 5, 1737, letter to Mr. Causton.

P. 48, "told her softly so that none could hear": JWJ MS, August 7, 1737.

P. 48, "Repelled!": JWD, August 7, 1737.

P. 48, "defaming [her] and refusing to administer the Lord's Supper": JWJ MS, August 8, 1737.

P. 49, fifty pound salary: JWJ MS, March 4, 1737.

P. 49, "purely ecclesiastical": JWJ MS, August 9, 1737.

P. 49, "a proud priest": JWJ MS, August 10, 1737.

P. 49, "spite and malice": Ibid.

P. 49, "add weight"; "general sense of the people": JWJ MS, August 17, 1737.

P. 50, "Being now only a prisoner at large": JWJ MS, December 2, 1737.

P. 50, "I went to America to convert the Indians": JWJ, December 24, 1737.

P. 51, "beloved obscurity": JWS, "On Laying of the Foundation of the New Chapel, Near the City-Road, London."

Chapter 5: Strangely Warmed

P. 53, "tossed to and fro. . .with every wind of doctrine": Ephesians 4:14.

P. 53, "the most dangerous": JW, Memorandum, January 25, 1738, published in JWJ, January 25, 1738. This memorandum is published as a footnote in *BWJW*, vol. 18, 212.

P. 54, "poisonous": JWJ, December 15, 1789.

P. 54, "The faith I want is": JWJ, February 1, 1738.

P. 54, "detained in London": JWS, "On Laying of the Foundation of the New Chapel, Near the City-Road, London."

P. 55, "mal-administration": Egmont Diary, II. 467, February 22, 1738. Quoted in editorial footnote in *BWJW*, vol. 18, 226.

P. 55, Trustees saw through to his hypocrisy: Ibid.

P. 55, he resolved once again: JWJ, March 2, 1738.

P. 55, preached multiple times a day: JWS, "On Laying of the Foundation of the New Chapel."

P. 55, "I was not to preach there anymore": JWJ, February 4, 1738. Cf.

February 12 and May 7, 1738.

P. 55, "Leave off preaching": JWJ, February 5, 1738.

P. 56, "My brother, my brother": JWJ, February 18, 1738.

P. 56, "Preach faith *till* you have it": JWJ, March 5, 1738.

P. 56, "Do not hide in the earth": JWJ, April 23, 1738.

P. 57, "justified by works": JWJ, August 27, 1739.

P. 57, "soul started back from the work": JWJ, March 6, 1738.

P. 57, "impossibility": Ibid.

P. 57, Wesley returned to preach: This assumes that the second man is the same as mentioned previously in Wesley's journal.

P. 57, "I am now ready to die": JWJ, March 27, 1738.

P. 57, "composed cheerfulness"; "perfect peace": Ibid.

P. 57, "only to believe that holy Scripture": The italics are those of JW, and he makes minor, skillful amendments to the original.

P. 58, the testimonies of multiple people: JWJ, April 22, 1738.

P. 58, Charles was downright angry: JWJ, April, 25, 1738.

P. 58, instantaneous conversion was possible: *CWJ*, April 25, 1738. It is interesting to note the two issues of dispute within the two brothers' journals.

P. 58, "in the faith": Ibid.

P. 59, "I love you greatly": Quoted in JWJ, May 10, 1738. The original is in Latin. This is JW's own translation.

P. 59, "O why is it that so great": JWJ, inserted just before May 24, 1738.

P. 59, "almost Christian": JWS, "The Almost Christian."

P. 59, "form of godliness": This is a favorite scripture reference of JW from 2 Timothy 3:5, which he uses throughout his corpus.

P. 59, "without Christ": *CWJ*, May 16, 1738.

P. 59, "he discovered": For this development, see *CWJ*, May 17, 1738.

P. 60, "In the name of Jesus of Nazareth, arise": *CWJ*, May 21, 1738.

P. 60, "strange palpitation of heart": Ibid.

P. 60, "almost believed the Holy Ghost was coming": *CWJ*, May 22, 1738.

P. 60, "purest Gospel": Ibid.

P. 61, "through faith in Christ": JWJ, May 24, 1738.

P. 61, "I felt my heart strangely warmed": Ibid.

P. 61, "a sure trust and confidence": Ibid. The italics are those of JW, and he makes minor, skillful amendments to the original.

P. 61, "I felt I did trust in Christ": JWJ, May 24, 1738.

P. 61, the subject of much speculation to this day: Randy L. Maddox, *Aldersgate Reconsidered* (Nashville: Kingswood, 1990).

P. 61, "justifying, saving faith": JWJ, May 24, 1738.

P. 62, "was but 'almost a Christian'": JWS, "The Almost Christian."

P. 62, "This he was as well assured of": Elizabeth Hutton to Samuel Wesley Jr., June 6, 1738, in Daniel Benham, *Memoirs of James Hutton Comprising of the Annals of His Life and Connection with The United Brethren* (London: Hamilton, Adams, 1856), 34–35.

P. 62, "have a care": Ibid.

P. 62, "the benefits received by the two sacraments": Ibid.

P. 62, the Reverend Tipping Sylvester preached at St. Mary's, Oxford: The sermon was preached February 6, 1738, against the Methodists referenced in Rev. Richard Green, *Anti-Methodist Publications Issued during the Eighteenth Century* (London: C. H. Kelly, 1902), 2.

P. 62, a baptized person is saved unless he or she commits apostasy: See Samuel Wesley Jr. to Elizabeth Hutton, June 17, 1738, in Benham, *Memoirs of James Hutton*, 36–37.

P. 62, "a great hypocrite": Elizabeth Hutton to Samuel Wesley Jr., June 6, 1738, in Benham, *Memoirs of James Hutton*, 34–35.

P. 62, "John seems to be turned a wild enthusiast": Ibid.

P. 63, "That I who went to America": JWJ, February 1, 1738, and footnote.

P. 63, "I am not sure of this": Ibid.

P. 63, "had then the faith of a *servant*": See also JWJ, April 25, 1738.

P. 64, merely the means to an end: JW to John Smith, June 25, 1746, in John Telford, *The Letters of John Wesley*, vol. 2, 75.

P. 64, repentance is the "porch": JW, "The Principles of a Methodist Farther Explained," IV, sec. 3, in *The Methodist Societies: History, Nature and Design*, vol. 9 of *BWJW*, ed. Rupert E. Davies, 227.

P. 64, rejecting his notion of true religion: See, for example, JWS, "The Lord Our Righteousness."

Chapter 6: Closed Doors

P. 67, "unwieldy crowds" and "unfashionable doctrine": JWS, "On Laying of the Foundation of the New Chapel, Near the City-Road, London."

P. 67, "as dead": See, for example, JWJ, May 9, 1739, and June 22, 1739, among others.

P. 67, layers of faith: JWS, "Salvation by Faith," I.

P. 67, "the faith of the heathen": Ibid.

P. 67, "the faith of the devil": Ibid.

P. 68, "is not barely a speculative, rational thing": Ibid., I, 4.

P. 68, "crack-brained": JWJ, July 17, 1739.

P. 68, "is, and must be, the foundation": JWS, "Salvation by Faith," III, 7.

P. 68, "the place where the Christians live": JWJ, July 22, 1738.

P. 68, "full power of faith": JWJ, June 7, 1738.

P. 69, "had now abundant opportunity": JWJ, August 1, 1738.

P. 69, "*homo perturbatus*": Daniel Benham, *Memoirs of James Hutton Comprising of the Annals of His Life and Connection with The United Brethren* (London: Hamilton, Adams, 1856), 40. Though many of Hutton's papers are put forth in this volume, it is difficult to ascertain how much is Hutton's view of the situation and how much is Benham's view, written more than a century later.

P. 69, "brooded over": Ibid.

P. 69, "had a desire to be the head of a party": Ibid.

P. 69, "spirit of meekness and love": JWL to Samuel Wesley Jr., July 6, 1738. See also JWL to CW, July 7, 1738.

P. 69, he withheld the criticisms: JWL to Moravian Church, September 27 and 28, 1738. See also JWJ.

P. 69, "for giving me to be an eyewitness of your faith": JWL to Count Zinzendorf, October 14–30, 1738. See also JWL to the Moravians, October 14–20, 1738.

P. 70, "while a great door and effectual": JWL to Count Zinzendorf, October 30, 1738.

P. 70, "the little flock": Ibid.

P. 70, grown to include more than fifty men: JWL to the Church in Herrnhut, October 14, 1738.

P. 70, "publish the word of reconciliation": Ibid.

P. 70, "a little revival": JWL to Charles Kinchin, November 16, 1738.

P. 70, "There is none besides": JWL to James Hutton, or "A Friend," December 1, 1738.

P. 71, "Our Lord's hand is not shortened": JWL to George Whitefield, February 26, 1739.

P. 71, "the fields after service": Ibid.

P. 71, "You spoke in buildings not consecrated": Samuel Wesley Jr. to JW, January 24, 1739, in JWL. The letter is mutilated, and there is some conjecture about Samuel's actual words. *BWJW* has editorial notes about the conjectures: "You spoke in build<ings not consecrated>" "not using the liturgy, and pray<ing extemporary>"

P. 72, "who was above measure enraged": JWJ, March 6, 1739.

P. 72, "extreme agony": Ibid.

P. 72, "from that hour, God": Ibid.

P. 72, "of the same spirit she had been of": JWJ, March 8, 1739.

P. 72, "labouring to pervert the truth of the gospel": Ibid.

P. 72, "as the less evil of the two": Ibid.

P. 72, "felt, as it were, the piercing of a sword": Ibid.

P. 72, "no sooner had we made our request known": Ibid.

Chapter 7: Open Fields

P. 73, Whitefield's voice could be heard: Benjamin Franklin made the scientific observation in Philadelphia, later writing that Whitefield "had a loud and clear Voice, and articulated his Words and Sentences so perfectly that he might be heard and understood at a great Distance, especially as his Auditors, however numerous, observ'd the most exact Silence. He preach'd one Evening from the Top of the Court House Steps, which are in the middle of Market Street, and on the West Side of Second Street which crosses it at right angles. Both Streets were fill'd with his Hearers to a considerable Distance. Being among the hindmost in Market Street, I had the Curiosity to learn how far he could be heard, by retiring backwards down the Street towards the River; and I found his Voice distinct till I came near Front Street, when some Noise in that Street, obscur'd it. Imagining then a Semicircle, of which my Distance should be the Radius, and that it were fill'd with Auditors, to each of whom I allow'd two square feet, I computed that he might well be heard by more than Thirty Thousand. This reconcil'd me to the Newspaper Accounts of his having preach'd to 25,000 People in the Fields, and to the ancient Histories of Generals haranguing whole Armies, of which I had sometimes doubted." See *Benjamin Franklin's Autobiography: An Authoritative Text*, ed. J. A. Leo Lemay and P. M. Zall (New York: Norton, 1986).

P. 73, "would not attend to the most pressing necessities": Adam

Clarke, *Memoirs of the Wesley Family* (London: J. & T. Clarke, 1823), vol. 2, 321.

P. 74, "There is a glorious door opened": GW to JW, March 3, 1739.

P. 74, imprisonment and even death were likely: *CWJ*, March 28, 1739.

P. 74, "speedy determination": JW, "The Principles of a Methodist Farther Explained," IV, sec. 3, in *The Methodist Societies: History, Nature and Design*, vol. 9 of *BWJW*, ed. Rupert E. Davies, 227.

P. 74, "opening the Bible": JWJ, March 28, 1739.

P. 75, "a new period": Ibid.

P. 75, "this *strange way* of preaching": JWJ, April 1, 1739. Emphasis in the original.

P. 75, "Oh how is God manifested": JWL to James Hutton, April 2, 1739.

P. 75, "one pretty remarkable instance": JWJ, April 1, 1739. Emphasis in the original.

P. 75, "tenacious of every point": JWJ, April 1, 1739.

P. 76, "a little eminence": JWJ, April 2, 1739.

P. 76, "unusual manner": JWJ, June 11, 1739.

P. 76, "should have thought the saving of souls": JWJ, March 29, 1739. Emphasis in the original.

P. 76, letter he wrote to a critic whose identity is not clear: It has been supposed that this letter was written to James Hervey on March 2, 1739—a month before Wesley's field preaching began—but both the date and the recipient have been called into question. Frank Baker, in his editorial notes to Wesley's letters in *BWJW* (vol. 1, 614–17), suggests the recipient to be Rev. John Clayton based on Wesley's diary entries in late March suggesting toil over crafting the letter, finally transcribed on March 28, the day before his departure from London to Bristol.

P. 76, "accept the cure of souls": JWL to Henry Stebbing, July 25, 1739.

P. 77, "I [cannot] be said": JWL to Rev. John Clayton (?), March 28, 1739.

P. 77, "God in Scripture commands me": Ibid.

P. 77, "I look upon *all the world as my parish*": Ibid. Emphasis in the original.

P. 77, "[In] whatever part of [the world] I am": Ibid.

P. 78, "white already to harvest": John 4:35.

P. 78, "the word of God ran as fire": JWL, June 17, 1746.

P. 78, "The clergy here": JWL to CW, April 9, 1739.

P. 78, "a metaphysical discourse": William Stephens, *A Journal of the Proceedings in Georgia* (3 vols.), quoted in Richard P. Heitzenrater, ed., *The Elusive Mr. Wesley*, 2nd ed. (Nashville: Abingdon, 2003), 249.

P. 79, "plain truths for plain people": JWS, "Preface," para. 3. This was reprinted in every edition of Wesley's collected sermons published during his lifetime.

P. 79, "the bulk of mankind": Ibid., para. 2.

P. 79, "Here thieves, prostitutes, fools": James Hutton in Daniel Benham, *Memoirs of James Hutton Comprising of the Annals of His Life and Connection with The United Brethren* (London: Hamilton, Adams, 1856), 42.

P. 79, "outward signs which had so often accompanied": JWJ, July 7, 1739.

P. 79, "a considerable part of the congregation": JWJ, August 28, 1748.

P. 79, "field preaching is a cross to me": JWJ, September 6, 1772.

P. 79, "What marvel the devil does not love": JWJ, June 24–27, 1759.

P. 80, "preached under tall spreading trees": Richard P. Heitzenrater, "John Wesley's Principles and Practice of Preaching," *Methodist History* 37, no. 2 (January 1999): 91–92.

P. 80, "to build a room large enough": JWJ, May 9, 1739. The building, dubbed "The New Room," remains the oldest Methodist building still in active use as of 2015.

P. 81, he took over management of the money: JWJ, May 9, 1739.

Chapter 8: Pursuit of Grace

P. 84, "strong in the faith and zealous": JWJ, November 1, 1739.

P. 84, "I observed every day more and more": JWJ, November 7, 1739.

P. 86, "neither *neglect* nor *rest in*": JWJ, November 15, 1739.

P. 86, "I had a long and particular conversation": JWJ, December 31, 1739.

P. 86, "As to [X]": Ibid.

P. 87, "true, Christian, Scriptural stillness": JWJ, January 1, 1740.

P. 87, "idle controversies and strife of words": JWJ, January 2, 1740.

P. 87, an affidavit circulated throughout Bristol: JWL to James Hutton, April 12, 1740.

P. 88, "closeness, darkness, [and] reserve": JWL to James Hutton, March 21, 1740.

P. 88, "describing things a little beyond the truth": JWJ, December 31, 1739.

P. 88, "poor brethren at Fetter Lane": JWJ, April 19, 1740.

P. 88, "new gospel": JWJ, April 25, 1740.

P. 88, "great antidote against this poison": JWJ, June 5, 1740.

P. 89, "Finding there was no time to delay": JWJ, June 22, 1740.

P. 89, "in their own opinions": JWJ, July 15, 1740.

P. 89, "for the Germans": JWJ, July 18, 1740.

P. 89, "I believe these assertions to be flatly contrary": JWJ, July 20, 1740.

P. 89, "uncouth heap of ruins": JW Tract, *Appeals to Men of Reason and Religion*, sec. 2.

Chapter 9: Free for All

P. 91, "the grace or love of God": JWS, "Free Grace."

P. 91, "author of sin": See, for example, JWL to Susanna Wesley, July 29, 1725.

P. 92, "horrible decree": John Calvin, *Institutes of Religion*, 3.23.7; JWS, "Free Grace."

P. 92, "the great decree of God": JWJ, May 21, 1741.

P. 92, "he that believeth shall be saved": Mark 16:16.

P. 92, "that if this were not the truth of God": JWJ, April 26, 1739.

P. 92, "Preach and print": JWL to James Hutton and the Fetter Lane Society, April 30, 1739.

P. 92, "I hear, honoured sir": GWL to JW, June 15, 1739.

P. 92, "I confess my spirit has been of late" "quite broken": GWL to JW, July 2, 1739.

P. 93, God the author of sin: See Susanna Wesley to JW, August 18, 1725.

P. 93, he could understand no reason or motivation to go forth: See JWS, "Free Grace," sec. 11.

P. 93, "to the very edge of Calvinism": *Conference Minutes*, 1745.

P. 93, "hair's breadth": JWL to John Newton, May 14, 1765.

P. 93, "antecedent to grace": Ibid.

P. 93, "method whereby God leads us": JW, *Explanatory Notes on the Bible*, Romans 8:30.

P. 94, "the first wish to please God": JWS, "On Working Out Our Own Salvation."

P. 94, "By justification we are saved": Ibid.

P. 94, "so free, so infinite": CW hymn, "And Can It Be?"

P. 94, "ten thousand times more convinced": GW to JW, March 26, 1740.

P. 94, "destroy brotherly love": Ibid.

P. 95, "God is sending a message": JWL to GW, August 9, 1740.

P. 95, "But neither will receive it": Ibid.

P. 95, "But when His time is come": Ibid.

P. 95, "the nation a-disputing": GW to JW, September 25, 1740.

P. 95, "rash and precipitant": Ibid.

P. 95, "I am willing to go with you to prison": GW to JW, November 9, 1740.

P. 96, "I went to Kingswood": JWJ, December 14, 1740.

P. 96, "we might again with one heart": Ibid.

P. 96, "cold" and resistant: JWJ, December 16, 1740.

P. 96, "You do not preach truth": JWJ, December 20, 1740.

P. 96, "had no ears to hear": JWJ, January 1, 1741. Emphasis in the original.

P. 97, "I will do just what I believe Mr. Whitefield would": JWJ, February 1, 1741.

P. 97, "*man's* faithfulness": JWJ, February 22, 1741.

P. 97, "bigots" for predestination: JWL to GW, August 9, 1740.

P. 97, "You should have told me of this before": JWJ, February 22, 1741.

P. 98, "Therefore, not for their opinions": JWJ, February 28, 1741.

P. 98, "If you had disliked my sermon": JWL to GW, April 27, 1741.

P. 99, "all the wrong expressions": Ibid.

P. 99, "Moral honesty does not allow of a treacherous wound": Ibid.

P. 99, "A Spaniard would have behaved": Ibid.

P. 99, "an open and probably irreparable breach": JWJ, April 4, 1741.

P. 99, "[Whitefield's] fair words are not to be trusted": CW to JW, March 16–17, 1741.

P. 99, "to hear him speak for himself": JWJ, March 28, 1741.

P. 99, "two different gospels": Ibid.

P. 99, "resolved publicly to preach against me": Ibid.

P. 100, "account of God's dealing with his soul": JWJ, August 31, 1741.

P. 100, "Though much may be said for my doing it": GW to JW, October 10, 1741.

P. 100, "I find I love you as much as ever": Ibid.

P. 100, "There are many doctrines of a less essential nature": JWS, "On the Death of the Rev. Mr. George Whitefield."

P. 101, "George Whitefield was so bright a star": John Fletcher Hurst, *John Wesley the Methodist: A Plain Account of His Life and Work* (New York: Eaton & Mains, 1903), 168.

Chapter 10: Thou Art beside Thyself

P. 103, "I was surprised": JWJ, May 28, 1742.

P. 104, "Thou art beside thyself": Acts 26:24. This text is the foundation of his sermon "The Nature of Enthusiasm."

P. 104, "cried out aloud": JWJ, April 17, 1739.

P. 104, "were seized with strong pain": Ibid.

P. 104, "a young man was suddenly seized": JWJ, April 21, 1739.

P. 104, "dropped on every side as thunderstruck": JWJ, April 26, 1739.

P. 104, "groanings": JWJ, May 1, 1739.

P. 104, "violent agonies": JWJ, May 2, 1739.

P. 104, "outward signs": JWJ, July 7, 1739.

P. 104, "The fact I nakedly relate": JWJ, October 23, 1739.

P. 105, "This fact, too": JWJ, October 25, 1739.

P. 105, "deeply offended": JWJ, February 25, 1739.

P. 105, "prayed that God": JWJ, July 15, 1739.

P. 105, "who knew his kingdom shook": JWJ, May 13, 1740; this is a favorite phrase of Wesley; cf. JWJ, March 12, 1743; October 27, 1739, "A Letter to Dr. Rutherford," III, 8, among others.

P. 105, "Sir, Our minister": JWJ, May 7, 1739.

P. 105, claiming dreams and visions: Elizabeth Hutton to Samuel Wesley Jr., June 6, 1738, in Daniel Benham, *Memoirs of James Hutton Comprising of the Annals of His Life and Connection with The United Brethren* (London: Hamilton, Adams, 1856), 34–35.

P. 105, "it is a convenient word": JW, *Farther Appeal to Men of Reason and Religion*, III, 1.

P. 106, "Enthusiasm is a false persuasion": Thomas Church, quoted in JW, "An Answer to the Rev. Mr. Church's Remarks on the Rev. Mr. John Wesley's Last Journal," III, 5.

P. 106, "The Nature of Enthusiasm": The scripture text on which the sermon is based (Acts 26:24), according to his incomplete diary and sermon register, was also the basis of sermons he preached May 30, 1741, and April 1, 1747.

P. 106, "a religious madness": JWS, "The Nature of Enthusiasm," sec. 12.

P. 106, "who imagine themselves Christians and are not." Ibid., sec. 16.

P. 107, initial interest and acceptance of such ecstasies: See, for example, JWJ, May 20, 1739.

P. 107, "tested the spirits": JWJ, January 28, 1739.

P. 107, trumped the written Word of God: See JWJ, May 1, 1741. These issues will return in Wesley's ministry in the 1760s with Thomas Maxfield and George Bell.

P. 107, "I told them they were not to judge": JWJ, June 22, 1739.

P. 107, "while I was speaking, one before me": Ibid.

P. 108, "great work of God": See Wesley's estimation of this work in JWJ, August 6, 1781; June 26, 1784; August 21, 1785; and JWS, "The Signs of the Times," among others.

P. 108, "Consider now": JW, "An Answer to the Rev. Mr. Church's Remarks on the Rev. Mr. John Wesley's Last Journal," II, sec. 18.

P. 108, "to declare to all mankind": Preface to JWJ, no.3.

P. 109, "in the heart, in the inmost soul": JW, *An Earnest Appeal to Men of Reason and Religion*, sec. 4.

P. 109, "We see—and who does not?": Ibid., sec. 2.

P. 109, "And this we conceive to be no other than love": Ibid.

P. 110, "the medicine of life": Ibid., sec. 3.

P. 110, join in the work: Ibid., sec. 17.

P. 110, "I scarce ever yet repented": JWL to Samuel Furly, March 10, 1763.

P. 111, "guilty of enthusiasm": JW, "An Answer to the Rev. Mr. Church's Remarks on the Rev. Mr. John Wesley's Last Journal," introduction, sec. 4.

P. 111, "a gentleman, a scholar, and a Christian": JW, "An Answer to Mr. Rowland Hill's 'Imposture Detected,'" sec. 13.

P. 111, "Your Lordship has": JW, "A Letter to the Lord Bishop of London Occasioned by His Lordship's Late Charge to His Clergy," IV, sec. 22.

P. 112, "My Lord, the time is short": Ibid.

P. 112, "a vulgar report got abroad": Henry Moore, *The Life of the Reverend John Wesley*, vol. 2 (New York: Bangs and Emory, 1824), 244.

P. 112, "[I] spent almost twenty days": JWJ, January 2, 1749.

P. 112, "Heavy work": JWJ, November 19, 1751.

Chapter 11: Method to the Madness

P. 115, "I go away, God willing": George Whitefield to JW, March 22, 1739.

P. 115, "I am but a novice": Ibid.

P. 116, "destroying Christian fellowship": JW, *Plain Account of the People Called Methodists*, I, sec. 11.

P. 116, "unholy men of all kinds": JWJ, February 6, 1740.

P. 117, "watching over each other's souls": JW, *Plain Account of the People Called Methodists*, I, sec. 8.

P. 117, "Are not the bulk of the parishioners": Ibid., I, sec. 11.

P. 117, "the forgiveness of sins": JW, *Rules of the Band Societies*.

P. 117, "to be on this and all other occasions": Ibid.

P. 117, "confess your faults one to another": James 5:16.

P. 118, "disorderly walkers": JWJ, February 24, 1741.

P. 118, "any reasonable objection was made": Ibid.

P. 118, "face to face with their accusers": Ibid.

P. 118, represent the Gospel in its fullness to a watching world: See JWL to "A Clerical Friend," March 11, 1745.

P. 118, "promised a better behavior": JWJ, February 24, 1741.

P. 118, penitent bands: JWJ, March 17, 1741.

P. 119, "commendatory letters": See Acts 18:27; 2 Corinthians 3:1; 1 Corinthians 16:3.

P. 119, "When any members of these": JWL to Thomas Church, June 17, 1746.

P. 120, "In a while, some of these informed me": JW, *Plain Account of the People Called Methodists*, II, sec. 3.

P. 121, "in order to inquire how their souls prosper": Ibid., II, sec. 5.

P. 121, "a desire to flee": JW, *Rules of the United Societies*, sec. 4.

P. 121, "the vilest offender": This phrase, though not Wesleyan in origin, is descriptive of JW's views.

P. 121, "will be shown by [their] fruits": JW, *Rules of the United Societies*, sec. 3.

P. 121, "Avoiding evil of every kind": Ibid., sec. 4.

P. 121, "Doing good of every possible sort": Ibid., sec. 5.

P. 121, "Attending upon all the ordinances of God": Ibid., sec. 6.

P. 122, "I had been often told": JWJ, March 9–11, 1747.

P. 123, overseen by twelve assistants: *Conference Minutes*, 1746.

P. 123, twelve circuits: Ibid., 1749.

P. 124, "connexion": JW spoke often of others in "connexion" with himself, which over time turned into a noun—"the connexion." See, for example, "Mr. Wesley's Last Will and Testament," February 20, 1789.: In Thomas Jackson ed., *The Works of John Wesley*, 3rd ed. (London: Wesleyan Methodist Book Room, 1872), vol. 4, 502.

P. 124, "make a trial": *Conference Minutes*, 1745.

P. 124, "almost all the seed has fallen by the wayside": Ibid., 1748.

P. 124, "The Preacher cannot give proper exhortations": Ibid.

P. 124, "preaching like an apostle": JWJ, August 25, 1763.

P. 124, "It is far easier to preach a good sermon": *Conference Minutes*, 1766.

P. 125, "try the parts and spirits": Ibid.

P. 125, prideful desire to found a party: Forming or becoming part of a "party" is a common concern of Whitefield's related to bigotry and zeal. See his letter and journals. For instance, GW to the Reverend Mr. E— J—, in Wales, October 6, 1742, in GW, *Letters of George Whitefield: For the Period 1734–1742* (Carlisle, PA: Banner of Truth, 1976), 446.

P. 125, "My brother Wesley acted wisely": Thomas Jackson, *The Centenary of Wesleyan Methodism: A Brief Sketch of the Rise, Progress and Present State of the Wesleyan-Methodist Societies throughout the World, Abridged* (London: John Mason, 1839), 52. See also Wesley's assessment, JW, *The Late Work of God in North America*, sec. 7.

P. 125, "I am not afraid": JW, "Thoughts upon Methodism," sec. 1.

Chapter 12: Love Lost

P. 129, "less perfect state": JW, "Account of an Amour," 67. This account was not published during Wesley's lifetime.

P. 129, "no design" to marry: Ibid., 78–79.

P. 129, neither would marry: CWJ, November 11, 1748.

P. 129, "unholy desires and inordinate affections": JW, "Account of an Amour," 74.

P. 130, "embryo intentions": CWJ, April 19, 1748.

P. 130, "neither opposed, nor much encouraged": Ibid.

P. 131, "an insatiable thirst for the salvation": Grace Murray, unpublished account in JW, "Account of an Amour," 25.

P. 131, "the remission of sins": Ibid., 73.

P. 131, "inside and out": Wesley uses the Latin phrase *"intus et in cute novi"* in JW, "Account of an Amour," 76.

P. 131, "observed her more narrowly": Ibid., 1.

P. 131, "sliding": Ibid.

P. 131, "This is all I could have wished for under heaven": Ibid.

P. 131, "I am convinced God has called you": Ibid., 2.

P. 131, "if we meet again": Ibid.

P. 131, "Rejoicing": Ibid.

P. 131, "no step" toward marriage: See JW, *The Rules of a Helper*.

P. 132, "consulted about every particular": *CWJ*, November 11, 1748.

P. 132, "My brother seemed": *CWJ*, April 8, 1749.

P. 132, "the affair between": JW, "Account of an Amour," 5.

P. 132, "I saw the work of God prosper in her hands": Ibid., 4–5.

P. 132, "She lightened my burden": Ibid.

P. 133, "the most useful woman in the kingdom": Ibid., 73.

P. 133, "a mutual promise or contract": "John Wesley's First Marriage," in *WHS*, vol. 36, 4, 110.

P. 133, "The people would not suffer you": JW, "Account of an Amour," 6.

P. 133, "thought it was not proper": Ibid., 7.

P. 134, "I am determined by conscience": Ibid., 9.

P. 134, he penned a letter to John Bennett: See JWL to John Bennett, September 7, 1748.

P. 134, "repeated requests" to "marry immediately": JW, "Account of an Amour," 14.

P. 134, "low born," a "servant": Ibid., 64.

P. 134, "break up all our Societies": Ibid.

P. 135, "inordinate affections": Ibid., 74, 82.

P. 135, "one of such importance": Ibid., 91.

P. 135, "Had not the Lord restrained you": Ibid., 91–92.

P. 135, "Mr. Wesley will have nothing": Ibid., 98.

P. 135, "that I might acknowledge my sin": Ibid., 96.

P. 136, "I should see her face": Ibid., 88.

P. 136, "If these things are so": Ibid., 98.

P. 136, proposing to some: CWL to Ed Perronet, November 4, 1749.

P. 136, "I am no longer of his council": Ibid.

P. 136, "ministry" of "deliverance": Ibid.

P. 136, "If I must break with him": CWL to Ed Perronet, October 30, 1749.

P. 136, "seemed pleased with the thought of parting": Ibid.

P. 137, "a woman of sorrowful spirit": *CWJ*, July 20, 1749.

P. 137, "I believe riding": JWL to Mary Vazeille, June 13, 1749.

P. 137, "Our different judgment of persons": CWL to James Hutton, July 30, 1786, quoted in Telford, *Letters of John Wesley*, vol. 8, 267.

P. 138, "resolved to marry": *CWJ*, February 2, 1751.

P. 138, "I was thunderstruck": Ibid.

P. 138, "Several days afterward": *CWJ*, February 17, 1751.

P. 138, "O how can we praise God enough": JWL to Mary Wesley, March 23, 1751.

P. 138, "You have surely a right": Ibid.

P. 138, "should not preach one sermon": Henry Moore, *The Life of the Reverend John Wesley*, vol. 2 (New York: Bangs and Emory, 1824), vol. 2, 104.

P. 138, "The more she travels, the better": JWL to Ebenezer Blackwell, April 16, 1752.

P. 139, "Oh what mystery is this!": JWL to Mary Wesley, March 30, 1751.

P. 139, his wife had an explosive temper: JWL to Mary Wesley, July 15, 1774.

P. 139, "it is an unhappiness almost peculiar": Susanna Wesley to JW, February 23, 1725.

P. 139, "Believe me, if you ever come": Emilia Wesley to JW, April 7, 1725, in Luke Tyerman, *The Life and Times of the Rev. John Wesley, M.A.*, vol. 1, 3rd ed. (London: Hodder and Stoughton, 1876), 33.

P. 140, defense of his marriage to the societies: *CWJ*, February 17, 1751, and March 1, 1751.

P. 140, "misspent his strength in trifles": *CWJ*, January 13, 1751.

P. 140, "my very best friend": See, for example, JWL to CW, May 25, 1764.

P. 140, he was holding together a fragile alliance: See JWL to CW, July 16, 1755.

P. 141, "might save my time and strength": Ibid.

P. 141, "Then I will go to Cornwall myself": Ibid.

P. 142, promising to stand with: See JWL to Sarah Ryan, November 8, 1757. Also see November 22.

P. 142, "stirring of resentment": JWL to Sarah Ryan, January 20, 1758.

P. 142, "The conversing with you": Ibid.

P. 142, "such a temper as I had not seen": JWL to Sarah Ryan, January 27, 1758.

P. 142, "After many severe words": Ibid.

P. 143, imprisoned in his own home: JWL to Mary Wesley, October 23, 1759.

P. 143, "from henceforth you may go": Ebenezer Blackwell to CW, January 22, 1753, in *WHS* vol. 36, 76.

P. 143, "vastly disappointed": Ebenezer Blackwell to CW, January 30, 1753, in *WHS* vol. 36, 77.

P. 143, "nothing to do in this affair": Ibid.

P. 144, "best friends": JWL to Ebenezer Blackwell, January 5, 1754.

P. 144, "improper" "cautious enough": Ebenezer Blackwell to JW, June 30, 1758, in *WHS*, vol. 36, 77.

P. 144, "When I have spoken to you" "[I] would even then": Ebenezer Blackwell to JW, March 2, 1759, in JWL, Telford.

P. 145, "Where you are I know not": JWL to CW, June 23, 1760.

P. 145, "diabolical lunacy": JWL to James Rouquet, March 30, 1761.

P. 145, did not think his life was safe with her: Ibid.

P. 145, Mary Wesley in a rage: Luke Tyerman, *The Life and Times of the Rev. Samuel Wesley, M.A.* (London: Simpkin, Marshall, 1866), vol. 2, 110–11.

P. 145, "My wife gains ground": JWL to CW, January 5, 1763.

P. 145, "continues in an amazing temper": JWL to CW, July 9, 1766.

P. 145, Mary proved a "cross" to him: JWL to Mary Bosanquet, January 15, 1770. Explaining that he would not pay for Mary to return to London from Newcastle, Wesley wrote, "I will not buy a cross, though I can bear it."

P. 145, "[H]is singular forbearance": Quoted in Telford, *Letters of John Wesley*, vol. 3, 64.

P. 145, "real or supposed": This is seen throughout their correspondence, but see esp. JWL to Mary Wesley, October 2, 1778.

P. 145, "not one or two intimates only": Ibid.

P. 146, "My brother is indeed an extraordinary man": This vignette was related by Sarah Wesley in Thomas Jackson, *The Life of the Rev. Charles Wesley*, vol. 2 (London: John Mason, 1841), 283.

P. 146, "Tell Sarah I will take her": Ibid.

P. 146, After accusing John of adultery: JWL to Mary Wesley, September 1, 1777.

P. 146, "without either anger or bitterness": JWL to Mary Wesley, October 2, 1778.

P. 147, "If you were to live a thousand years": Ibid.

Chapter 13: Love Your Enemies

P. 149, "slender thread": Jonathan Edwards's sermon, "Sinners in the Hands of an Angry God."

P. 149, "Now you have the extraordinary opportunity": Ibid.

P. 149, "a little crack brained": JWJ, July 17, 1739.

P. 150, "How is the faithful city become an harlot!": Isaiah 1:21.

P. 150, "an instance of love to our neighbor": JWS, introduction to "Hypocrisy in Oxford," sec. 3.

P. 150, "how faithful [Oxford]": Ibid., sec. 5.

P. 150, "all here are so prejudiced": JWJ, June 18, 1741.

P. 150, "whether they will hear: Ibid.

P. 150, "almost Christian" and "altogether Christian": JWS, "The Almost Christian." The contrast between an "almost" and "altogether" Christian is the basis of this classic sermon.

P. 150, "experience what it is to be": Ibid., III, sec. 11.

P. 151, "so many of you are *triflers*": JWS, "Scriptural Christianity," IV, sec. 10.

P. 151, "the last messengers of God": Ibid., IV, sec. 11.

P. 151, "I preached, I suppose": JWJ, August 24, 1744.

P. 151, "I am now clear of the blood": Ibid.

P. 151, "I have fully delivered my soul": Ibid.

P. 152, "the scum of Cornwall": JW, *A Farther Appeal to Men of Reason and Religion*, III, sec. 12.

P. 152, "The beast was wiser than his drivers": JWJ, March 12, 1742.

P. 152, "came in among us as lions": JWJ, September 16, 1740.

P. 153, "I wonder if the devil has not wisdom enough": Ibid.

P. 153, "soft hair": JWJ, October 20, 1743.

P. 153, "rule, confirmed by long experience": JWJ, August 6, 1746.

P. 153, "filled with love": JWJ, May 20, 1749.

P. 154, "softer": Ibid.

P. 154, "love your enemies": These words are also recorded in Luke 6:27, 35. Wesley does not give a citation in his journal, merely the words.

P. 154, "A Catholic Spirit": JWS, "A Catholic Spirit," had 2 Kings 10:15 as its main text, which was also the main text from sermons he preached at the Foundery on November 23, 1740; in Newcastle on September 8, 1749; and in Bristol on November 3, 1749. It is impossible to know whether the printed sermon is the same as what he preached on these occasions.

P. 154, "a difference in opinions or modes of worship": Ibid., introduction, sec. 4.

P. 154, "general": Ibid., I, sec. 8.

P. 154, "main branches of Christian doctrine": Ibid., III, sec. 1.

P. 154, "Do you 'love your enemies'?": Ibid., I, sec. 17.

P. 154, "Love me": Ibid., II, sec. 3.

P. 155, "Love me, with a very tender affection": Ibid.

P. 155, "provokes to love and good works": Ibid., II, sec. 6.

P. 155, "so far as in conscience": Ibid., II, sec. 7.

P. 1555, "join with me in the work of God": Ibid.

P. 155, "think and let think": This idea permeates his thinking from early on to late in his ministry. See JWJ, May 29, 1745; December 3, 1776; May 18, 1788; JWS, "The Lord Our Righteousness," II, sec. 20, among many instances.

P. 155, "I overtook a serious man": JWJ, May 22, 1742.

P. 155, "as one who had happened upon a snake": Ibid.

P. 155, "But being the better mounted of the two": Ibid.

P. 156, "His love resembles that of him": JWL to Dr. Conyers Middleton, January 4, 1749.

P. 157, "several of the bishops began to speak against us": JWJ, March 11, 1745.

P. 157, "in such a manner": JW open letter, "A Letter to the Right Reverend Lord Bishop of London," sec. 2.

P. 157, "the time is short": Ibid., sec. 22.

P. 157, "great work of God": JWS, "The Signs of the Times" II, sec. 2.

P. 157, "a great man, indeed": JWS, "On Laying of the Foundation of the New Chapel, Near the City-Road, London," sec. 2.

P. 157, "heavy work": JWJ, October 19, 1751.

P. 158, "I was well pleased to partake": JWJ, August 29, 1762.

P. 158, "If your Lordship should think": JW, "A Letter to the Bishop of Gloucester," III.

P. 158, "I was a little surprised": JWL to CW, January 5, 1763.

Chapter 14: Least of These

P. 159, "outcasts of men": *Farther Appeals*, III, pt. III, sec. 35.

P. 159, "seek and to save that which was lost": Luke 19:10.

P. 159, "The rich, the honourable": *Farther Appeals*, III, pt. III, sec. 35.

P. 159, "necessities of life": JWS, "The Causes of the Inefficacy of Christianity," sec. 10.

P. 160, "experience, reading, and reflection": JWS, "The Use of Money," I, sec. 8.

P. 160, "Do not throw it away in idle expenses": Ibid., II, sec. 1.

P. 160, "by superfluous or expensive furniture": Ibid., II, sec. 3.

P. 160, "farther end": Ibid., III, sec. 1.

P. 160, "When the Possessor of heaven": Ibid.

P. 161, "not a tenth, not a third": Ibid., III, sec. 6.

P. 161, "I look up on all this revenue": JW, *Plain Account of the People Called Methodists*, XV, sec. 6.

P. 161, "If I leave behind me ten pounds": JW, *An Earnest Appeal to Men of Reason and Religion*, sec. 96.

P. 161, Gaston Jean Baptiste de Renty: See JW, *The Life of Monsieur de Renty*, sec. 2, §1.

P. 161, "A poor wretch cries to me for an alms": JWS, "On Pleasing All Men," II, sec. 5.

P. 162, "the itch": JWL to Dr. Andrew Wilson, July 8, 1774, in *WHS*, vol. 36, 30.

P. 162, he relentlessly gave to beggars: Samuel Bradburn, *A Farther Account of That Illustrious Man of God*, 19, appended to Richard Rodda, *A Discourse Delivered at the Chapel in Oldham Street, Manchester, March 13th, 1791. On Occasion of the Death of the Rev. John Wesley, A.M.* (Manchester, UK: J. Radford, 1791).

P. 162, never gave away less than £1,000 per year: Ibid., 17. This confidant, Samuel Bradford, claims to have witnessed Wesley giving away £1,400 from 1780 to 1781, as a member of his "Family" in London.

P. 162, "Let those animating words be written on your hearts": JWS, "The Reward of Righteousness," III, sec. 3.

P. 163, The Kingswood School: JWJ, August 24, 1753.

P. 163, "carding and spinning of cotton": JWJ, May 7, 1741.

P. 163, lending stock: JW, *Plain Account of the People Called Methodists*, XV, sec. 2. See also "The Foundery Lending Stock" by R. Green, in *WHS*, vol. 3, 197–98.

P. 163, "as a comfortable earnest": JW, *Plain Account of the People Called Methodists*, XIII, sec. 2.

P. 164, there is no distinction "Christ is all and in all": Colossians 3:11.

P. 164, "I bear the rich": JWL to Ann Foard, September 29, 1764.

P. 164, "Diligence and frugality must produce riches": JWS, "Causes of the Inefficacy of Christianity," sec. 19.

P. 164, "possessing everything": JWL to Dr. Wrangel, January 30, 1770.

P. 164, "beget and to increase": JWS, "Dangers of Riches," I, sec. 12.

P. 164, "Money never stays with me": JWL to Mrs. Hall, October 6, 1768.

P. 165, "inefficacy of Christianity": JWS, "The Cause of the Inefficacy of Christianity," sec. 1.

P. 165, "Reverend Sir": Quoted in Telford, *Letters of John Wesley*, vol. 6, 230.

P. 165, "I have *two* silver teaspoons": JWL to the Officer of Excise, September 1776.

P. 166, "For upwards of eighty-six years": Luke Tyerman, *The Life and Times of the Rev. Samuel Wesley, M.A.* (London: Simpkin, Marshall, 1866), vol. 1, 436.

Chapter 15: Sovereign Remedy

P. 167, 32,500 patients: George Rudé, *Hanoverian London: 1714–1808* (Berkeley: University of California Press, 1971), 85. Rudé cites a May 1748 *Gentleman's Magazine* which reported on "the Numbers of Objects under Cure."

P. 167, "I saw the poor people pining away": JW, *Plain Account of the People Called Methodists*, XII, sec. 1.

P. 167, "desperate expedient": Ibid.

P. 167, "I had often observed": JWJ, September 8, 1736.

P. 168, "settling a regular method": JWL to CW, April 21, 1741.

P. 168, "many of our brethren": JWJ, May 7, 1741.

P. 168, "To inquire into the state of their souls": JW, *Plain Account of the People Called Methodists*, XI, sec. 4.

P. 169, **"spiritual weakness"**: JWS, "On Visiting the Sick," sec. 1.

P. 169, **"I thought out of the desperate expedient"**: JW, *Plain Account of the People Called Methodists*, XII, sec. 2.

P. 170, *Primitive Physick*: The *k* was dropped in later editions, which offers a more natural reading to a modern audience. This was an expanded edition, with an important preface of the 1745 pamphlet, JW, *A Collection of Receipts for the Use of the Poor* (Bristol, UK: F. Farley, 1775).

P. 170, **"hoped to soften the evils of life"**: JW, preface to *Primitive Physick*, sec. 3

P. 170, **"animal food"**: See JWJ, December 29, 1746; August 1, 1748, among other instances.

P. 170, **"vegetable diet"**: JWJ, December 29, 1746.

P. 170, **"soul and body"**: Ibid.

P. 170, **"poison"**: See JWS, "Discource Eight on the Sermon on the Mount," sec. 23, JW, *Thoughts on Nervous Disorders, Lowness of Spirits*, sec. 3, among others.

P. 170, **"one grand preventative of pain"**: JW, *Primitive Physick*, sec. 3.

P. 170, **"chamber-horse"**: See JWL to his niece Sarah Wesley, August 18, 1790; JWL to Mrs. Christian, July 17, 1785; and JWL to Samuel Bradburn, March 13, 1788.

P. 171, **"electrical experiments"**: JWJ, October 16, 1747.

P. 171, **"troubled many years"**: JWJ, January 20, 1753.

P. 171, **"decry of medicine"**: Ibid. It is not clear if his pun was intended or not.

P. 171, **"try the virtue of this surprising medicine"**: JWJ, November 9, 1756.

P. 171, **"found an immediate, some a gradual cure"**: Ibid.

P. 172, **"How much sickness"**: JW, preface to *The Desideratum; or Electricity Made Plain and Useful*, sec. 3.

P. 172, **"the general and rarely failing remedy"**: Ibid., sec. 7.

P. 172, **"the noblest medicine yet known"**: Ibid., sec. 53.

P. 172, **"Never start at its being a quack medicine"**: JWL to CW, December 26, 1761.

P. 172, **"Rub the part, morning and evening"**: JW, *Primitive Physick*, sec. 11.

P. 173, **"Give one or two drams of distilled verdigris"**: JWL to the *Gazetteer*, December 28, 1775.

P. 173, printing error: JWL to *Lloyd's Evening Post*, January 1, 1776.

P. 173, "an unfeeling quack": Fly-Flap (pseudonym), "To the Rev. Mr. Wesley." *The Gazetteer*, January 1, 1776.

P. 173, "calm, dispassionate": JW, "To the Editor of Lloyd's Evening Post." *Lloyd's Evening Post*, and *British Chronicle*, January 26–29, 1776.

P. 173, "Fifty years ago, I imagined": Ibid.

P. 173, "makes many inquire concerning": JW, "To the Printer of the Gazetteer," *The Gazetteer*, January 31, 1776.

P. 173, "shewing that a great number": This is simply part of an overlong subtitle to *An Examination of Mr. John Wesley's Primitive Physick*, published in London in 1776 by William Hawes. The full text of the subtitle reads as follows: *showing that a great number of the prescriptions therein contained are founded on ignorance of the medical art, and of the power and operations of medicines; and that it is a publication calculated to do essential injury to the health of those persons who may place confidence in it. Interspersed with medical remarks and practical observations.*

P. 174, "The love of God, as it is the sovereign remedy": JW, preface to *Primitive Physick,*
VI, sec. 4.

P. 174, "fears God": Ibid.

P. 174, "which are of infinitely greater importance": JWS, "On Visiting the Sick," I, sec. 2.

P. 174, "higher end": Ibid., III, sec. 3.

Chapter 16: Perfect Love

P. 177, "We had, I believe, pretty near": *JWJ*, January 1, 1762.

P. 177, "Your day of Pentecost": JWJ, October 28, 1762.

P. 177, "Any unprejudiced reader": Ibid.

P. 177, "I now stood and looked back": JWJ, December 31, 1762.

P. 177, "What the end will be I know not": Ibid.

P. 178, The journey was filled with ambiguities: See Mark K. Olson's helpful book, *John Wesley's Theology of Christian Perfection: Developments in Doctrine and Theological System* (Fenwick, MI: Truth in Heart, 2007).

P. 178, "Be ye therefore perfect": Matthew 5:48.

P. 178, "Herein is our love made perfect": 1 John 4:17.

P. 178, "Not as though I had already attained": Philippians 3:12, 15.

P. 179, "That ye may stand perfect and complete": Colossians 4:12.

P. 179, "seeing they are the words of God": JWS, "Christian Perfection," sec. 3.

P. 179, he did not mean perfection in knowledge: Ibid., I.

P. 179, "made free from outward sin": Ibid., II, 3.

P. 179, "a fond conceit": GW to JW, September 25, 1740, in JWL.

P. 179, "even though all men should be offended": JWS, introduction to "Christian Perfection," sec. 2.

P. 179, "voluntary transgressions of a known law": JW, *Plain Account of Christian Perfection*, sec. 19.

P. 180, "the heaviest trial": See Charles Atmore, *The Methodist Memorial: being an impartial sketch of the lives and characters of the preachers. . .among the people called Methodists* (Bristol, UK: Richard Edwards, 1801), 268–69. One can hardly imagine it being a greater trial than his marriage.

P. 180, "son in the gospel": See, for example, *Conference Minutes*, 1766, Q. 29, 3.

P. 180, "seem to have tasted of the same blessing": See JWJ, April 28, 1764.

P. 180, "perfect as an angel": JWL to Thomas Maxfield, November 2, 1762.

P. 181, "remove any misunderstandings": JWJ, December 27, 1761.

P. 181, "witnesses of the great salvation": JWJ, July 26, 1762.

P. 181, "none who dreamed of being immortal": Ibid.

P. 181, met with Maxfield: JWJ, August 21, 1762.

P. 181, "disliked": Ibid.

P. 181, "littleness of love": JWL to Thomas Maxfield, November 2, 1762.

P. 181, "bear-garden": JWL to CW, December 11, 1762.

P. 181, "unscriptural, enthusiastic expressions": Ibid.

P. 181, "mend them or end them": Ibid.

Pp. 181–82, "The reproach of Christ I am willing to bear": JWJ, December 22, 1762.

P. 182, "as from God, what I knew God had not spoken": JWJ, December 26, 1762.

P. 182, "convince him of his mistakes": JWJ, January 7, 1763.

P. 182, "as unmoved as a rock": Ibid.

P. 182, no longer in "connexion": JWL to the editor of the *London*

Chronicle, February 9, 1763, in Telford.

P. 182, "the utter absurdity": JWJ, February 28, 1763.

P. 182, "I went to bed at my usual time": Ibid.

P. 182, "confused and distressed": JWJ, May 2, 1763.

P. 182, "My point was still": Ibid.

Pp. 183–84, "laying claim to almost every apostolic gift": See Richard Green, *The Works of John and Charles Wesley* (London: C. H. Kelly, 1896), 123. Wesley's reply is discussed in more detail in chapter 13.

P. 183, "sin remains [in believers] still": JWS, "On Sin in Believers," IV, 8.

P. 183, "watch against the flesh: Ibid., V, 1.

P. 183, "always abiding": JW, *Plain Account of Christian Perfection*, sec. 26, 1.

P. 183, "that *monstrous doctrine of sinless perfection*": George Whitefield letter, June 2, 1766, quoted in Luke Tyerman, *The Life and Times of the Rev. Samuel Wesley, M.A.* (London: Simpkin, Marshall, 1866), vol. 2, 562.

P. 183, he rarely spoke about the state of his own soul: Samuel Bradburn, *A Farther Account of the Illustrious Man of God*, 22.

P. 183, "necessary correlation": Ibid.

P. 184, "chief conductors": JWL to CW, February 28, 1766.

P. 184, "has spread so far": JWL to CW, June 21, 1767.

P. 184, "If we were more holy in heart and life": Ibid.

P. 184, "I do not love God": JWL to CW, June 27, 1766. Where the word *evidence* is used, Wesley has the Greek word ελεγχος, from Hebrews 11:1.

P. 184, "I find rather an increase": Ibid.

P. 185, "I have told all the world": JWL to the editor of *Lloyd's Evening Post*, March 5, 1767.

Chapter 17: A Thousand Tongues

P. 187, "My chains fell off": CW hymn, "And Can It Be?"

P. 187, "challenge the world together": JWL to CW, July 16, 1755.

P. 187, nine thousand hymns: For this estimate of the number of Charles Wesley hymns, see Frank Baker, "Charles Wesley's Productivity as a Religious Poet," in *WHS*, vol. 47, 2.

P. 188, "born in song": See the influential preface to *The Methodist Hymn-Book with Tunes* (London: Methodist Conference Office, 1933), which reads: "Methodism was born in song. Charles Wesley wrote the first hymns of the Evangelical Revival during the great Whitsuntide of 1738 when his brother and he were 'filled with the Spirit,' and from that time onwards the Methodists have never ceased to sing. Their characteristic poet is still Charles Wesley. While for half a century hymns poured continually from his pen on almost every subject within the compass of Christianity, and while no part of the New Testament escaped him, most of all he sang the 'gospel according to St. Paul.' He is the poet of the Evangelical faith. In consequence Methodism has always been able to sing its creed."

P. 188, "A man may be orthodox in every point": JWS, "The Way to the Kingdom."

P. 188, "Orthodoxy, or right opinion, is but a slender part": JW, *Plain Account of the People Called Methodists*, I, 2.

P. 188, "a form of godliness": 2 Timothy 3:5 is one of Wesley's favorite biblical quotations.

P. 189, "*homo unius libri*": JW, preface to *Sermons on Several Occasions*, vol. 1.

P. 189, "to find the way to heaven": Ibid.

P. 189, "to spend at least an hour a day reading": JWL to Sarah Wesley, September 8, 1781.

P. 189, "Israel's strength and consolation": CW hymn, "Come, Thou Long-Expected Jesus."

P. 190, "what is of infinitely more moment": JW, preface to *Collections of Hymns for the People Called Methodists*.

P. 190, A book on the doctrine of the Trinity, by the Reverend William Jones: William Jones, *The Catholic Doctrine of a Trinity proved by above an hundred clear arguments, expressed in the terms of the Holy Scriptures* (Oxford: Theatre, 1756).

P. 190, "Mr. Jones's book on the Trinity": JWL to Mary Bishop, April 17, 1776.

P. 191, that he did not approve of all the hymns: Richard Green, *The Works of John and Charles Wesley*, 66.

P. 191, "a spirit of universal love": JW, preface to *Hymns and Spiritual Songs*, 2.

P. 192, 6,200 scriptural hymns: For this approximation, see Baker, "Charles Wesley's Productivity as a Religious Poet" in *WHS*, vol. 47, 1–7.

P. 192, He was also keenly aware: See JWL to "A Friend," September 20, 1757.

P. 192, "How shall we guard more effectually against formality": JW, *Conference Minutes*, 1746.

P. 192, "careful choice of hymns": Ibid.

P. 192, "those complex tunes": Ibid., 1768.

P. 192, "Exhort every one in the congregation to sing": Ibid., 1780.

P. 192, "this part of divine worship": *BWJW*, vol. 7, app. H, "Directions for Singing."

P. 193, greatest "variety" of hymns: JW, preface to *A Collection of Hymns for the Use of the People Called Methodists*.

P. 193, "O for a thousand tongues to sing": CW hymn, "O for a Thousand Tongues."

P. 193, "Had I a thousand tongues": *BWJW*, vol. 7, 80.

Chapter 18: Shaking Hell's Gates

P. 195, "to reform the nation, and in particular, the Church": *Conference Minutes*, Large Minutes 1763.

P. 195, "save their own souls": JWJ, June 25, 1744.

P. 195, "That all things be considered": *Conference Minutes*, 1744.

P. 196, "Are lay assistants allowable?": Ibid.

P. 196, "Seeing life and health are things of so great importance": JWL to a clergyman, May 4, 1748.

Pp. 197–98, "Be diligent" and "Be serious": "Twelve Rules of an Assistant," *Conference Minutes*, 1744. These rules were later revised, as the following will show.

P. 198, "learners rather than teachers": *Conference Minutes*, 1746.

P. 198, "to provide a complete library": JWL to Ebenezer Blackwell, August 14, 1748.

P. 198, "To expound every morning and evening": *Conference Minutes*, 1744.

P. 199, *Directions Concerning Annunciation and Gesture*: In Thomas Jackson, ed., *The Works of John Wesley*, 3rd ed. (London: Wesleyan Methodist Book Room, 1872), vol. 8, 518–27.

P. 199, "You have nothing to do but to save souls": *Conference Minutes*, 1745.

P. 199, "it is plain God has blessed": JW, *Plain Account of the People Called Methodists*, II, 12.

Pp. 199–200, "remarkably wanting in gifts or grace": Ibid.

P. 200, "prefer grace before gifts": JWL to CW, July 24, 1751.

P. 200, "purge. . .the laborers": CW to John Bennett, August 11, 1751, in *BWJW*, vol. 10, 241.

P. 200, "I am told from Bristol: Charles Wesley apparently wrote this on a letter from JW to himself and sent it back with the note. See JWL to CW, August 17, 1751, in *BWJW*, vol. 26, 476.

P. 200, "break [John's] power": Quoted in *BWJW*, vol. 26, 479.

Pp. 200–201, "I am quite ready to part": JWL to CW, December 4, 1751.

P. 201, "their advice concerning the best method": *Conference Minutes*, 1766.

P. 201, "I did not seek any part of this power": Ibid.

P. 201, "Give me one hundred preachers": Luke Tyerman, *The Life and Times of the Rev. Samuel Wesley, M.A.* (London: Simpkin, Marshall, 1866), vol. 3, 632. Tyerman cites James Sigston's *Life of Bramwell* as the source, which cannot be correct. Though the letter seems authentic, it is not cited in Telford, *Letters of John Wesley*.

P. 202, "tyrannical" "despotic": See *Conference Minutes*, 1766.

P. 202, "thought as well of them": JW, *Thoughts upon Some Late Occurrences*, March 3, 1785.

P. 202, "work in which they were unitedly engaged": Quoted in *BWJW*, vol. 10, 548.

P. 203, "assume any superiority over your brethren": JW "To the Methodist Conference," in *Conference Minutes*, 1791. Dated April 7, 1785.

P. 207, "You see then in all the pains I have taken": JW, *Thoughts upon Some Late Occurrences*, March 3, 1785.

Chapter 19: Setting Up the Kingdom

P. 207, 130,000 strong at his death in 1791: *Conference Minutes*, 1791.

P. 207, "shake the gates of hell": Luke Tyerman, *The Life and Times of the Rev. Samuel Wesley, M.A.* (London: Simpkin, Marshall, 1866), vol. 3, 632.

P. 207, Christianity starts with individuals: This is the outline of JWS, "Scriptural Christianity."

P. 207, "set up His Kingdom among men": JWS, "The Way of the Kingdom," I, 13.

P. 207, **"God takes unto Himself":** Ibid., I, 12.

P. 208, **"Not only thy friend":** Ibid., I, 9.

P. 208, **"the poisonous writers":** JWL to Sarah Wesley, September 26, 1788.

P. 208, **"Sir, you wish to serve God":** Thomas Coke and Henry Moore, *The Life of the Rev. John Wesley, M.A., including an Account of the Great Revival of Religion,* 2nd ed. (London: G. Paramore, 1792), 53.

P. 208, **"Christianity is essentially a social religion":** JWS, "Fourth Discourse on the Sermon on the Mount," I, 1.

P. 208, **"cannot possibly have a being":** Ibid., I, 3.

Pp. 208–9, **"it is true that the root of religion lies in the heart":** Ibid., III, 1.

P. 209, **"a very different book":** JWJ, February 12, 1772.

P. 209, **"rise and progress":** Ibid.

P. 209, **"that execrable sum of all villainies":** Ibid.

P. 209, **"When shall the Sun of Righteousness arise":** JWJ, July 31, 1736. This is an echo of Malachi 4:2.

P. 209, **Anthony Benezet was impressed by the tract's pathos:** Benezet uses the term *pathetic,* which had an entirely different meaning in the eighteenth century. See Anthony Benezet to JW, May 23, 1774, in *Arminian Magazine,* 1787.

P. 210, **"remarkably horrid, dreary, and barren land":** *Thoughts upon Slavery,* II, sec. 1.

P. 210, **"Did the Creator intend":** Ibid., III, sec. 7.

P. 210, **"what punishment have these *Law-makers*":** Ibid., III, sec. 9.

P. 210, **"setting the Bible out of the question":** Ibid., IV, sec. 1.

P. 210, **"defended, on the principles of even heathen honesty":** Ibid.

P. 210, **"absolute necessity":** Ibid., IV, sec. 5.

P. 210, **"I deny that villainy is ever necessary":** Ibid.

P. 211, **"To the captains employed in this trade":** Ibid., V, sec. 2.

P. 211, **"Is there a God?":** Ibid., V, sec. 3.

P. 211, **"Has gold entirely blinded your eyes":** Ibid., V, sec. 4.

P. 211, **"the spring that puts all the rest":** Ibid., V, sec. 5.

P. 211, **"O, whatever it costs, put a stop":** Ibid.

P. 211, **"Liberty is the right of every human":** Ibid., V, sec. 6.

P. 212, **"a picture of hell on earth":** JWJ, February 2, 1753.

P. 212, **1,100 French prisoners:** JWJ, October 15, 1759.

P. 212, **prison-reformer John Howard:** See JWJ, June 28, 1787; JWL to

Walter Churchney, June 20, 1789.

P. 213, "What an amazing way of deciding controversies!": JW, *A Seasonable Address to the More Serious Part of the Inhabitants of Great Britain.*

P. 213, "I am of neither side": JWL to CW, March 1, 1775.

P. 213, New printing of *Thoughts upon Slavery*: See JWL to Thomas Clarkson, August 1787.

P. 213, "filled with high and low": JWJ, March 3, 1787.

P. 213, "Satan [who] fought": Ibid.

P. 214, "The first time I was here": JWJ, August 18, 1789.

P. 215, "Unless the divine power has raised you up": JWL to William Wilberforce, February 24, 1791. The Latin phrase translates: "Athanasius against the world."

P. 215, "poor African": Ibid.

About the Author

Jake Hanson is a graduate of Wheaton College (B.A.) and Beeson Divinity School (MDiv). A preacher, teacher, and retreat speaker, Jake also operates a website (TheDecidedLife.com) devoted to biography, Bible study, and theology. He is the author of *Igniting the Fire: The Movements and Mentors Who Shaped Billy Graham*. He lives near Birmingham, Alabama.

Also available by Jake Hanson

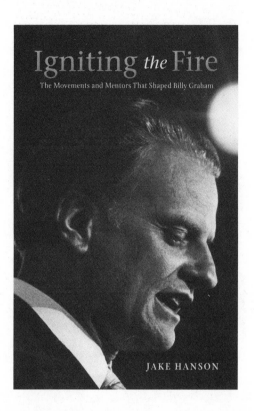

Focusing on Billy Graham's formative years, from his
boyhood through college, to his bursting onto the national
scene in 1949, author Jake Hanson has drawn upon scores
of original documents and new interviews to detail the
environment, the movements, and the mentors that
fueled Billy Graham's passion for the Gospel.